No Rattling of Sabers

AN ANTHOLOGY OF ISRAELI WAR POETRY

D0880329

Modern Middle East
Literature in Translation
Series

No Rattling of Sabers
An Anthology of Israeli War Poetry

Translation and Introduction

by

Esther Raizen

Center for Middle Eastern Studies
The University of Texas at Austin

Library of Congress Catalogue Card Number: 95-83542

ISBN 0-292-77071-5

Printed in the United States of America

Cover drawing: Dina Pozniak

Cover design: Diane Watts

Book designer: Helen-Jo Jakusz Hewitt

Series editor: Annes McCann-Baker

Distributed by arrangement with University of Texas Press/Box 7819
Austin Texas 78713

© Rights to the Hebrew poems are reserved to the poets or to ACUM.
We thank Sifriyat Poalim for permission to publish *At a Time Like This* by L. Alex and *Eulogy* by Amichai Israeli (Border Crossing, 1983), *Teacher of Defeated Hebrew Language* and *1936-1986* by Eitan Kalinski (Poems, 1989).
We thank Ruvik Rosenthal for permission to publish *Only 20 Years Old* by Gideon Rosenthal.

o

The splendidly verbal HJJH

Contents

Contents ix

Author's Preface

American interest in Israeli literature is on the rise—the works of prominent writers, especially those using the medium of prose, are often available in English translation in the United States shortly after they have been published in Israel. Quite a few poetry collections of individual poets and a number of anthologies of translated Hebrew poetry are available in the United States, some of them in bilingual form.

Such collections often tend to minimize the inclusion of political poems, considered by many to be an inferior branch of the art because of its subordination of imagery and aesthetic values to social messages. Since such poems are very often written in response to specific incidents, understanding them may well depend on historical information, and their existential significance is, at most, limited. A corresponding critical attitude is non-existent when prose is concerned: writers expressing explicit political views in their works, such as A.B. Yehoshua or Amos Oz, have little difficulty maintaining their prominence in the Israeli literary pantheon.

Although war poems are not necessarily political in nature, only a high degree of aesthetic camouflage applied to their imagery makes their acceptance as significant pieces of poetry possible. The overt messages in "I have lived twenty years upon this earth. It was good, and I want to keep on, simply keep on living" (Rosenthal, *Only Twenty Years Old*) or "Not thirsting for battle did we go to war" (Sarig, *Return*) are considered a disadvantage when compared to the covert message in *Again a Drab Khaki Light Is Coming Down* (Wieseltier), a poem whose significance is revealed only by its repeated reference to the color of military uniform. Rosenthal and Sarig are too emotional, too sentimental. The reader who knows that both lost their lives in battle is even more so. This, again, is a disadvantage when the prevailing standards of the medium favor the suppression and disguise of emotions, with their revelation only in the least direct manner.

Thus, considerations of artistic value may well explain the absence of war poetry from collections of translated poems. American readers are therefore rarely familiar with the work of Israeli poets who write such poems. Because their work is popular with the general public, and possibly because many of their poems were set to music, as is very often the case with war poetry or poetry of protest, these writers have been frequently referred to in Israeli literary circles as "versifiers," in an apparent attempt to distinguish them from "real" poets. Writers like Aryeh Sivan, Ramy Ditzanny, or Eli Alon, who produced a significant body of political poetry, have often been referred to as "enlisted poets," a semi-derogatory epithet which was originally applied to poets serving as spokesmen for the Israeli political mainstream, and now to those who write political poetry in general, be it associated with the political mainstream or, as is often the case, in opposition to it.

Political poetry is, however, a legitimate, compelling manifestation of human experience. The role of war poetry in conveying such experience, both individual and collective, is of special significance where Israel, a country in which the realities of war are ineradicably engraved in the collective psyche, is concerned. The constant threat to the nation's existence, the never-ending sacrifice of the young, the uncertainties brought about by the political instability in the region, and the constant need to test the values of democracy and justice against the effects of long-term friction with the hostile population in the territories gained after the 1967 war, are intensely reflected in Israeli poetry. Israeli poets have provided notable representation of the elemental experiences and emotions associated with life under constant duress, coupled with memories of historical catastrophes. The study of Israeli war poetry may serve, therefore, as a window into a prime constituent of Israeli existence, with a significance reaching beyond that of poetry per se.

Dedicated to war poetry of the last fifty years, *No Rattling of Sabers* includes the works of both poets of prominence and those less known. Selection did not solely involve poetic merit as judged by aesthetic criteria, but also recognition of a common need among ordinary people to express themselves in the medium of poetry, an inclination that seems to grow at times of national strife. In addition to poems taken from collections by individual poets, this book draws on sources not readily available to readers outside Israel—newspapers, magazines, journals, and memorial volumes. Thus, this compilation reflects a wide variety of emotions associ-

ated with a virtually permanent state of war, and represents varied levels
of aesthetic awareness and expression. Thematic consideration was given
to three salient points: war as viewed by the fighting soldier; war as
viewed by civilians, including reflections of the world of parents, wives,
children, and teachers; and, war as a force giving rise to poetic impulses.
Another principle of selection stems from an endeavor to illustrate inter-
relatedness among works written throughout the period. This interrela-
tionship, manifested by duplication in imagery and expression, is readily
recognized by readers capable of handling the Hebrew text, and, to some
extent, by readers of the translated poems as well.

Poems are presented in a loose chronological order that illustrates both
the continuation and the changes of attitudes and themes in the course of
some fifty years and seven major wars: the War of Independence, 1947–
1949; the Sinai (Kadesh) War, 1956; the Six Day War, 1967; the War of At-
trition, 1967–1970; the Yom Kippur (October) War, 1973; the Lebanon War,
1982; and the Gulf War, 1991.

Translation is an art which involves a great deal of compromise. Some
poems were excluded from this anthology only because they would not
lend themselves to translation. In others, included, the compactness of the
Hebrew mode of expression, the uniqueness of its idiom, and the many in-
tentional ambiguities that are inherent in the language and often serve as
the basis of its kaleidoscopic imagery were at times compromised for the
sake of clearer communication with the English-speaking reader. Sense
took precedence over sound, so no attempt was made to replicate the oc-
casional use of rhyme and rhythm, to the detriment, in some cases, of the
effect of the poem. Lexical choice, manipulation of imagery, and line
structure were maintained as closely as possible to the original, with the
intent to present the poems as poetry rather than prose translation. Bibli-
cal quotations and allusions, typical of Hebrew poetry, were preserved
whenever possible, with wording based on the Revised Standard Version
or the King James. References to pertinent Biblical verses are included
with the notes for some poems.

My sister Dina Pozniak searched for many small details of information that helped me in my research, and I am indebted to her. I am grateful to W.P. Lehmann of Austin for his guidance and support, to Annes McCann-Baker and Diane Watts of the Center for Middle Eastern Studies at the University of Texas at Austin, to John Merritt of Austin for assistance with military terminology in English, to Sharon Laor who worked with me in Israel, to Hani Moshe of ACUM, to Chaya Hoffman of the Institute for the Translation of Hebrew Literature, to Gavriela Gilboa, and to the poets who read portions of the manuscript and helped me bring it to its final form—Ramy Ditzanny, Aliza Greenberg Tur-Malka, Aryeh Sivan, Meir Wieseltier, Nathan Yonathan, Alex Liban, Eli Alon, and T. Carmi.

The book was published with the assistance of a grant from The Institute for the Translation of Hebrew Literature, Israel.

Introduction

January of 1991 found the State of Israel in the agonizing position of a sitting duck. Directly impacted by the Gulf War, yet prevented by political circumstances from providing their own defense against SCUD missiles flying in from Iraq, the Israelis were repeatedly rushed into makeshift sealed rooms in anticipation of incoming missiles carrying chemical warheads. They watched with horror unfamiliar scenes of local destruction and mass exodus from potential target areas, and, like the rest of the world at that time, turned to the international and local media for information, advice, and succour. "What are our writers doing at a time like this?" was a favorite topic of discussion in Israeli newspapers during that period of turbulent routine.

Writers, like everyone else in Israel, struggled to maintain their mental equilibrium and withstand the pressures of war. They were interviewed frequently, and they wrote—mostly about writing and reading preferences. Ruth Almog stated in an interview:

> I do not respond to current events, and what is happening today will be expressed in writing only years from now, if at all. I do not wish to think about writing right now—this does not seem to be a good time. Now one just needs to survive (Hameiri 1991).

Nathan Yonathan wrote:

> Strong sheets of plastic belong to life more than any word or poem do. Yet there, in the chill of the bomb-shelter, after everything has been sealed, emanates a strong, almost erotic need for the touch of words (Yonathan 1991).

Indeed, newspapers were bombarded with contributions, often the outpourings of civilians-turned-poets, and literary critics were busy debating what and how one should write during wartime. Moshe ben Shaul decried the barrage of poetry on "the situation":

> What is written now about now, today about today … with no perspective, even that of a few hours … remains meaningless. What is meaningless will be soon forgotten (ben Shaul 1991).

And the critic Orzion Bartana explicitly declared that literature is not among the areas which tend to flourish in wartime, when writers are

forced to provide a high degree of externalized imagery "in order to en-
sure their coverage by the media" (Bartana 1991).

The emotional pressure during war, lack of perspective, and tenacious
adherence to certain themes and communicative effects were generally
viewed as detrimental to the creation of good poetry, in particular the
political poetry and war poetry written concurrently with the war itself.
Only the poet David Avidan, who in the course of some forty years of an
active career had achieved mastery in highly publicized, externalized
writing, challenged openly: "The concept of political poetry as poetry
marching towards politics, in a sacrifice-like act—and at the expense of the
values of poetry per se—is not acceptable," he wrote , and called for open-
ness of mentality, energy, and language to allow the gain of enrichment by
"extra-poetic" language materials (Avidan 1991).

That exchange to some extent echoed a well-known controversy which
took place some fifty years earlier, when the onslaught of World War II
brought about a heated public debate between the three prominent
Hebrew poets of that time: Leah Goldberg, Abraham Shlonsky, and
Nathan Alterman. Goldberg maintained it was a poet's duty to write
during times of catastrophe and great despair, thus giving both expression
and support to the good and exalted dimension of the human spirit. She
viewed the realities of war, however, as undeserving of poetic attention.
"Forever," she wrote, "is a field of wheat greater and more beautiful than
desolate land, run over by tanks, be the aim of these tanks as lofty as it
may be" (Dorman 1990). Abraham Shlonsky—sensitized by the Soviet
methods of creating mass culture and popular support for the
government—like Goldberg, renounced the creation of war poetry.
Moreover, he insisted that in times of war poetry should not be written at
all, "just as one should not play music in a house of mourning, just as one
should not turn on the lights in a besieged city. Because total blackout is
imperative for defense" (ibid.).

Unlike his two contemporaries, Nathan Alterman declared it necessary
to give expression to the realities of war, like all other realities. "Good lit-
erature," he wrote, "is never a step-mother to her poems, war poems in-
cluded" (ibid.). In retrospect, the popularity of Alterman's political poems
in his newspaper columns attests to his keen sensitivity to national senti-

ments, which demanded and actively sought both representation and guidance from writers of prose and poetry. Nevertheless, the critical stance that puts aesthetics above all else clashed with Alterman's popularity, opening a line of criticism which since the 1950s was used in support of challenges to his dominance and merit as a poet. As a matter of routine literary critics have considered it necessary to search for evidence of absolute aesthetic quality in war poems lest those be considered merely popular, sentimental, or immature.

Debate on the duty of the poet as a citizen periodically arises in circumstances of national stress, and while poets generally tend to withdraw from mixing poetic expression and public activity, demand on part of the general public for such expression is strong and inescapable. Writers are often reminded that

> … they are obliged to simply do their work, like the soldiers and bureaucrats, like rabbis and prostitutes…the question whether … writers, instead of drenching themselves in tears, should douse themselves in gasoline and in the city square, is a good question. And the answer is: Yes. And let them blaze… (Edeliest 1990)

Conflicts between poets and their potential public and debates over the merit of war poems are by no means limited to Israel. Indeed, they were quite prevalent in the Western world during and after each of the World Wars. The romantic perspective, which emphasized theme and idea as expressed by a writer, gave way at the beginning of the 20th century to the evaluation of prose and poetry through their aesthetic structure and poetics. Study of poetry via the perspective of personal or social circumstances had gone into eclipse. Because of their special nature, war poems have never lent themselves completely to this line of criticism, and have remained in something of a gray area. For example, while the need for "having been there" was never a prerequisite for acceptance of war poems (Edward Hirsch, Andrew Hudgins, and Mary Jo Salter were all born in the 1950s, yet wrote recognized war poetry painting the horrors of World War II), actual wartime experience has always been a bonus point, and statements such as "Archibald MacLeish served as a captain of field artillery in World War I," or "Richard Hugo flew thirty five missions as a bombardier in Italy," or "Robert Lowell was a conscientious objector during the Second World War," (Stokesbury 1990) are very common in the literature.

World War I was fought between many nations, involved millions of people, and demonstrated the enormous impact of new weapons of mass destruction. The magnitude of horror revealed during the war gave birth to poetry of great distress, which struggled with a need to define the nightmarish experience in existential rather than personal or national terms and portrayed war in all its senselessness as an absurd, suffocating reality.

The universal tones of World War I poetry were generally replaced by more personal and private avenues of thought in the work of World War II poets. Those writers met with pressure to produce poems, pressure from readers whose expectations were based on familiarity with World War I poetry. They were faced with the need to repeat a message already fully delivered during that earlier conflict. While the need to express the repeated and manifold-magnified horror was there, the capability to do so seemed to have been hindered both by the fact that patriotism and hero- ism were diminished by the recurrent catastrophes that proved the world had learned nothing, and by a language usage which had become too dull to express in new terms what had already been obvious two decades be- fore. As a result, poetry of World War II, being written during the high tide of modernism, was largely characterized by a nonchalant, cool, la- conic, wry, and often sarcastic tone. With time, however, this tone mel- lowed and shifted back to the more straightforward, dramatic tone: some of the best American poems pertaining to World War II were written ex post facto, even a generation or two after that war. The time lapse and subsequent violent events such as the Vietnam War gave the artists ample opportunity to immerse themselves in the magnitude of the calamity and come out with a bold, direct expression thereof.

In one way or another the two World Wars and the Middle East wars fought during the 20th century touched the core of Jewish existence and became central components of the national experience. World War I, which had no significant "Jewish accent" to it, took place during years of great agitation within the Jewish national movements, and highlighted the scattered and alienated existence of Jews, who often found themselves fighting on opposite sides in the war. This reality added a special histori- cal perspective to the war experience of the Jewish soldier, who was hard-pressed to decide whether that war, with all its cruelty and senselessness, was *his* war at all. Such contemplation forcefully inserted a measure of historical "sense" into the crumbling world. The historical perspective—which was dramatically highlighted by the realities of World War II and the Holocaust, and which progressively coincided with the developing sense of urgency within the Zionist movement—added a positive element to an experience which was, in essence, negative.

The Holocaust brought forth a strengthened national identity, which eventually led to the creation of the State of Israel, a symbol to many of strength, independence, stability, and hope. The Jewish poet could not, therefore, relate to the horror only—the historical significance of the war demanded expression as well. And indeed, Hebrew war poetry written during World War II and in the early years of the Jewish State was characterized by the need for synthesis of the horror with the message of deliverance. This need gave birth to poems that, although not ignoring the death and the agony, tended to minimize them by weighing them against national necessities and gains. Statehood and independence were seen as dramatically offered to the nation by those who had died, and accepted with solemn appreciation and promises to cherish their memory. The strong ties between soldiers, expressed as a solid, sublime entity in the term *re'ut* (camaraderie), were second only to the bond with the land.

Thus, while in the wider external literary milieu patriotic images gave way to a cynical and wry tone, Hebrew war poetry was anything but cynical. Yet the exalted imagery was generally subdued and stern, and symbols such as "kingdom," "domination," or "holy hearts" (as in the poetry of Greenberg and Tur-Malka) were rare. Simplicity, which was one of the trademarks of the Palmach (the pre-statehood elite military unit) dominated the imagery:

> The yoke, as simple as earth,
> They carried without a backward look.
> No shofar was sounded before them,
> Nor were their heads stroked on a winter night.
> No. With sleeves tied around the neck from behind,
> Only their sweaters embraced them.
>
> (Alterman, *Around the Campfire*)

> Ten boys,
> They are like the homeland: rough, with stammering manners,
>   plain stride, in love,
> There are wise ones, and there are buffoons, and there are ones
>   weighty with integrity, knotty!
> Yet the heart of all is laughing!
>   Because it lives!
>
> Not battle heroes,
> No fancy uniform nor splendor,
> But in the rugged tunic, the spiked boot,
>   In the knitted Palmach cap!

(Omer, *A Squad in the Land*)

Death was recognized in its totality, and so was bereavement. The forever-young dead became a cherished, exclusive group, a source of inspiration for generations of schoolchildren, who, year after year, would recite Alterman's *Silver Platter* or Gouri's *Behold, Our Bodies Are Laid Out* and *Prayer*. Camaraderie carried with it the promise of immortality, which somewhat eased the pain over the loss of life. Like it, poetic expression in itself was viewed as a step towards immortality, a commemoration fitting for the young dead as well as from their living comrades, a link between worlds which are ultimately separate. The Ministry of Defense, for example, published a series of official memorial volumes, *Parchments of Fire,* that included numerous poems and prose pieces written by fallen soldiers. As the years passed, however, the other side of this bond between the cherished dead and the living became apparent: the ever-demanding, almost threatening existence of the dead became something of a trial in the collective memory:

> And this is your sign: because you were cut off as if by a sickle
> At the feet of the nation, with your arms spread as if towards
>   happiness—
> That nation will not run away from foes, it will not be able to run,
> Because your hands will be clasping its feet in the dark ...

(Alterman, *In the Month of Aviv*)

The glory of the dead was often painted in ominous colors (Tur-Malka, *For the Fighters—A Lament*, Gouri, *Behold, Our Bodies Are Laid Out*), and the power of words proved to be disappointingly weak, both in offering consolation and in preventing normal life from unfolding without the constant reminder of the dead and their sacrifice (Zelda, *How Much a Word Could Help*; Omer, *To the Memory of a Comrade*). Although the existence of Israel as an independent state fulfilled the expectations of the Jewish people, statehood failed to answer the hopes for peace. The early fifties were marred by terrorist attacks from across its borders, and the 1956 Sinai War was soon to follow. While morale boosters such as Hefer's *Sappers* or Mohar's *Anonymous Squad* were extremely popular, Israeli war poetry from the late fifties on became increasingly characterized by understatement, cynicism, and skepticism, much like poetry of World War II, and also by bitter self-criticism. The constant need to fight became a recognized fact of life, without much glory attached to it:

> The sickle cuts and the sword cuts
> Our lives are a harvest in the morning of a nation,
> He who carries sheaves in the shimmering field
> Also carries another sheaf— his life— for his people.

> (Mohar, *Between Sickle and Sword*)

The 1967 war, however, transformed the mood within the Israeli populace. The feeling of a trapped country that must fight for its existence gave way to enormous relief and a sense of power and vindication. Nevertheless, even amidst the victory celebrations, a book was conceived which gave expression to the apprehension, doubts, and shock of the young soldier faced with the horrors of war and resenting the constant need to fight. *Siach Lochamim* (published in English as *The Seventh Day*) was decried by many as a defeatist document, but opened the way for other forms of written expression that reflected a wide range of sentiments, from doubt to outright criticism. The war, which produced an endless parade of victory albums and memorabilia, also gave rise to poems by Eli Alon, Yehudah Amichai, and others who, perhaps much earlier than the rest of Israeli society, realized the enormous cost of the victory and boldly challenged the happiness and feeling of comfort prevalent in the Israel of that time.

The long War of Attrition which followed the 1967 war gave rise to a protest movement in which many artists, among them poets, were actively involved. The surprise and near-catastrophe of the 1973 war, and the strong opposition to Israel's involvement in Lebanon during the early 1980s, brought about great despair. At the same time the events encouraged strong political involvement on the part of poets, who explicitly criticized the politics of the Israeli government while denouncing the horrors of endless bloodshed and sacrifice. War poetry adopted, as a result, a strongly political stance, which had been uncommon before the 1970s. The 1973 war produced Reuven ben Yoseph's *Voices in the Golan Heights,* a collection of war poems which openly challenged the highly cherished call for individual sacrifice for the sake of the nation:

> And greater than the readiness to sacrifice
> Is the eagerness to kill, and you have no compunction
> When a tank swells in the gun-sight and your finger
> Releases its diminutive shells to drive
> The enemy from the land, but you have to stop,
> For the tanks are fleeing and the halftrack is still and you
> Are looking forever to the heavens and knowing there is naught
> Greater than the readiness for sacrifice.

(ben Yoseph, On the Readiness for Sacrifice)

Although diverse political positions were taken by Israeli poets, most of them had identified with the political strata represented by the labor movement. Poets of the fifties and sixties, who showed growing dissatisfaction with the path taken by the Labor party, often chose to limit the scope of their poetic response to political events, perhaps by that means expressing their dissatisfaction and, perhaps, trying to avoid the image of popular versifiers. The 1977 elections which brought into power the right-wing government propelled Israeli poets into action. They also gave life to the Israeli peace movement which had been marginal prior to that time.

The main wave of political poetry hit Israeli society during and after the 1982 Lebanon War, the first war openly protested while it was still in full sway. Poets found themselves obligated to fight against the "irresponsiveness and plotted silence which are found at times even among those opposing the war... against the narcotic jargon of the official media" (Hever and Ron 1982, Epilogue). The massacre by Christian militia of hundreds of Palestinians in the Sabra and Shatilah refugee camps, which drew into the streets of Tel Aviv some 400,000 demonstrators against the Israeli involvement in Lebanon, was also a catalyst for poets like Dahlia Ravikovitch, who wrote *You Don't Kill Babies Twice,* one of the most widely recited poems of the 1982 war and a strong indication of the political turn taken by war poetry. Other prominent poets, such as Natan Zach and Yehudah Amichai, openly broke the taboo on writing war poetry and publishing it while events were still in progress. Two anthologies, *No End to Battle and Killing* and *Border Crossing*, published shortly after the war, were openly critical of everything—from the political decisions, to the behavior of the Israeli soldier, to the indifference of the Israeli public. In mid-1983, after the release of the government-sponsored commission of inquiry report on the Sabra and Shatilah massacre, and with the Israeli army deeply involved in guerrilla war inside Lebanon, a force led by families of soldiers emerged within the peace movement—Parents Against Silence. More than any other single event, Prime Minister Menahem Begin's statement on television, claiming that "the Beaufort [fortress] was captured without [Israeli] casualties," mobilized parents and friends of soldiers who were killed in that battle and became a high point of mistrust in the government and of disillusionment. Yaakov Gutterman, a bereaved father, published an open letter to Begin in which he urged him to resign, and to accept full responsibility for the death of his son and his comrades. A vigil lasting for some five months in front of Begin's house announced daily the number of Israeli soldiers killed in the war. Raiah Harnik, whose son Guni was also among the fallen in the battle for Beaufort, became a leading figure in the protest movement, and expressed, in her painful lines addressed to a grandchild who would never be born, the trauma of a nation which had lost trust in its leadership and hope for a future:

> Your father, my child, was carried off by the wind
> Of the mountain. In a foreign land
> Your father remained, my child.
> Somebody made a mistake, my beautiful son
> And now you will not be.

(Harnik, *And at Night*)

Yet poetry of protest, which surged in the early 1980s, did not last long as a form of expression for most of the poets. Many of them again resorted to lyricism, perhaps as a sign of despair, of recognition that words can barely provide outlet, let alone help. Among the few who still continued to write war poetry and political poetry were Ramy Ditzanny, Eitan Kalinski, and Aryeh Sivan, who asked in his *A Poet's Dilemma*:

> What will a poet, who suspects that his king
> Is nothing but a demon, do?
> Will he sit at his desk, write a good poem
> In which he will expand his testimony, enrich and improve it,
> And will express in it, in imagery concocted in exact dosage
> Of revealing and hiding—
> As required by the art of correct poetry—
> The horror which crawls upon its belly in it
> Like a viper?

This open challenge to "the art of correct poetry" has remained unanswered. During the Gulf War, David Avidan and Pinhas Sadeh were among the only veteran poets who found it necessary to express themselves in regard to the situation, and the arena was largely left to younger poets like Ilan Sheinfeld or to "amateurs."

The special circumstances of the Gulf War transformed the nature of Israeli war poetry. The distress and despair typical of earlier poetry were still there, yet the poems were clean of cynicism and self-criticism and their political overtones were muted. The solemn, somber tone of early poetry returned with a twist: the Gulf War was the first in which the feeling of historical inevitability, for better or worse, was replaced by the sense of helplessness. The rush to the sealed rooms and the use of gas masks gave rise to apocalyptic imagery and strong allusions to the Holocaust, allusions which up to that time had been largely kept out of war poetry. Poems turned inward, became locked in,

> Now I will close myself for the night in my sealed room,
> With the haunting voices which came to visit me
> From the time we were burnt in Auschwitz.

> (Sheinfeld, *War Night 6*)

and, while in earlier decades hope was vested in the future, during and after the Gulf War eyes were turned to the dark past:

> At us, the eyes of our fathers and mothers are gazing.
> Innumerable eyes, for two thousand years now, from the ghettos of Worms and Mainz,
> Toledo, Nemirov, Kishinev, Treblinka, Auschwitz.
> And their eyes—what do they say? Their eyes are saying: Children of ours, grandchildren, happy are you.
> For you do not dig grave-holes for yourselves in the snow, nor burn in furnaces of fire, like us.

For you are not torn apart by the teeth of dogs, nor impaled within
    your mother's belly.
For you have power, and you dwell upon your own land.
You are our consolation… insofar as any kind of consolation is
    possible.

(Sadeh, *At Nightfall*)

War poetry of the early nineties is characterized by great fatigue and
quiet despair. Memorial Day of 1994 was marked by Amichai's painful
dirge entitled *Now Who Will Remember the Ones That Remember?*
Haiim Gouri's *Like Beirut*, which concludes our anthology, summarizes
both the personal perspective of a poet who has struggled with war for
over fifty years, and the collective emotions of a nation which is desperate
for change:

Like Beirut I worship other gods,
Half-destroyed.
Growing deaf, growing gray.
And there is no sign in me of a cease-fire, of a short respite,
Of sharpshooters' repose.

Various sentiments are associated with war, and many of the universal
as well as the particular are reflected in this volume of Israeli war poetry.
It provides insight into the moods of a nation troubled by memories of his-
torical catastrophes, strongly driven to survive and prosper in the turbu-
lent Middle East, and fully comprehending the price of living in a constant
state of war. Determination to survive, and live by the sword if need be,
and going to battle against one's will have always co-existed in the Israeli
psyche. This special combination has produced poetry which is perhaps
best characterized by what is absent from it—there is no rattling of
sabers. Israeli war poetry is that of quiet strength, simple words, and
emotions which are expressed on the "revealing" rather than the "hiding"
side. As such, even if not quite in line with "the art of correct poetry," it is
presented here for the reader.

Esther Raizen
November 1995

Poems

Prayer
Haiim Gouri

Bestow a blessing on the young men, because the time has come;
See them, silent and ready,
Their eyes burning.
Look, evening is falling,
Wind in the treetops, pines aquiver.
There will be battle tonight. And they are so very few.
Bless them, because the time has come.
Stars are enkindling
As the many troops gather from all about.
Who will see the light of day?
Who will have fallen and died?
Will there be victory or, instead, defeat and the grave?
Bless them, bless those going out to the battle.
Bless their weaponry that it may not miss, bless their homes.
Bless this nation, its youth and its fighters,
Until war is done.
Behold— they have left, quiet, their footsteps become lost
Darkness is thick, and night upon the mountains.
Bless them, because the time has come.
Bestow a blessing on the young men.   ℬ

The Death Of The Man In The Field
Haiim Gouri

Send not your wild supplications to the gods dwelling in their lofty abodes.
Nor stand in wait at the steps of their temples with eyes yearning for sleep.
Last stars. Last stars in the world
And strong winds in the mountains. Opaque darkness.

There yonder, on the border of the living, they found you lying, a human bundle.
Your flesh they carried off for sale, your soul to the markets.
Your hair yet wet and warm, your hands slowly moving
And your eyes wide, seeking cascading fireworks.

תְּפִלָּה
חיים גורי

הָבֵא בְּרָכָה לַנְּעָרִים, כִּי בָּאָה עֵת.
רְאֵה אוֹתָם שׁוֹתְקִים וּנְכוֹנִים,
וְעֵינֵיהֶם דּוֹלְקוֹת.
רְאֵה, יוֹרֵד הָעֶרֶב,
רוּחַ בַּצַּמָּרוֹת, הָאָרֶץ מְרַטֵּט.
קְרָב יִהְיֶה הַלַּיְלָה. וְהֵמָּה מְעַטִּים מְאֹד.
בָּרְכֵם, כִּי בָּאָה עֵת.
כּוֹכְבִים הֵצִתוּ,
וּמַחֲנוֹת רַבִּים נֶאֱסָפִים מֵעֵבֶר.
מִי יִרְאֶה אוֹר-יוֹם!
מִי נָפַל וָמֵת?
הַנִּצָּחוֹן אוֹ אִם תְּבוּסָה וָקֶבֶר?
בָּרְכֵם, בֶּרֶךְ יוֹצְאֵי לַמִּלְחָמָה.
בֶּרֶךְ נִשְׁקָם לְבַל יַחְטִיא, בֶּרֶךְ בֵּיתָם.
בֶּרֶךְ אֶת זֶה הָעָם, אֶת נְעָרָיו וְלוֹחֲמָיו
עַד קְרָב יִתָּם.
הִנֵּה יָצְאוּ שְׁקֵטִים וְצַעֲדָם אוֹבֵד
וַעֲלָטָה כְּבֵדָה וְלַיְלָה בֶּהָרִים.
בָּרְכֵם, כִּי בָּאָה עֵת.
הָבֵא בְּרָכָה לַנְּעָרִים.

מוֹתוֹ שֶׁל הָאִישׁ בַּשָּׂדֶה
חיים גורי

אַל תִּשְׁלַח תְּחִנָּתְךָ הַפְּרוּעָה לָאֵלִים הַשּׁוֹכְנִים בִּזְבוּלָם.
אַל תִּנְצֹר מַדְרֵגוֹת הֵיכָלָם בְּעֵינַיִם כָּלוֹת לִתְנוּמָה.
כּוֹכָבִים אַחֲרוֹנִים. כּוֹכָבִים אַחֲרוֹנִים בָּעוֹלָם
וְרוּחוֹת חֲזָקוֹת בֶּהָרִים. אֲפֵלָה אֲטוּמָה.

שָׁם, עַל גְּבוּל הַחַיִּים, מְצָאוּךָ מֻטָּל, צְרוּר אָדָם.
אֶת בְּשָׂרְךָ הֵם נָשְׂאוּ לְמִמְכָּר, נִשְׁמָתְךָ לַשְּׁוָקִים.
שְׂעָרְךָ עוֹד רָטֹב וְחַמִּים, וְיָדֶיךָ נָעוֹת לְאַט
וְעֵינֶיךָ תְּרוֹת לִרְוָחָה מַפְּלֵי זִיקוּקִין.

Women had primped in response to your presence. Yet it will not be women
   crying over your death.
Spring burgeons in the fields of others, but your field is nettles, nettles.
"Once on a time, in that huddle of wooden houses he was born to good luck, a
   male child,
And sent forth his first cry into the gulf of cerulean skies."

Clods, clods, dew falling, trees and shadows.
Moments of terrible anticipation, the clarity of a sparkling firefly.
A head of a man. The murmur of a distant city.
Who would listen to the dimming of the heartbeat that breaks the silence?   ৯০

BEHOLD, OUR BODIES ARE LAID OUT
Haiim Gouri

   To Dani and his friends

Behold, our bodies are laid out— a long, long row.
Our faces are altered. Death looks out of our eyes. We do not breathe.
Twilight dwindles and evening falls over the mountain.
Look— we do not come upright to tread the roads in the last light of sunset.
We do not make love, we do not strum strings in softly gentle sound,
We do not shout in the groves when the wind comes streaming through the forest.

Behold, our mothers are stooped and silent, and our comrades hold back from
   weeping,
And there are explosions of grenades nearby and fire and signs of an impending
   storm!
Will you indeed bury us now?
We would rise, coming out as before, and we would live again.
We would stagger, awesome and great and rushing to help,
For all within us is still living, and racing in the arteries, and fervid.

We did not break faith. See, our weapons are held close with their cartridges
   empty, out of bullets.
They remember our words to the very last. Their barrels are still hot
And our blood is splattered along the paths step upon step.
All we could, we did, until the very last one fell, no more to rise.
Will we indeed be blamed if we remain dead at evening time
With our lips fixed to the hard stony ground?

נָשִׁים הִתְיַפּוּ לְמוּלְךָ, לֹא נָשִׁים יִתְיַפְּחוּ עַל מוֹתְךָ.
הָאָבִיב בִּשְׂדוֹתָם שֶׁל זָרִים, וְשָׂדְךָ חֲרוּלִים חֲרוּלִים.
"אֵי-פַעַם, בִּשְׁכוּנַת הַצְּרִיפִים, הוּא נוֹלַד לְמַזָּל, בֶּן זָכָר,
וְשָׁלַח אֶת בִּכְיוֹ הָרִאשׁוֹן אֶל עָמְקָם שֶׁל שָׁמַיִם תְּכֵלִים."

רְגָבִים, רְגָבִים, טַל נוֹפֵל, אִילָנוֹת וּצְלָלִים.
רְגָעִים אֲיֻמֵּי צִפִּיָּה, גַּחְלִילִית בְּהִירָה וְדוֹלֶקֶת.
רֹאשׁ אָדָם. רַעַשׁ עִיר רְחוֹקָה.
מִי מַקְשִׁיב לְעִמְעוּם הַלְמוּתוֹ שֶׁל הַלֵּב הַשּׁוֹבֵר אֶת הַשֶּׁקֶט?

הִנֵּה מֻטָּלוֹת גּוּפוֹתֵינוּ

חיים גורי

לדני וחבריו

רְאֵה, הִנֵּה מֻטָּלוֹת גּוּפוֹתֵינוּ שׁוּרָה אֲרֻכָּה, אֲרֻכָּה.
פָּנֵינוּ שֻׁנּוּ. הַמָּוֶת נִשְׁקָף מֵעֵינֵינוּ. אֵינֶנּוּ נוֹשְׁמִים.
כָּבִים נְגוֹהוֹת אַחֲרוֹנִים וְהָעֶרֶב צוֹנֵחַ בָּהָר.
רְאֵה, לֹא נָקוּם לְהַלֵּךְ בַּדְּרָכִים לְאוֹרָהּ שֶׁל שְׁקִיעָה רְחוֹקָה.
לֹא נֶאֱהַב, לֹא נַרְעִיד לֹא נַרְעִיד בְּצְלִילִים עֲגִים וּדְמוּמִים,
לֹא נִשְׁאַג בַּגַּנִּים עֵת הָרוּחַ עוֹבֶרֶת בַּיַּעַר.

רְאֵה, אִמּוֹתֵינוּ שְׁחוֹחוֹת וְשׁוֹתְקוֹת, וְרֵעֵינוּ חוֹנְקִים אֶת בִּכְיָם,
וּמִפָּץ רִמּוֹנִים מִקָּרוֹב וּדְלֵקָה וְאוֹתוֹת מְבַשְּׂרִים סְעָרָה!
הַאֻמְנָם תַּטְמִינוּנוּ כָּעֵת?
הֵן נָקוּם, וְהֵגַחְנוּ שֵׁנִית כְּמוֹ אָז, וְשַׁבְנוּ שֵׁנִית לִתְחִיָּה.
נְדַדֶּה אֲיֻמִּים וּגְדוֹלִים וְאָצִים לְעֶזְרָה,
כִּי הַכֹּל בְּקִרְבֵּנוּ עוֹד חַי וְשׁוֹצֵף בָּעוֹרְקִים וְלוֹהֵט.

לֹא בָּגַדְנוּ. רְאֵה, נִשְׁקֵנוּ צָמוּד וּמֵרֻקָּן כַּדּוּרִים, אַשְׁפָּתֵנוּ רֵיקָה.
הוּא זוֹכֵר מְלוֹתֵינוּ עַד תֹּם. עוֹד קָנָיו לוֹהֲטִים
וְדָמֵנוּ מֵתָז בַּשְּׁבִילִים שַׁעַל-שַׁעַל.
עָשִׂינוּ כְּכֹל שֶׁנּוּכַל, עַד נָפַל הָאַחֲרוֹן וְלֹא קָם.
הַאֻמְנָם נֵאָשֵׁם אִם נוֹתַרְנוּ עִם עֶרֶב מֵתִים
וּשְׂפָתֵינוּ צְמוּדוֹת אֶל אַדְמַת הַסְּלָעִים הַקָּשָׁה?

Look— what a great wide night.
Look— the blossom of stars in the dark.
Scent of pines. You will bury us now, with clods of dirt on our faces.
Here, among the bristling barbed wire, the trenches, here we are all together.
New day, do not forget! Do not forget!!
Because we carried your name until death closed our eyes.

Behold our bodies are laid out, a long row, and we are not breathing.
But the wind, full of breath, is strong in the mountains.
Morning is born, and dew-bringing sunset exults.
We will still come back, we will meet, and return like red flowers.
You will recognize us at once, as the voiceless "Mountain Platoon."
Then will we blossom. When the scream of the last shot shall have fallen to
    silence in the mountains.   🙠

The Ones Forgotten
Haiim Gouri

I remember them.
They were my comrades.
Such is the way of time: to swirl columns of dust,
To extinguish with them the ember of remembrance.
And this is the secret of blood: to gush forth and splatter
On rock and dirt
And fade into oblivion at the firstborn of rains.
But they were my friends.
Those, who glow like hot ashes
At the breath from my nostrils.
Those, who are lofty as God's heavens.
Those heroes who feed maggots in the pestilential stench,
Make a meal for buzzards and hyenas.
Knife-men with hard fists, with beauty of stature,
Whose quiffs were the abode of birds
And whose hearts, the abode of love.
Sons of dynamite at insane barricades
Of barbed wire and fury.
Numbers without names on the army forms.
Calcined bones in the torrid oven

רְאֵה אֵיזֶה לַיְלָה גָּדוֹל וְרָחָב.
רְאֵה, פְּרִיחַת כּוֹכָבִים בַּמַּחְשָׁךְ.
נִיחוֹחֵי אֳרָנִים. תִּקְבְּרוּנוּ כָּעֵת, וְרִגְבֵי הֶעָפָר עַל פָּנֵינוּ.
פֹּה הַתַּיִל סָמוּר, חֲפִירוֹת, פֹּה כֻּלָּנוּ יַחְדָּיו.
יוֹם חָדָשׁ, אַל תִּשָׁכַח! אַל תִּשָּׁכַח!
כִּי נָשָׂאנוּ שִׁמְךָ, עַד הַמָּוֶת עָצַם אֶת עֵינֵינוּ.

הִנֵּה מֻטָּלוֹת גוּפוֹתֵינוּ שׁוּרָה אֲרֻכָּה, וְאֵינֶנּוּ נוֹשְׁמִים.
אַךְ הָרוּחַ עַזָּה בֶּהָרִים וְנוֹשֶׁמֶת.
וְהַבֹּקֶר נוֹלָד, וּזְרִיחַת הַטְּלָלִים רוֹנֶנֶת.
עוֹד נָשׁוּב, נִפָּגֵשׁ, נַחְזֹר כִּפְרָחִים אֲדֻמִּים.
תַּכִּירוּנוּ מִיָּד, זוֹ "מַחְלֶקֶת הָהָר" הָאִלֶּמֶת.
אָז נִפְרַח. עֵת תִּדֹּם בֶּהָרִים זַעֲקַת יְרִיָּה אַחֲרוֹנָה.

הַנִּשְׁכָּחִים
חיים גורי

אֲנִי זוֹכֵר אוֹתָם.
הֵם הָיוּ רֵעַי.
זוֹ דֶּרֶךְ הָעִתִּים: עַרְבֵּל תִּמְרוֹת אָבָק,
כַּבּוֹת בָּם עַד תֻּמָּה גַּחֶלֶת זִכָּרוֹן.
וְזֶהוּ סוֹד הַדָּם: פָּרוֹץ וְהִנָּתֵז
עַל סֶלַע וְעָפָר
וּגְוֹעַ נְשִׁיָּה עִם בְּכוֹר הַסַּגְרִירִים.
אַךְ הֵם הָיוּ רֵעַי.
הַלָּלוּ, הַזּוֹרְחִים כְּרֶמֶץ אֲדַמְדָּם
עִם נְשִׁימַת אַפִּי.
הַלָּלוּ, הַגְּבֹהִים כִּשְׁמֵי הָאֱלֹהִים.
רְמַת הַגִּבּוֹרִים בְּקֶטֶב הָרֵיחוֹת
וּסְעֻדַּת הַבַּז וְהַצְּבוֹעִים.
סַכִּינָאִים נוּקְשֵׁי-אֶגְרוֹף, יְפֵי קוֹמָה,
שֶׁבְּלוֹרִיתָם מִשְׁכַּן הַצִּפֳּרִים
וּלְבָבָם מִשְׁכַּן הָאַהֲבָה.
יַלְדֵי הַדִּינָמִיט אֶל מַחְסוֹמֵי תִּזְזִית
שֶׁל תַּיִל וְחָרוֹן.
סְפָרוֹת לְלֹא כִּנּוּי בְּטֹפֶס הַצָּבָא.
עַצְמוֹת הַגִּיר בְּמִשְׂרְפוֹת חַמָּה

Of the sun of the East.
Lead and flesh.
I remember them.   &

To The Memory Of A Comrade
Hillel Omer

> *To Haiim ben Dor, of blessed memory*

Haiim,
Behold you have returned to your Mother,
To this earth that you loved.
And we your comrades stand and ponder: There now— Haiim is gone.
None of us weeps. We are men who do not cry.
— Perhaps my eyes are a little moist, so be it, I am the sentimental one in the
    group.

Haiim,
You have returned to your Mother,
Entering the cycle of her blossomings and harvests, the eternal cycle.
Alas, you will no longer be with us.
You will not join in our parties,
You will not experience joy, you will not laugh, nor smoke your pipe.

But we, we will be happy again for many more years;
And it is possible that we may not always remember you!

Greatgodalmighty!
It is possible that we will forget you!

Indeed you will laugh no more. Nor will we have your jokes to laugh at;
For you have returned to your Mother that you loved.
And never again will we say to you: On Saturday at ten we meet, if only it does
    not rain!
Nor will you again say: Saturday is Saturday!

Haiim,
We loved you.
In a poem one does not write that you were loved,
But you were!

שֶׁל שֶׁמֶשׁ הַמִּזְרָח.
עוֹפֶרֶת וּבָשָׂר.
אֲנִי זוֹכֵר אוֹתָם.

לְנִשְׁמַת רֵעַ

ע. הלל

לחיים בן-דור ז״ל

חַיִּים,
הִנֵּה שַׁבְתָּ אֶל אִמְּךָ,
אֶל הָאֲדָמָה הַזֹּאת שֶׁאָהַבְתָּ.
וַאֲנַחְנוּ רֵעֶיךָ עוֹמְדִים וְתוֹהִים: הִנֵּה חַיִּים הָלַךְ.
וְאִישׁ מֵאִתָּנוּ אֵינֶנּוּ בּוֹכֶה. אֲנַחְנוּ אֲנָשִׁים שֶׁאֵינָם בּוֹכִים.
— אוּלַי עֵינַי רְטֻבּוֹת מְעַט, מֵילָא, אֲנִי הָרַגְשָׁן שֶׁבַּחֲבוּרָה.

חַיִּים,
אַתָּה שַׁבְתָּ אֶל אִמְּךָ,
וְאַתָּה נִכְנָס לְמַעְגַּל פְּרִיחוֹתֶיהָ וּתְנוּבוֹתֶיהָ, מַעְגַּל-הַנֶּצַח.
אֲבָל אִתָּנוּ לֹא תִּהְיֶה.
לֹא תָסֵב בִּמְסִבּוֹתֵינוּ,
לֹא תִשְׂמַח עוֹד, לֹא תִּצְחַק, וְלֹא תְעַשֵּׁן מִקְטֶרֶת.

וַאֲנַחְנוּ נָשׁוּב וְנִשְׂמַח עוֹד שָׁנִים רַבּוֹת;
וְאֶפְשָׁר שֶׁלֹּא נִזְכֹּר אוֹתְךָ תָּמִיד!

אֵל אֱלֹהִים!
אֶפְשָׁר שֶׁנִּשְׁכַּח אוֹתְךָ!

כֵּן. אַתָּה לֹא תִּצְחַק עוֹד. וְאָנוּ לֹא נִצְחַק לַהֲלָצוֹתֶיךָ;
הֲלֹא שַׁבְתָּ אֶל אִמְּךָ אֲשֶׁר אָהַבְתָּ.
וּכְבָר לֹא נֹאמַר לְךָ: בְּשַׁבָּת בְּעֶשֶׂר נִפָּגְשִׁים, וְרַק שֶׁלֹּא יֵרֵד גֶּשֶׁם!
וְאַתָּה כְּבָר לֹא תֹּאמַר: שַׁבָּת זֶה שַׁבָּת!

חַיִּים,
אֲנַחְנוּ אָהַבְנוּ אוֹתְךָ,
בְּשִׁיר לֹא כּוֹתְבִים שֶׁהָיִיתָ אָהוּב,
אֲבָל הָיִיתָ אָהוּב!

We did not weep for you,
But our souls did.
Our souls are not soldiers, and they cry upon the death of their sister-soul.
You will surely forgive them.

Oh, our souls are not soldiers, and are not inured to war:
They weep when they are distressed,
They are little girls.

Haiim,
You were a child.
You were just an ordinary person: a man,
You loved!
And it is possible that you did not see the pillar of love that went before you;
We did!
A pity that we had not told you that before.
And yet it is possible that we could not.
We are ordinary people, sparing of compliments.

A pillar of love!
It is not a shelter from fire!
Today one does not win with love. Perhaps tomorrow, or the day after.

May it be so!   ℘

WORD FROM THE GRAY SOLDIERS
Hillel Omer

The things that our hearts wish to say to our girls,
We shall speak in the stillness of a whisper.
Because the words are greater than the strength of our hearts,
And our hearts whisper a shout— shouters of love are we.
We are the gray soldiers, devotees of blood.
We shout-shout, because we have feeling hearts in our chests.

O girls,
We cherish all that is beautiful in you.
Because we love the beautiful:
Because we are ardent men.

לֹא בָּכִינוּ עָלֶיךָ,
אֲבָל נַפְשׁוֹתֵינוּ הָיוּ בּוֹכוֹת.
נַפְשׁוֹתֵינוּ אֵינָן אַנְשֵׁי-צָבָא, וְהֵן בּוֹכוֹת בְּמוֹת אֲחוֹתָן.
הֲלֹא תִּסָּלַח לָהֶן.

הוֹ, נַפְשׁוֹתֵינוּ אֵינָן אַנְשֵׁי-צָבָא, וְאֵינָן לְמוּדוֹת-מִלְחָמָה:
הֵן בּוֹכוֹת בַּצַּר לָהֶן,
הֵן יְלָדוֹת קְטַנּוֹת.

חַיִּים,
אַתָּה הָיִיתָ יֶלֶד.
הָיִיתָ פָּשׁוּט: אָדָם,
אָהַבְתָּ!
וְאֶפְשָׁר שֶׁלֹּא רָאִיתָ אֶת עֲנַן-הָאַהֲבָה שֶׁהָלַךְ לְפָנֶיךָ;
אֲנַחְנוּ רָאִינוּ!
חֲבָל שֶׁלֹּא אָמַרְנוּ לְךָ זֹאת קֹדֶם.
וְאוּלַי אֶפְשָׁר שֶׁלֹּא יָכֹלְנוּ לוֹמַר.
אֲנַחְנוּ אֲנָשִׁים פְּשׁוּטִים, וּמְקַמְּצִים בְּמַחֲמָאוֹת.

עֲנַן שֶׁל אַהֲבָה!
אֵינוֹ מַחֲסֶה-מָגֵן מִפְּנֵי-אֵשׁ!
הַיּוֹם אֵין מְנַצְּחִים בְּאַהֲבָה. אֶפְשָׁר שֶׁמָּחָר-מָחֳרָתַיִם.

מִי יִתֵּן!

זֶבַר הַחַיָּלִים הָאֲפֹרִים
ע. הלל

אֶת הַדְּבָרִים אֲשֶׁר יֵשׁ עַל לִבֵּנוּ לוֹמַר לְנַעֲרוֹתֵינוּ,
נֹאמַר בְּדוּמִיַּת לַחַשׁ.
כִּי הַדְּבָרִים גְּדוֹלִים מִכֹּחַ לִבֵּנוּ,
וְלִבֵּנוּ מְלַחֵשׁ צְעָקָה — צוֹעֲקֵי-אַהֲבָה אֲנַחְנוּ.
אֲנַחְנוּ הַחַיָּלִים הָאֲפֹרִים, עוֹבְדֵי-הַדָּם.
צוֹעֲקִים-צוֹעֲקִים אֲנַחְנוּ, כִּי לֵב לָנוּ בְּחָזוֹתֵינוּ.

הַנְּעָרוֹת,
אוֹהֲבִים אָנוּ אֶת כָּל הַיָּפֶה שֶׁבָּכֶן.
כִּי עַל-כֵּן אוֹהֲבִים אָנוּ אֶת הַיָּפֶה:
כִּי עַל-כֵּן אֲנָשִׁים אוֹהֲבִים אֲנַחְנוּ.

We are the gray soldiers, the ones whose hands are battle-blackened,
Whose nostrils are death-stenched, whose tongues are parched by the trek.
We shout love into the depths of your souls,
> To the narcissus of your laughter,
> To the melancholy of your blue eyes,
> To the myrrh and aloes of your bodies,
Oh, to such living marble!

For you are more beautiful than the strength of our hearts
And we are more resistant than fire. Like the stones of this land.
But like rock gushing forth a spring when struck by a staff,
We outpour love when you strike longings within us.
Therefore listen, O girls, to the stillness of the night,
To the whispering distances.
This is truly our voice which comes and enfolds you with love
This is truly the beat of our hearts that yearn unfulfilled toward you.

O girls
Listen to the night,
At night, at night, from the north, from the strongholds of the Mountain of God
> From the distances of the moon-struck Negev,
For you our souls are scented with tears.
For you— drunk-drunk with flowers.
The rock did not desiccate the spring,
So how shall we desiccate our souls?

We were not blunted by death. Only our appearance turned gray.
Because, devotees of blood, we were to fight for a homeland.

Homeland,
This is the name given to your love;
Because there is a threshold, which we will reach at the end of all blood.
Within our bodies or without them, we will reach it:
Like butterflies touching the lips of a lily,
Or eagles aloft to the lips of sunset,
We shall reach your beloved lips,
Like the beloved lilies and like the setting sun.

אֲנַחְנוּ הַחַיָּלִים הָאֲפֹרִים, שֶׁיָּדֵינוּ שְׁחוֹרוֹת-מִלְחָמָה,
שֶׁנֶּחְרַיְרֵינוּ צְחוּנֵי-מָוֶת, שֶׁלְּשׁוֹנֵנוּ נֶחֱרָה מִדֶּרֶךְ.
צוֹעֲקִים אָנוּ אַהֲבָה אֶל תּוֹכְכֵי נַפְשׁוֹתֵיכֶן,
אֶל נַרְקִיסֵי צְחוֹקְכֶן,
אֶל תּוּגַת עֵינֵיכֶן הַכְּחֻלּוֹת,
אֶל מוֹר-אָהֳלוֹת גּוּפְכֶן,
הוֹי, אֶל הַשַּׁיִשׁ הֶחָי הַזֶּה!

כִּי יָפִיתֶן מִכֹּחַ לִבֵּנוּ,
וְאָנוּ קָשִׁים מִן הָאֵשׁ. כְּסַלְעֵי הָאָרֶץ הַזֹּאת.
אַךְ כְּמוֹ סֶלַע יָקָר מַעְיָן בְּהַכּוֹת בּוֹ מַטֶּה,
כֵּן נָקַר אַהֲבָה בְּהַכּוֹתְכֶן בָּנוּ כְּסוּפִים.
עַל כֵּן הַקְשֵׁבְנָה, הַנְּעָרוֹת, אֶל דּוּמִיַּת הַלַּיְלָה,
אֶל הַמֶּרְחָבִים הַמִּתְלַחֲשִׁים.
הֲלֹא זֶה קוֹלֵנוּ הַבָּא וּמְסוֹבְבְכֶן אַהֲבָה,
הֲלֹא זוֹ פְּעִימַת לִבֵּנוּ הַנִּשְׁבָּר לִקְרַאתְכֶן.

הַנְּעָרוֹת
הַקְשֵׁבְנָה, לַלַּיְלָה.
בַּלַּיְלָה, בַּלַּיְלָה, מִן הַצָּפוֹן, מִמִּשְׁלָטֵי הַר-הָאֱלֹהִים,
מִמֶּרְחַקֵּי הַנֶּגֶב הַסּוֹהֵר,
אֲלֵיכֶן נַפְשׁוֹתֵינוּ נִיחוֹחוֹת-בֶּכִי.
אֲלֵיכֶן שְׁכוּרוֹת-שְׁכוּרוֹת פְּרָחִים.
הֵן סֶלַע לֹא הוֹבִישׁ מַעְיָן,
וְאֵיךְ נוֹבִישׁ נִשְׁמוֹתֵינוּ?

הֵן לֹא קָהִינוּ מִמָּוֶת. רַק מַרְאֵינוּ הֶאֱפִיר.
כִּי עוֹבְדֵי-דָם הָיִינוּ לִלְחֹם אֶל מוֹלֶדֶת.

מוֹלֶדֶת,
זֶה שֵׁם קָרָא לְאַהֲבַתְכֶן;
כִּי יֵשׁ מִפְתָּן, אֵלָיו נַגִּיעַ בְּאַחֲרִית כָּל דָּם.
בְּגוּפוֹתֵינוּ נַגִּיעַ, אוֹ בִּבְלִי הֱיוֹתָם:
כְּפַרְפָּרִים יַגִּיעוּ עַד שְׂפָתֵי שׁוֹשַׁנָּה,
אוֹ כַּנְּשָׁרִים עַד שְׂפָתֵי הַשְּׁקִיעָה,
נַגִּיעַ עַד שִׂפְתוֹתֵיכֶן הָאֲהוּבוֹת,
כַּשּׁוֹשַׁנִּים הָאֲהוּבוֹת וְכַשֶּׁמֶשׁ הַשּׁוֹקַעַת.

We shall reach them! Because for that we spilled much blood,
                    Blood of comrades and blood of enemies.
And in blood we wrote war— a book cruel of days.

O girls!
Our girls in the villages and cities, waiting at many doorsteps.
Hold for us the bindings of your love— these are the bindings of the power
                    Which extends from you to the far ends of the homeland.

O girls!
Our girls beloved-to-the-depths-of-the-abyss-and-the-god of our hearts!
Listen to the stillness of our shouting hearts!
Lend your ears to the word from the gray soldiers
Oh, open the gates of love for us,
Break for us the locks of all gardens.   ℘

A Squad In The Land
Hillel Omer

Let me sing of ten comrades,
Of an undefeated squad of boys!
— — — — — — — — — —

The mountains of night are high,
And the stars surpassingly strong.
No wind travels, no cricket sings;
In the wadi, covertly, the squad of boys paces, armed,
                    Hand on rifle butt.

Ten boys,
They are like the homeland: rough, with stammering manners, plain stride, in
    love,
There are wise ones, and there are buffoons, and there are ones weighty with
    integrity, knotty!
Yet the heart of all is laughing!
        Because it lives!

Not battle heroes,
No fancy uniform nor splendor,

נַגִּיעַ! כִּי עַל כֵּן שָׁפַכְנוּ דָּם הַרְבֵּה.
דַּם רֵעִים וְדַם אוֹיְבִים.
וּבְדַם כָּתַבְנוּ מִלְחָמָה — סֵפֶר אַכְזָרִי-יָמִים.

הַנְּעָרוֹת!
נַעֲרוֹתֵינוּ בַּכְּפָרִים וּבַקְּרָיוֹת, הַמְחַכּוֹת עַל מִפְתָּנִים רַבִּים.
אֲחַזְנָה לָנוּ כַּבְלֵי אַהֲבַתְכֶן — הֵן אֵלֶּה הֵם כַּבְלֵי הַכֹּחַ
הַנִּמְתָּח מִכֶּן אֶל יַרְכְּתֵי מוֹלֶדֶת.

הַנְּעָרוֹת!
נַעֲרוֹתֵינוּ הָאֲהוּבוֹת עַד-שְׁאוֹל-וֵאלֹהֵי הַלֵּב!
הַקְשַׁבְנָה אֶל הַדּוּמִיָּה שֶׁבְּלִבֵּנוּ הַצּוֹעֵק!
כְּרֶינָה אָזְנֵיכֶן לִדְבַר הַחַיָּלִים הָאֲפֹרִים
הוֹ, פִּתְחֶנָה לָנוּ שַׁעֲרֵי-הָאַהֲבָה.
שַׁבְרֶנָה לָנוּ מַנְעוּלֵי כָּל הַגַּנִּים.

כִּתָּה בָּאָרֶץ
ע. הלל

הָבָה אָשִׁיר עַל עֲשָׂרָה רֵעִים,
עַל כִּתַּת-נְעָרִים לֹא-נֻצָּחָה!
- - - - - - - - - -

גְּבוֹהִים הָרֵי הַלַּיְלָה,
וַעֲצוּמִים מְאֹד הַכּוֹכָבִים.
לֹא רוּחַ שָׁט, לֹא שִׁיר הַצְּרָצָרִים;
בַּנְּדִי, בְּהֶסְתֵּר כִּתַּת הַנְּעָרִים פּוֹסַעַת, חֲמִשָּׁה,
יָדָהּ עַל קַת.

עֲשֶׂרֶת נְעָרִים,
כְּמוֹתָם, כַּמָּכוֹרָה: קַשִּׁיחִים, עֶלְגֵּי נִמּוּס, פְּשׁוּטֵי הַלּוּךְ, מְאֹהָבִים,
יֵשׁ חֲכָמִים, וְיֵשׁ לֵצִים, וְיֵשׁ כְּבְדֵי-יַשְׁרוּת, מְסֻקְסִים!
אַךְ לֵב כֻּלָּם צוֹחֵק!
כִּי חַי!

לֹא גִּבּוֹרֵי קְרָבוֹת,
לֹא שְׂרָד וְלֹא הָדָר,

But in the rugged tunic, the spiked boot,
                    In the knitted Palmach cap!
My ten friends are pacing, a squad,
                    A squad in the Land!
A march of ones in love— as simple as it sounds— with this land,
                                        With this wadi!
With this mountain and its bristling stones.

Ten boys. Of no one kind is their ammunition,
Nor was it only one girl who enchanted their souls.
Each with his unique laughter,
Each with his secret, in the book or the vineyard, in melody or argument,
Ten boys, but their heart is one—
                    And it is molded from Earth!

Therefore they will not despise Her in the muddiness of shoe and garment;
There is no spite nor praise.
For She is with them forever,
In that She is their mother to the end,
Whole like the night.

The uniform is not "nonsense" to them,
Nor is their essence in bloodiness and hurrahs,
But in the jokes, whispered in the dark rhythm of their steps,
And in the artless and unaffected smiles!

The mountains of night are high,
And the stars surpassingly strong.
No wind travels, no cricket sings;
In the wadi, covertly, the squad of boys paces,
                    Armed,
                    The march of those who love!

Arise, arise, my ten comrades!
Pour forth your laughter in lead, my comrades!
Pour forth your song in fire!
And, in the rugged tunic, in the spiked boot,
                    In the knitted Palmach cap!
Arise, O undefeated squad!

Not the army of Goliath with his mighty boast,
                    With armor, with scales!

כָּךְ, בִּמְעִיל הַגַּס, בַּנַּעַל הַסְּמוּרָה,
בַּגֶּרֶב הַפַּלְמָחִי הַזָּקוּר!
פּוֹסְעִים עֲשֶׂרֶת יְדִידַי, כִּתָּה,
כִּתָּה בָּאָרֶץ!
מַסַּע מְאֹהָבִים, פְּשׁוּטוֹ כְּמַשְׁמָעוֹ, בָּאֲדָמָה הַזֹּאת,
בְּזֶה הַוָּדִי!
בְּזֶה הָהָר סוֹמֵר-הַטֶּרֶשׁ.

עֲשֶׂרֶת נְעָרִים, לֹא תִּחְמָשְׁתָּם אַחַת,
וְלֹא אַחַת הַנַּעֲרָה אֲשֶׁר קָסְמָה נַפְשָׁם.
אִישׁ-אִישׁ וְנִיב צְחוֹקוֹ,
אִישׁ-אִישׁ וְכִבְשׁוֹנוֹ, בְּסֵפֶר אוֹ בַכֶּרֶם בַּצְּלִיל אוֹ בְּכוֹחַ,
עֲשֶׂרֶת נְעָרִים , אַךְ לְבָבָם אֶחָד —
וְהוּא יָצוּק מֵאֲדָמָה!

עַל כֵּן לֹא בּוֹז יָבוֹזוּ לָהּ בְּרִפְשׁוֹנָהּ בַּנַּעַל וּבַבֶּגֶד;
לֹא בּוּז וְלֹא הֵלֶל.
שֶׁהִיא עִמָּם עַד קֵץ,
שֶׁהִיא אִמָּם עַד תֹּם,
אַחַת כְּמוֹ הַלֵּיל.

לֹא הֶבֶל הַמַּדִּים לָהֶם.
לֹא עִקָּרָם בַּדָּם וּבְהֵידָד,
כִּי עִקָּרָם בַּהֲלָצָה, שֶׁנִּתְלַחֲשָׁה בַּקֶּצֶב הָאָפֵל,
וּבַחִיּוּךְ הָעַרְמוּמִי וְהַתָּמִים!

גְּבוֹהִים הָרֵי הַלַּיְלָה,
וַעֲצוּמִים מְאֹד הַכּוֹכָבִים.
לֹא רוּחַ שָׁט, לֹא שִׁיר הַצַּרְצָרִים;
בַּוָּדִי, בְּהֶסְתֵּר כִּתַּת הַנְּעָרִים פּוֹסַעַת,
חֲמִשָּׁה,
מַסַּע הָאוֹהֲבִים!

עוּרוּ, עוּרוּ, עֲשֶׂרֶת רֵעַי!
תְּנוּ צְחוֹקְכֶם בָּעוֹפֶרֶת, רֵעַי!
תְּנוּ מִזְמוֹרְכֶם בָּאֵשׁ!
כָּךְ, בִּמְעִיל הַגַּס, בַּנַּעַל הַסְּמוּרָה,
בַּגֶּרֶב הַפַּלְמָחִי הַזָּקוּר!
עוּרִי הַכִּתָּה הַלֹּא-נֻצָּחָה!

לֹא צָבָא גָּלְיָת אַדִּיר הָרַהַב,
בְּשִׁרְיוֹן, בְּקַשְׂקַשִׂים!

Not so!
But the sons of a shepherd-nation, the ones who left the sheep in their pens,
This is the army of David!
    And he is beautiful of eyes!
To him alone,
To him alone the singing women answer:
    He has slain, slain his ten thousands

And King David is the sweet singer of Israel!   ෨

AROUND THE CAMPFIRE
Nathan Alterman

For seven years of the Palmach, Nisan 5708

Their nation was no mother to them.
Nor did she know of it when they went out on the road.
It was a deep and breathing night
As always in the month of Nisan.
And in it a group of nameless young men sat
With uncovered elbows and knees.

They listened, attending in quietness,
Or wove an argument into the discussion.
In front of them, over some blazing logs
A campfire curvetted in the wind.
Nothing more. But in the stubborn history of the nation
That night became engraved in Time.

The yoke, as simple as earth,
They carried without a backward look.
No shofar was sounded before them,
Nor were their heads stroked on a winter night.
No. With sleeves tied around the neck from behind,
Only their sweaters embraced them.

Stiff boots, knapsacks,
A meal of olives and dates,

כִּי לֹא!
כִּי בְּנֵי אֲמָה-רוֹעָה, נוֹטְשֵׁי הַצֹּאן בַּמִּכְלָאוֹת,
זֶה צְבָא דָוִד!
וְ ה וּ א יְ פֵ ה - עֵ י נָ יִ ם!
אַךְ לוֹ,
אַךְ לוֹ תַּעֲנֶינָה הַנָּשִׁים הַמְשַׂחֲקוֹת:
הִ כָּ ה, הִ כָּ ה בְּ ר ְ ב ְ ב וֹ תָ י ו

וְהַמֶּלֶךְ דָוִד נְעִים-זְמִירוֹת-יִשְׂרָאֵל!

מְסַבִּיב לַמְּדוּרָה
נתן אלתרמן

עם שבע שנים לפלמ"ח, ניסן תשי"ח

אֲמָתָם לֹא הָיְתָה לָהֶם אֵם.
לֹא יָדְעָה בְּצֵאתָם לַדֶּרֶךְ.
הָיָה לַיְלָה עָמֹק וְנוֹשֵׁם
כְּתָמִיד בְּנִיסָן-הַיָּרֵחַ.
וְיָשְׁבָה בּוֹ עֲדַת נְעָרִים בְּנֵי-בְּלִי-שֵׁם,
חֲשׂוּפֵי מַרְפְּקִים וָבֶרֶךְ.

הֵם הִקְשִׁיבוּ הַקְשֵׁב וְהַחֲרֵשׁ
אוֹ שִׁלְּבוּ בְשִׂיחָה דְּבַר-וְכֹחַ.
לִפְנֵיהֶם, עֲלֵי רֶגֶל שֶׁל אֵשׁ,
מְדוּרָה חָגָה-נָעָה בָּרוּחַ.
לֹא יוֹתֵר.   אַךְ בִּכְתָב הָאֻמָּה הֶעָקֵשׁ
אוֹתוֹ-לַיְלָה נֶחֱרַת עֲלֵי לוּחַ.

אֶת הָעֹל הַפָּשׁוּט כְּעָפָר
הֵם נָשְׂאוּ בְּלִי הַבֵּט אָחוֹרָה.
לֹא תָּקַע לִפְנֵיהֶם הַשּׁוֹפָר,
לֹא לֵטַף קָדְקֳדָם בְּלֵיל-חֹרֶף.
לֹא.   בִּשְׁנֵי שַׂרְווּלִים הַקְּשׁוּרִים לַצַּנָּאר
רַק הַסְּוֶדֶר חִבְּקָם מֵעֹרֶף.

נַעֲלַיִם נֻקְשׁוֹת, יַלְקוּטִים,
סְעֻדָּה שֶׁל זֵיתִים וּפְרִי-תָּמָר,

Battered aluminum cups
Camaraderie— and sacrifice beyond all saying.
What more can we add?… Of such small things
Are legends born. This is The Real Stuff.

What shall we sing of them— what shall we sing?
They do it better than we.
They themselves compose their own verses;
Even books, they have already penned…
Such is the quality of the Palmach. It leaves
No task for those who are "not of ours"…

Now this must be said:
Young man, let it be known—
Among the great jubilations of this era
There is nothing beyond the beauty of your humble celebration.
Facing you the nation on the verge of freedom
Bows. And weeps. Understand her.   ⁊

THE SILVER PLATTER
Nathan Alterman

> 'A state is not served to a people on a silver platter'
> Haiim Weizmann

…The land is hushed, a reddening sun
Slowly dims
Over smoking borders.
And a Nation stands— heart-torn yet alive … —
To encounter the miracle
The only miracle…

In preparation for ceremony she rises athwart the moon's crescent
And stands, before daybreak, swathed in celebration and awe.
— — Then from afar come
A maid and a youth
And slowly, slowly they pace towards the Nation.

וְסִפְלֵי אֲלוּמִינְיוּם קְמוּטִים
וְרֵעוּת, וְקָרְבָּן לְאֵין אֹמֶר.
מַה נּוֹסִיף וְנֹאמַר?.. מִדְּבָרִים פְּעוּטִים
נוֹצָרוֹת אַגָּדוֹת. זֶה הַחֹמֶר.

מַה נָּשִׁיר עֲלֵיהֶם? מַה נָּשִׁיר?
הֵם עוֹשִׂים זֹאת יָפֶה מֵאִתָּנוּ.
בְּעַצְמָם הֵם כּוֹתְבִים לָהֶם שִׁיר,
וַאֲפִלּוּ סְפָרִים כְּבָר נָתְנוּ ...
זֶהוּ טִיב הַפַּלְמָ"ח. הוּא אֵינֶנּוּ מַשְׁאִיר
כָּל מְלָאכָה לְ"שֶּׁלֹּא מִשֶּׁלָּנוּ" ...

אֲבָל כָּכָה יֻגַּד נָא לֵאמֹר:
נְעָרִים, לֶהֱוֵי נָא יָדוּעַ —
בֵּין חַגָּיו הַגְּדוֹלִים שֶׁל הַדּוֹר
אֵין יָפֶה מֵחַגְּכֶם הַצָּנוּעַ.
לְמוּלְכֶם הָאֻמָּה עַל סִפּוֹ שֶׁל הַדְּרוֹר
מִשְׁתַּחֲוָה. וּבוֹכָה. הֲבִינוּהָ.

מַגָּשׁ הַכֶּסֶף
נתן אלתרמן

"אין מדינה נתנת לעם על מגש של כסף"
חיים וייצמן

... וְהָאָרֶץ תִּשְׁקֹט. עֵין שָׁמַיִם אוֹדֶמֶת
תְּעַמְעֵם לְאִטָּהּ
עַל גְּבוּלוֹת עֲשֵׁנִים.
וְאֻמָּה תַּעֲמֹד — קְרוּעַת לֵב אַךְ נוֹשֶׁמֶת ... —
לְקַבֵּל אֶת הַנֵּס
הָאֶחָד אֵין שֵׁנִי ...

הִיא לַטֶּקֶס תִּכּוֹן. הִיא תָקוּם לְמוּל סַהַר
וְעָמְדָה, טֶרֶם-יוֹם, עוֹטָה חַג וְאֵימָה.
— — אָז מִנֶּגֶד יֵצְאוּ
נַעֲרָה וָנַעַר
וְאַט-אַט יִצְעֲדוּ הֵם אֶל מוּל הָאֻמָּה.

Clad in ordinary attire but with military harness and heavy-booted,
In the path they proceed,
Advancing without speaking.
They have not changed their clothing nor yet laved-away with water
The marks of the day of toil and the night in the line of fire.

Infinitely weary, withdrawn from rest,
Dripping with the dew of Hebrew youth— —
Quietly the two approach
Then stand motionless,
And there is no sign whether they yet live or have been shot.

Then the Nation asks, flooded by tears and wonderment,
Who are you? and the two softly
Answer her: We are the silver platter
Upon which was served to you the Jewish state.

Thus they say, and fall at her feet, shrouded with shadow.
And the rest shall be told in the history of Israel.   ೞ

MEMORIAL
Uri Zvi Greenberg

Dedicated to IDF pilot David Tamir

He who knew to serve as one of the ordinary soldiers
And was like a resolute, tractable weapon
May his body be counted among the exalted ones come lofty days of kingdom;
To his name shall a poet attach the best poem.
He who withdrew his feet from the dances of youth
And his mouth, as his bosom, from the pleasures of this world —
May his steps be led atop roses
To the topmost Inner Chamber, where his life rings its voice
In an everlasting song of happiness, for it has achieved all:
In that conquest of the heart, by one principle of longing,
To one holy landscape for which, only second in place, there is:
The one mother.   ೞ

לוֹבְשֵׁי חֹל וַחֲגוֹר, וְכִבְדֵי נַעֲלַיִם,
בַּנְּתִיב יַעֲלוּ הֵם
הָלוֹךְ וְהַחֲרֵשׁ.
לֹא הֶחֱלִיפוּ בְגָדָם, לֹא מָחוּ עוֹד בַּמַּיִם
אֶת עִקְבוֹת יוֹם-הַפֶּרֶךְ וְלֵיל קַו-הָאֵשׁ.

עֲיֵפִים עַד בְּלִי קֵץ, נְזִירִים מִמַּרְגּוֹעַ,
וְנוֹטְפִים טַלְלֵי נְעוּרִים עִבְרִיִּים — —
דֹם הַשְּׁנַיִם יִגְּשׁוּ,
וְעָמְדוּ לִבְלִי-נוֹעַ.
וְאֵין אוֹת אִם חַיִּים הֵם אוֹ אִם יְרוּיִים.

אָז תִּשְׁאַל הָאֻמָּה, שְׁטוּפַת דֶּמַע-וָקֶסֶם
וְאָמְרָה: מִי אַתֶּם? וְהַשְּׁנַיִם, שׁוֹקְטִים,
יַעֲנוּ לָהּ: אֲנַחְנוּ מַגַּשׁ הַכֶּסֶף
שֶׁעָלָיו לָךְ נִתְּנָה מְדִינַת-הַיְּהוּדִים.

כָּךְ יֹאמְרוּ. וְנָפְלוּ לְרַגְלָהּ עוֹטְפֵי-צֵל.
וְהַשְּׁאָר יְסֻפַּר בְּתוֹלְדוֹת יִשְׂרָאֵל.

אזכרה
אורי צבי גרינברג

הוקדש לדוד תמיר, טייס צבא הגנה לישראל

אֲשֶׁר יָדַע לְשָׁרֵת כְּאַחַד הַחַיָּלִים הַפְּשׁוּטִים
וַיְהִי כִּכְלִי זַיִן חַד-מַעַשׂ, צַיְתָן,
גוּפוֹ יִהְיֶה בֵּין גְּבֹהִים בִּימֵי מַלְכוּת גְּבֹהִים;
בְּמֵיטַב הַשִּׁיר יְשַׁבְּחֵנּוּ פַּיְטָן.
אֲשֶׁר מָנַע אֶת רַגְלָיו מִמְּחוֹלוֹת הַבַּחֲרוּת
וּפִיו, כְּחֵיקוֹ, מִמַּנְעַמֵּי עוֹלָם —
רַגְלָיו תּוּבַלְנָה עֲלֵי שׁוֹשַׁנִּים לַהֵיכָל
הָעֶלְיוֹן, שָׁם חַיָּיו מְ נ ַ ג ְ נ ִ י ם בְּ ק וֹ ל ָ ם
שִׁיר-אֲשֶׁר-נִצְחִי, כִּ י הַ שִּׂ י ג ּ וּ הַ כֹּ ל :
בְּזֶה כִּבּוּשׁ הַלֵּב בְּ ח ֹ ק כֹּ ס ֶ ף אֶ ח ָ ד
לְנוֹף קֹדֶשׁ אֶחָד, שֶׁשְּׁנִיָּה בְּמַעֲלָה לוֹ:
הָ אֵ ם הָ אַ ח ַ ת .

SPLENDOR FROM THE SPLENDID
Uri Zvi Greenberg

Those who go forth with weapons to the war of their people
Love their lives much more
Than those who do not go forth with sword
And are happy at dawn and mournful at dusk ..

And because life is so precious to the warriors,
They go forth to sacrifice their lives for the sake of their people
Splendor from the splendid is their giving .. there is nothing more:
Their blood — —

Every warrior is a man of happiness, even if his clothing is faded
And his shoes are worn out, he is prepared for the coming of a glorious time,
As, to that end, he has drawn sword from sheath ..

Nourished not by bread, nurtured not by wine,
But by the glorious deed for the sake of Jerusalem.
Mastery is in his body. He will not be driven to his knees.
The image of David he has in his eyes — —

Thus was ancient Israel in the days of Canaan.
Thus is young Israel come days of strife—   ౮

POEM OF BLESSING
Uri Zvi Greenberg

Blessed are the ones going forth, happy are they that they are armed Jews
Upon the land of Israel, under the vault of heaven.
Marching on in strength, tree-sturdy, warm-hearted ..
          And they are like fire prevailing even over waters.
The ones advancing and spreading towards Negev and Galilee
          The ones marching out and going up to Jerusalem
In their young flesh the song of longing and the murmur of sorrows subdued.

With them stride in soldiers' pace the ancient warriors of the Lord
Like shadows of pine trees, like scents of pines at the time of evening .. in the
          warmth of twilight.
And with them stride shadows of Jews— soldiers in alien armies

הַיָּקָר מִן הַיָּקָר
אורי צבי גרינברג

הַיּוֹצְאִים עִם כֵּלִים לְמִלְחֶמֶת עַמָּם
אוֹהֲבִים חַיֵּיהֶם פִּי כַמָּה וְכַמָּה
מֵאֵלֶּה שֶׁאֵינָם יוֹצְאִים בְּחַרְבָּם
וְהֵם שְׂמֵחִים בְּשַׁחְרָם וְנוּגִים בְּעַרְבָּם ..

וּמֵחֲמַת שֶׁיְּקָרִים חַיֵּיהֶם לַלּוֹחֲמִים,
הֵם יוֹצְאִים לְהַקְרִיב חַיֵּיהֶם לְעַמָּם
אֶת הַיָּקָר מִיָּקָר הֵם נוֹתְנִים .. אֵין בִּלְתּוֹ:
זֶה דָּמָם — —

כָּל לוֹחֵם אִישׁ-חֶדְוָה הוּא, אַף אִם בֶּגֶד דֵּהֶה לוֹ
וּנְעָלָיו רְפוּטוֹת, הוּא נָכוֹן לְהוֹד זְמַן,
כִּי לְשֵׁם כָּךְ שָׁלַף חֶרֶב מִנְּדָן ..

נָזוֹן לֹא מִפַּת הוּא, גָּדֵל לֹא מִיַּיִן,
אֲבָל מִזִּיו מַעַשׂ בִּגְלַל יְרוּשָׁלַיִם.
אַדְנוּת בְּגוּפוֹ. לֹא יַעֲמֹד עַל בִּרְכַּיִם.
בְּבוֹאַת דָּוִד לוֹ בְּבָבַת הָעַיִן — —

כָּזֶה יִשְׂרָאֵל הַקַּדְמוֹן בִּימֵי כְּנַעַן.
כָּזֶה יִשְׂרָאֵל הַצָּעִיר בִּימֵי לַעַן —

שִׁיר הַבְּרָכָה
אורי צבי גרינברג

בְּרוּכִים הַהוֹלְכִים, אַשְׁרֵיהֶם כִּי הֵם יְהוּדִים חֲמוּשִׁים,
עַל אַדְמַת יִשְׂרָאֵל תַּחַת כִּפַּת הַשָּׁמַיִם.
דּוֹרְכֵי-עֹז קְשֵׁי-מַעַשׂ, אִילָנִיִּים, חַמֵּי לֵב ..
וְהֵם כְּמוֹ אֵשׁ גּוֹבֶרֶת עַל כָּל מַיִם.
הַהוֹלְכִים וּפוֹשְׁטִים אֱלֵי נֶגֶב וְגָלִיל
הַהוֹלְכִים וְעוֹלִים לִירוּשָׁלַיִם
וּבִבְשָׂרָם הַצָּעִיר רִנַּת כְּסוּפִים וְהֶמְיַת יְגוֹנִים כְּבוּשִׁים.

אַתֶּם הַהוֹלְכִים בְּמִצְעָד-חַיָּלִים לוֹחֲמֵי הַשֵּׁם הַקַּדְמוֹנִים
כְּצִלְלֵי אֲרָנִים וְרֵיחוֹת אֲרָנִים לְעֵת עֶרֶב .. בְּחֶמַת דְּמָדוּמִים
וְהוֹלְכִים אַתֶּם צֶאֱלֵי יְהוּדִים חַיָּלִים מִן צִבְאוֹת זָרִים

Who fell in foreign killing fields for the glory and exaltation of emperors'
    banners..

God knows the anguish of their heart, knows that they have lifted their eyes to
    those mountains' heights.

Also with them stride those who yearned for deliverance, who craved a miracle,

Who have found in *this* time their respite, after weapon-deprived deaths,

In the weapons of these young men of Israel now in the mountains of Jerusalem

And down in the Negev and up in the Galilee and near the ascent of Ephraim..

Jews, heroic with their swords of honor, under the vault of heaven.   ဆ

THE ONES LIVING BY THEIR VIRTUE SAY
Uri Zvi Greenberg

They were the choicest ones, full of life .. their voice has grown silent.

Sons of the race of David, those who fell with their sword in hand.

Simple and lovely like David the lad from a shepherd's family ..

And they will praise you from the dust, O Lord!

The dust which encases them is not the dust of death ..

Of that kind of dust you had aforetime created mankind.

Of that kind is the Temple Mount, the Dust, and the Rock.

Like that Dust they will praise you .. they are immortality!

There is no truth but them, no glory but them.

And we in the world— without them— we

Live by naught but their virtue, by their splendor we prosper.

Whosoever looks upon their grave is no longer enslaved— —   ဆ

HAGOMEL
Uriel Ofeq

I know not what my merit may have been, that I returned at dawn,

I know not the hand which had touched me by chance.

Nor do I know if my gratitude will reach the right gate—

The Gate of God, or of a blind miracle.

When bullets became drunk in their wild dance

And the scythe of Bereavement arose to reap from them;

שֶׁנָּפְלוּ בִּשְׂדֵה-קְטֶל נָכְרִי לְמַעַן הוֹד וּכְבוֹד דֶּגֶל קֵיסָרִים ..
אֶת עֶצֶב דָּמָם יוֹדֵעַ אֵל, כִּי נָשְׂאוּ עֵינֵיהֶם אֶל רוּם הָרִים.
וְהוֹלְכִים אַתָּם כְּמֵהֵי גְאֻלָּה וְצוֹפֵי-לַנֵּס עֲדֵי כִלְיוֹן עַיִן
שֶׁמָּצְאוּ תִּקּוּנָם עַכְשָׁו, אַחֲרֵי הַרְבֵּה-מְאֹד-מֵת לִבְלִי כְּלֵי זַיִן,
בִּכְלֵי זֵינָם וְרִכְבָּם שֶׁל צְעִירֵי יִשְׂרָאֵל עַכְשָׁו בְּהָרֵי יְרוּשָׁלַיִם
וּבַנֶּגֶב מַטָּה וּבַגָּלִיל מַעְלָה וּבְסָמוּךְ לְמַעֲלוֹת אֶפְרַיִם ..
יְהוּדֵי גְבוּרוֹת עַל חֶרֶב כְּבוֹדָם תַּחַת כִּפַּת הַשָּׁמַיִם.

הַחַיִּים - בִּזְכוּתָם אוֹמְרִים
אוּרִי צְבִי גְרִינְבֶּרְג

הֵם הָיוּ בְּחִירִים, רוֹנְנִים .. קוֹלָם נָדַם.
בְּנֵי גֶזַע דָּוִד שֶׁנָּפְלוּ וְחַרְבָּם בְּיָדָם.
וּפְשׁוּטִים וַחֲמוּדִים כְּדָוִד הַנַּעַר מִמִּשְׁפַּחַת הָרוֹעִים ..
וְהֵם י ו ד וּ ךָ , עָ פָ ר , אֱלֹהִים!
עֲפַר גוּלָּמָם אֵינוּ עֲפַר מָוֶת ..
מִמִּין-זֶה-עָפָר יָצַרְתָּ-קֶדֶם-קֶדֶם אָדָם.
מִמִּין-זֶה הַר הַבַּיִת, הֶ עָ פָ ר ו ה ס ל ע.
הֵם יוֹדוּךָ-עָפָר-מִמִּין-זֶה .. הֵם אַלְמֻתָּם!
אֵין אֱמֶת זוּלָתָם וְאֵין הוֹד מִלְּבַדָּם.
וַאֲנַחְנוּ בַיְקוּם — זוּלָתָם — אֵינָם אֶלָּא
חַ יִּ י ם - בִּ ז כ וּ ת ם , בְּזֵינָם גַּם נִזְבָּד.

הַמַּבִּיט לְקִבְרָם חָדֵל לִהְיוֹת עֶבֶד — —

הַגּוֹמֵל
אוּרִיאֵל אוֹפֶק

לֹא אֵדַע מַה זְּכוּתִי כִּי חָזַרְתִּי עִם שַׁחַר.
לֹא אֵדַע אֶת הַיָּד בִּי נָגְעָה לְתֻמָּהּ.
לֹא אֵדַע אִם תִּמָּצֵא תּוֹדָתִי אֶת הַשַּׁעַר -
שַׁעֲרוֹ שֶׁל הָאֵל, אוֹ שֶׁל פֶּלֶא סוּמָא.

עֵת שָׂכְרוּ כַדּוּרִים בְּמָחוֹלָם הַפָּרוּעַ
וְחֶרְמֵשׁ מְשֻׁכָּל הִתְנַשֵּׂא בָּם לִקְצֹר;

When arms cradled my wounded comrade,
At that point I cried to the advancing Bereavement: "Stop!"

"Oh, come not near," I pleaded, "this is not the night,
It is still early, so early! You should not dare to take me.
For at dawn I will return; because in the thicket are a ram's horns.
And you would be left empty-handed."

I know not whether my gratitude has reached the Gate.
Nor would I recognize the hand that had guarded my brow;
But that ineffable one who had stayed with me until dawn—
To his portal my blessing reaches.   ৪০

AND MY BROTHER WAS SILENT
Amir Gilboa

My brother came from the field
In gray attire.
And I feared that this dream of mine would not come true
And I immediately started to count his wounds.
And my brother was silent.

I dug into the pockets of his trench coat
And found a small bandage with a dried stain.
And on a much-worn postcard, her name
Under a painting of poppies.
And my brother was silent.

Then I untied the pack
And took out his possessions, memory by memory.
Hurrah, my brother, my brother the hero,
Behold I found your decorations!
Hurrah, my brother, my brother the hero,
I shall proudly sing a hymn to your name
And my brother was silent.
My brother was silent.

And his blood from the ground cries.   ৪০

עֵת חָבְקוּ הַזְּרוֹעוֹת אֶת רֵעִי הַפָּצוּעַ -
אָז זָעַקְתִּי לַשְּׁכוֹל הַפּוֹסֵעַ: "עֲצֹר!"

"אַל תִּקְרַב," הִתְחַנַּנְתִּי, "לֹא זֶהוּ הַלַּיְל.
עוֹד מֻקְדָּם, כֹּה מֻקְדָּם! לֹא תָעֵז בִּי לִזְכּוֹת.
כִּי עִם שַׁחַר אָשׁוּב; כִּי בַּסְבָךְ קַרְנֵי אַיִל.
וְאַתָּה תִּנָּתֵר וְכַפֶּיךָ רֵיקוֹת."

לֹא נוֹדַע אִם מָצְאָה תּוֹדָתִי אֶת הַשַּׁעַר.
לֹא אַכִּיר אֶת הַיָּד שֶׁנָּצְרָה רַקָּתִי;
אַךְ אוֹתוֹ נֶעֱלָם שֶׁלִּוַּנִי עִם שַׁחַר -
אֶל פִּתְחוֹ מַשִּׁיקָה בִּרְכָתִי.

וְאָחִי שׁוֹתֵק
אמיר גלבע

אָחִי חָזַר מִן הַשָּׂדֶה
בְּבֶגֶד אָפֹר.
וַאֲנִי חָשַׁשְׁתִּי שֶׁמָּא חֲלוֹמִי יִתְבַּדֶּה
וְהִתְחַלְתִּי מִיָּד אֶת פְּצָעָיו לִסְפֹּר.
וְאָחִי שׁוֹתֵק.

אַחַר חִטַּטְתִּי בְּכִיסֵי הַסַּגִּין
וּמָצָאתִי אִסְפְּלָנִית שֶׁיָּבֵשׁ כִּתְמָהּ.
וּבִגְלוּיָה שְׁחוּקָה אֶת שְׁמָהּ
תַּחַת לְצִיּוּר שֶׁל פְּרָגִים.
וְאָחִי שׁוֹתֵק.

אָז הִתַּרְתִּי אֶת הַצְּרוֹר
וְהוֹצֵאתִי חֲפָצָיו, זֵכֶר אַחַר זֵכֶר.
הֵידָד, אָחִי, אָחִי ה ג ב ו ר,
הִנֵּה מָצָאתִי אוֹתוֹתֶיךָ!
הֵידָד, אָחִי, אָחִי ה ג ב ו ר,
אָשִׁיר גַּאֲוָה לִשְׁמֶךָ!
וְאָחִי שׁוֹתֵק.
וְאָחִי שׁוֹתֵק.

וְדָמוֹ מִן הָאֲדָמָה זוֹעֵק.

Forced March In Summer
Yehoshua Zafrir

Again we went out, O one who bore me, to the forced march in summer
With our magazines full, to the only road that we could take.
And the hearts of all of us, Mother, a wall of protection and a barrier,
A sukkah of peace and preservation from churning dread.

You do know, O one who bore me, I am not a man of fine words
And in telling things my brothers were better than me
The story that I have held-close within myself for you
Was shattered upon our surging against the fire of cannons.

When my comrades return, in quietness they will tell you
About your son who had left for the forced march in summer.
And how in his khaki shirt he advanced against the bullets—
So that such do not cross your doorstep, Mother, there at home.

Open are my eyes, Mother, tranquil as the sky,
Upon the ebbing of the gathered storm and thundered lightning.
I and my Land have made an eternal covenant— there is no barrier between us.
As witness to my oath— these silent piles of earth …   ℘

The Sappers
Haiim Hefer

Night is already falling, enfolding the mountain,
And the jackal is howling in the groves,
Along the steep path descending to the village
Again a squad of sappers marches.

Our packs are heavy with dynamite,
The way, rigorous and rugged.
"Three more kilometers, so hang in there, sapper,
For then dynamite will speak!"

To the villages of the enemy we take destruction,
With mine and detonator and fuse,
Many a target will be blown up in the air,
When sappers set off the explosives.

מַסַּע הַקַּיִץ
יְהוֹשֻׁעַ צְפָרִיר

שׁוּב יָצָאנוּ, הוֹרָתִי, אֶל מַסַּע הַקַּיִץ,
וְאַשְׁפּוֹתֵינוּ מְלֵאוֹת, לַדֶּרֶךְ אֵין־אַחֶרֶת.
וּלְבַב כֻּלָּנוּ, אִמָּא, חוֹמַת מָגֵן וָחַיִץ,
סֻכַּת־שָׁלוֹם וָיֶשַׁע מוּל אֵימָה נִסְעֶרֶת.

הֵן יָדַעְתְּ, אִמִּי, לֹא אִישׁ־דְּבָרִים אָנֹכִי
וּלְסַפֵּר הֵיטִיבוּ זֹאת מִמֶּנִּי הָאַחִים.
הַסִּפּוּר שֶׁעֲבוּרֵךְ נָצַרְתִּי בְּתוֹכִי
נִקְרַע בְּעֵת זִנַּקְנוּ מוּל אֵשׁ הַתּוֹתָחִים.

כְּשֶׁרֵעַי יָשׁוּבוּ, יָסִיחוּ לָךְ בְּדָמִי
עַל בְּנֵךְ אֲשֶׁר יָצָא לְמַסָּע בַּקַּיִץ.
וּבְחָקִי־כֻּתָּנְתּוֹ הוּא רָץ לְמוּל קְלִיעִים —
לְבַל יַעַבְרוּ סִפֵּךְ, אִמָּא, שָׁם בַּבַּיִת.

פְּקוּחוֹת עֵינֵינוּ, אִמָּא, רוֹגְעוֹת כְּמוֹ שָׁמַיִם,
בְּשׁוֹךְ חַשְׁרַת־סוּפָה וְרַעַם הַבְּרָקִים.
אֲנִי וְאַדְמָתִי כָּרַתְנוּ בְּרִית־אֵין־חַיִץ.
עֵדִים לִשְׁבוּעָתִי — תִּלֵּי עָפָר שׁוֹתְקִים ...

הַחַבְּלָנִים
חַיִּים חֶפֶר

כְּבָר הַלַּיְלָה יוֹרֵד וְעוֹטֵף אֶת הָהָר,
וְהַתַּן מְיַלֵּל בַּגְּנָנִים,
בַּמִּשְׁעוֹל הַתָּלוּל הַיּוֹרֵד אֶל הַכְּפָר
שׁוּב צוֹעֶדֶת כִּתַּת חַבְּלָנִים.

הַתַּרְמִיל עַל גַּבֵּנוּ כָּבֵד בַּמִּטְעָן,
וְהַדֶּרֶךְ קָשָׁה וְטַרְשִׁית.
"עוֹד שְׁלֹשָׁה קִילוֹמֶטֶר, מַעְלֵשׁ יָא חַבְּלָן,
וַאֲזַי יְדַבֵּר דִּינָמִיט!"

אֶל כְּפָרֵי הָאוֹיֵב אֶת הַהֶרֶס נָבִיא
בְּמוֹקֵשׁ וּבַדְּטוֹ, בַּפְּתִיל,
עוֹד אוֹבְּיֶקְט לֹא אֶחָד יְנֻשָּׂא בָּאֲוִיר,
עֵת חַבְּלָן אֶת הַחֹמֶר יַפְעִיל.

Then if it happens that we return to the base,
And the wind still gusts in the groves—
Again, when evening comes, we will hoist the deadly burden,
And it's, "Take to the road, sapper squad!"   ∽

WE LEFT SLOWLY
Haiim Hefer

We left slowly. The night was pale.
In the distance the lights flickered.
And you were all loveliness like your two eyes
With tears cupped in them.

The jackal howled as you went to the vineyard
Your tears flowing like sap from a tree.
And you remembered the hours before
We went out to battle by the narrow path.

You remembered our laughter like a stream.
You remembered a dance and a lilting harmonica.
You remembered the haystack,
And the hand's touch of the only one… ·

And if you are left, with loneliness enfolding,
And you walk in the vineyards slowly—
You will wait. Therefore, in such silence
We parted with a smile in our eyes.   ∽

EULOGY
Moshe Tabenkin

Bereavement revolves in our garden like a sword.
Bereavement visits us, the home of Mother and Father.
At dawn our boy went out— There was evening— —
Morning came. Day was over— he did not return.

וְהָיָה אִם נָשׁוּב וְנַחֲזֹר לַבָּסִיס,
וְהָרוּחַ תִּרְעַשׁ בַּגַּנִּים —
שׁוּב, עֵת עֶרֶב יָבוֹא, הַמַּטְעָן נַעֲמִיס,
וְ"לַדֶּרֶךְ, כִּתַּת חַבְּלָנִים!"

יָצָאנוּ אַט

חיים חפר

יָצָאנוּ אַט. חִוֵּר הָיָה הַלַּיִל.
בַּמֶּרְחַקִּים הִבְלִיחוּ הָאוֹרוֹת.
וְאַתְּ הָיִית יָפָה כִּשְׁתֵּי עֵינַיִךְ
עֵת הַדְּמָעוֹת הָיוּ בָּן עֲצוּרוֹת.

יְלֵל הַתָּן. וְאַתְּ הָלַכְתְּ לַכֶּרֶם.
וְדִמְעָתֵךְ נָשְׁרָה כְּמוֹ שָׂרָף.
וְאַתְּ זָכַרְתְּ אֶת הַשָּׁעוֹת בְּטֶרֶם
יָצָאנוּ בַּמִּשְׁעוֹל הַצַּר לַקְּרָב.

וְאַתְּ זָכַרְתְּ צְחוֹקֵנוּ כְּמוֹ נַחַל.
וְאַתְּ זָכַרְתְּ נִגּוּן וּמַפּוּחִית.
וְאַתְּ זָכַרְתְּ אֶת עֲרֵמַת הַשַּׁחַת.
וְאֶת מַגַּע יָדוֹ שֶׁל הַיָּחִיד ...

וְאִם נוֹתַרְתְּ, וְהַבְּדִידוּת חוֹבֶקֶת.
וְאַתְּ פּוֹסַעַת בַּכְּרָמִים לְאַט —
אַתְּ תְּחַכִּי. עַל-כֵּן, כָּל-כָּךְ בְּשֶׁקֶט
נִפְרַדְנוּ וְחִיַּכְנוּ בְּמַבָּט.

מִסְפֵּד

משה טבנקין

הַשְּׁכוֹל מִתְהַפֵּךְ בְּגַנֵּנוּ כְּחֶרֶב.
פָּקַדְנוּ הַשְּׁכוֹל, בֵּית-אֵם וּבֵית-אָב.
עִם שַׁחַר יָצָא נַעֲרֵנוּ — עִם עֶרֶב — —
בָּא בֹקֶר. תַּם יוֹם — הוּא לֹא שָׁב.

Our boy was— a silvery olive tree,
Was— a poplar with dreamy leaves.
Our boy was— a branching oak.
Was the tallest of palms!

Our boy was born in the shade of Gilbo'a,
Laved was our boy in the spring of Harod,
Our boy, the good, the tall.
We loved you to the limits of laughter and tears!

Our boy was— a field of verdant crops.
Was— opening of eyelids in early morning.
Was— like laughing blossom of apple
Was the most fragrant of buds!

Our boy was weaned to light and to blue skies.
Our boy was destined to be full of years.
Our proud boy, our cypress-sapling lad,
How fearlessly he advanced against the scythe of blood!

Our boy was— like a pine in the woodlands.
Was— a fig tree putting forth its figs.
Our boy was— a myrtle of dense roots.
Was the most fiery of poppies!

Our boy was the apple of the eye of Izre'el,
Blue skies, cool rains, and dog-day heat nurtured him.
This valley— his friend— was looking forward to the fulfillment of his life,
Anticipating with an assurance not without fair cause!

Our boy was— like the rocks of Gilbo'a.
Was— like the soaring of its magnificent eagles—
Strong and daring and talltalltall.
To the very last of his moments against the enemy.

Bereavement finds shelter in the depth of our dwellings
In our path bereavement is like a companion—
Carrying in its hands to the darkness of our mourners
A candle of agony, a candle of pride— an ever-burning flame.   ℘

הָיָה נַעֲרֵנוּ — עֵץ זַיִת מַכְסִיף,
הָיָה — צַפְצָפָה חֲלוּמַת הֶעָלִים.
הָיָה נַעֲרֵנוּ — אַלּוֹן מַעֲנִיף.
הָיָה הַתָּמִיר בַּדְּקָלִים!

נוֹלַד נַעֲרֵנוּ בְּצֵל הַגִּלְבֹּעַ.
רֻחַץ נַעֲרֵנוּ בְּנַחַל חֲרֹד.
נַעֲרֵנוּ שֶׁלָּנוּ הַטּוֹב, הַגָּבוֹהַּ.
אֲהַבְנוּךָ עַד צְחוֹק וּדְמָעוֹת!

הָיָה נַעֲרֵנוּ — שְׂדֵה פַּלְחָה מוֹרֶקֶת.
הָיָה — עַפְעַפֵּי שַׁחֲרִית נִקְרָעִים.
הָיָה — כִּתְפָּרַחַת תַּפּוּחַ צוֹחֶקֶת.
הָיָה הַבָּשׂוֹם בַּפְּקָעִים!

נִגְמַל נַעֲרֵנוּ לְאוֹר וְלִתְכֵלֶת.
נוֹעַד נַעֲרֵנוּ לִשְׂבֹּעַ יָמִים.
נַעֲרֵנוּ הַגֵּא, נַעֲרֵנוּ בְּרוֹשׁ-יֶלֶד,
אֵיךְ זָנַק מוּל חֶרְמֵשׁ הַדָּמִים!

הָיָה נַעֲרֵנוּ — כְּאֹרֶן הַחֹרֶשׁ.
הָיָה — תְּאֵנָה הַחוֹנֶטֶת פַּגִּים.
הָיָה נַעֲרֵנוּ — הֲדַס סְבוּךְ הַשֹּׁרֶשׁ.
הָיָה הַלּוֹהֵט בַּפְּרָגִים!

הָיָה נַעֲרֵנוּ — בְּבַת-יִזְרְעֶאל,
טִפְּחוּהוּ תְּכוֹל-שַׁחַק, מָטָר וְשָׂרָב.
לְפֹעַל-חַיָּיו עֵמֶק-רַע יִחֵל,
יִחֵל וּבָטַח. לֹא לַשָּׁוְא! —

הָיָה נַעֲרֵנוּ — כְּצוּק הַגִּלְבֹּעַ,
הָיָה — כִּמְעוֹף נְשָׁרָיו נֶאְדָּר —
אַמִּיץ וְנוֹעָז וְגָבוֹהַּ-גָּבוֹהַּ
עַד אַחֲרוֹן רְגָעָיו מוּל הַצָּר.

הַשַּׁכּוֹל מִסְתּוֹפֵף בְּעִמְקֵי אָהֳלֵינוּ.
הָיָה בִּנְתִיבֵנוּ הַשַּׁכּוֹל כְּעָמִית —
נוֹשֵׂא בְּכַפָּיו אֶל חֶשְׁכַת אָבֵלֵינוּ
נֵר יָגוֹן, נֵר גָּאוֹן — אֵשׁ-תָּמִיד.

GOD HAS MERCY ON KINDERGARTEN CHILDREN
Yehudah Amichai

God has mercy on kindergarteners,
Less so on school children,
And for the grown he has no more mercy,
He leaves them alone,
So sometimes they must crawl on all fours
In the scorching sand,
In order to reach the triage unit
While their blood is seeping away.

Perhaps to the ones who truly love
He will extend mercy— have pity and provide shade
Like a tree to someone asleep on a bench
Along the boulevard.

Perhaps to them we too will bring out
The last coins of grace
Which mother left us,
So that their happiness will succour us
Now and in other days.   ∞

TWO POEMS
ABOUT THE FIRST BATTLES
Yehudah Amichai

A.
The first battles brought forth
Awesome flowers of love
With shells as near-deadly kisses.
In the beautiful buses of our city
Our young-boy-soldiers are being led out:
Every bus line— No. 12, No. 8, No. 5,
Goes to the front.

B.
On the way to the front we slept in a kindergarten,
Under my head I put a wooly teddy bear,

אֱלֹהִים מְרַחֵם עַל יַלְדֵי הַגַּן
יהודה עמיחי

אֱלֹהִים מְרַחֵם עַל יַלְדֵי הַגָּן,
פָּחוֹת מִזֶּה עַל יַלְדֵי בֵּית-הַסֵּפֶר.
וְעַל הַגְּדוֹלִים לֹא יְרַחֵם עוֹד,
יַשְׁאִירֵם לְבַדָּם,
וְלִפְעָמִים יִצְטָרְכוּ לִזְחֹל עַל אַרְבַּע
בַּחוֹל הַלּוֹהֵט,
כְּדֵי לְהַגִּיעַ לְתַחֲנַת הָאִסוּף
וְהֵם שׁוֹתְתֵי דָם.

אוּלַי עַל הָאוֹהֲבִים-בֶּאֱמֶת
יִתֵּן רַחֲמִים וְיָחוּס וְיָצֵל
כְּאִילָן עַל הַיָּשֵׁן בַּסַּפְסָל
שֶׁבַּשְּׂדֵרָה הַצִּבּוּרִית.

אוּלַי לָהֶם גַּם אֲנַחְנוּ נוֹצִיא
אֶת מַטְבְּעוֹת הַחֶסֶד הָאַחֲרוֹנוֹת
שֶׁהוֹרִישָׁה לָנוּ אִמָּא,
כְּדֵי שֶׁאָשְׁרָם יָגֵן עָלֵינוּ
עַכְשָׁו וּבַיָּמִים הָאֲחֵרִים.

שְׁנֵי שִׁירִים
עַל הַקְּרָבוֹת הָרִאשׁוֹנִים
יהודה עמיחי

[א]
הַקְּרָבוֹת הָרִאשׁוֹנִים הֶעֱלוּ
פִּרְחֵי אַהֲבָה נוֹרָאִים
עִם נְשִׁיקוֹת כְּמַעַט-מְמִיתוֹת כַּפְּגָזִים.
בָּאוֹטוֹבּוּסִים הַיָּפִים שֶׁל עִירֵנוּ
מוּבָלִים הַנְּעָרִים-הַחַיָּלִים:
כָּל הַקַּוִּים 12, 8, 5,
נוֹסְעִים אֶל הַחֲזִית.

[ב]
בַּדֶּרֶךְ לַחֲזִית לָנוּ בְּגַן-יְלָדִים,
לִמְרַאֲשׁוֹתַי שַׂמְתִּי דֻּבּוֹן צֶמֶר,

Onto my tired face came down tops
And trumpets and dolls—
Not angels;
My feet, in their heavy boots,
Toppled a tower of bright-colored blocks
Stacked one atop the other,
Each block smaller than the one beneath it.
And in my head were memories great and small in turmoil
And they made dreams in it.

And out across from the window there were fires …
And also in my eyes, even under their lids.   ⬧

RAIN ON THE BATTLEFIELD
Yehudah Amichai

   To the memory of Dicki

Rain falls on the faces of my comrades;
On the faces of my living comrades, who
Cover their heads with a blanket—
And on the faces of my dead comrades, who
No longer cover.   ⬧

AN ANONYMOUS SQUAD
Yehiel Mohar

The mountains are roaring and the road is fearful.
And the enemy hears the joyful shouts:
Here marches a unit of soldiers on the border.
And that border is in the heart of every soldier.

May a song arise for an anonymous squad.
Strong like hewed stones
Its soul is a flame, and its banner is love
Kissing the skies of past and future.

אֶל פְּנֵי הָעֲיֵפוֹת יָרְדוּ סְבִיבוֹנִים
וַחֲצוֹצְרוֹת וּבֻבּוֹת —
לֹא מַלְאָכִים,
רַגְלִי, בַּנַּעֲלַיִם הַכְּבֵדוֹת,
הִפִּילוּ מִגְדַּל קֻבִּיּוֹת צִבְעוֹנִיּוֹת
שֶׁעָמְדוּ זוֹ עַל זוֹ,
כָּל קֻבִּיָּה קְטַנָּה מִזּוֹ שֶׁתַּחְתֶּיהָ.
וּבְרָאשֵׁי הָיוּ זִכְרוֹנוֹת גְּדוֹלִים וּקְטַנִּים בְּעִרְבּוּבְיָה
וְעָשׂוּ בּוֹ חֲלוֹמוֹת.

וּמֵעֵבֶר לַחַלּוֹן הָיוּ שְׂרֵפוֹת ...
וְכֵן בְּעֵינַי שֶׁמִּתַּחַת לִשְׁמוּרוֹתַי.

גֶּשֶׁם בִּשְׂדֵה הַקְּרָב
יהודה עמיחי

לזכר דיקי

גֶּשֶׁם יוֹרֵד עַל פְּנֵי רֵעַי;
עַל פְּנֵי רֵעַי הַחַיִּים, אֲשֶׁר
מְכַסִּים רָאשֵׁיהֶם בַּשְּׂמִיכָה —
וְעַל פְּנֵי רֵעַי הַמֵּתִים, אֲשֶׁר
אֵינָם מְכַסִּים עוֹד.

כִּתָּה אַלְמוֹנִית
יחיאל מוהר

הֶהָרִים יִרְעֲמוּ וְהַדֶּרֶךְ תָּחוּל,
וְיַקְשִׁיב הָאוֹיֵב לַמִּצְהָל:
כָּאן צוֹעֶדֶת כִּתַּת חַיָּלִים עַל הַגְּבוּל,
וְהַגְּבוּל הוּא בְּלֵב כָּל חַיָּל.

יַעַל שִׁיר לְכִתָּה אַלְמוֹנִית,
אֵיתָנָה כְּאַבְנֵי הַגְּזִית,
נִשְׁמָתָהּ לְהָבָה, וְדִגְלָהּ אַהֲבָה
הַנּוֹשֵׁק שְׁמֵי עָבָר וְעָתִיד.

On the roads of the Galilee, in the environs of Eilat,
In the nights of the desolate desert,
The squad is marching, hand on rifle butt,
Oh, glory, glory without a name.

How beautiful is the squad in the simplicity of its trek,
In the laughter that has not deserted its mouth,
Through wearying days of march and burden,
As it watched over field and village.

A song to the beauty of lads in the file,
To the flame which is a hymn in their eyes
Because from time immemorial and forever only such an anonymous squad
Advances its nation to freedom.   ଽ

BETWEEN SICKLE AND SWORD
Yehiel Mohar

Our lives unfold between the sickle and the sword.
Our lives are intertwined with spears and grain.
Behold how we have been woven of such warp and woof:
Blushing flowers and white-hot steel.

That same hand that grasps the weapon
Thrusts mowers' teeth into the standing grain.
Ancient songs there are, about the covenant with each rock—
Their echo still rises from the stones of the wall.

Because for us the sickle is the sword
And for us a sword is like a sickle.
With us, legends at eventide
Still tell of blood and dew together.

And again against the whiteness of our dwellings
Night comes on, a shadow is moon-cast,
Therefore always our lives unfold
In the light of a sword and a sickle.

בִּשְׁבִילֵי הַגָּלִיל, בְּנוֹפָהּ שֶׁל אֵילַת,
בְּלֵילוֹת הַמִּדְבָּר הַשּׁוֹמֵם,
צוֹעֶדֶת הַכִּתָּה, וְיָדָהּ עַל הַקֵּת,
תִּפְאָרָה, תִּפְאָרָה לְלֹא שֵׁם.

מַה יָּפְתָה הַכִּתָּה בְּפַשְׁטוּת מִצְעָדָהּ,
בִּצְחוֹקָהּ שֶׁמְּפִיהָ לֹא סָר,
בְּיָמִים יְגֵעִים שֶׁל מַסָּע וּמַשָּׂא,
בְּשָׁמְרָה עַל שָׂדֶה וְעַל כְּפָר.

עַל יְפִי נְעָרִים בַּשּׁוּרָה הָעַרְפִּית,
עַל הָאֵשׁ בָּעֵינַיִם מִזְמוֹר,
כִּי מֵאָז וְתָמִיד רַק כִּתָּה אַלְמוֹנִית
מַפְסִיעָה אֶת עַמָּהּ אֱלֵי דְרוֹר.

בֵּין מַגָּל וָחֶרֶב
יחיאל מוהר

חַיֵּינוּ עוֹלִים בֵּין מַגָּל וּבֵין חֶרֶב,
חַיֵּינוּ שְׁזוּרִים חֲנִיתוֹת וְדָגָן,
הִנֵּה אֵיךְ נִקְלַעְנוּ גַּם שְׁתִי וְגַם עֵרֶב
פְּרָחִים אֲדֻמִּים וּבַרְזֶל מִלְבָן.

הַיָּד הָאַחַת הָאוֹחֶזֶת בַּשֶּׁלַח
שְׁנֵי מַקְצָרוֹת הִיא תִּנְעַץ בַּקָּמָה.
שִׁירִים עַתִּיקִים עַל הַבְּרִית עִם כָּל סֶלַע —
הַדָּם שׁוּב עוֹלֶה מֵאַבְנֵי הַחוֹמָה.

כִּי לָנוּ הַמַּגָּל הוּא הַחֶרֶב
וְלָנוּ חֶרֶב כְּמַגָּל.
אֶצְלֵנוּ אַגָּדוֹת עִם עֶרֶב
עוֹד מְסַפְּרוֹת עַל דָּם וָטָל.

וְשׁוּב מוּל לִבֵּן אֹהָלֵינוּ
הַלַּיְלָה גָּח, הַצֵּל מֻטָּל,
עַל כֵּן תָּמִיד עוֹלִים חַיֵּינוּ
בְּאוֹר שֶׁל חֶרֶב וּמַגָּל.

The sickle cuts and the sword cuts
Our lives are a harvest in the morning of a nation,
He who carries sheaves in the shimmering field
Also carries another sheaf— his life— for his people.

It is indeed a singular event on a road
That never ever meets any other
That the hand which sows in toil
Shall raise its offering on the tip of spears.   ഔ

FOR THE FIGHTERS— A LAMENT
Ayin Tur-Malka

Look at the faces of these sleeping ones
For they are the faces of those who have turned inward
And not the faces of the ones who are missing—
Their mouths are sealed. Their eyes are agape.
Their ears are like the curled cavern of a sea shell.
Upon their death hide, oh please, their faces!
Because black fire burns at their mouths
And yellowness of fire licks off their eyes.
Their ears resound only to the drum of death.

Holy their hearts will forever remain.   ഔ

HERALDS OF NEW JERUSALEM
Ayin Tur-Malka

> To the memory of the glorious Ariela from the
> Lechi brigade, may God avenge her blood

Were there amongst us bridegrooms and brides
For the New Jerusalem?
Were we under a canopy at the taking of an oath to Jerusalem?
Did stars gleam in the midst of Jerusalem's soil?
Were there constellations like pavement under the feet
Of those who sanctified Jerusalem in their life and death?

קוֹצֵר הַמַּגָּל וְהַחֶרֶב קוֹצֶרֶת
חַיֵּינוּ קָצִיר בְּבִקְרָהּ שֶׁל אֵמָּה,
הַנּוֹשֵׂא אֲלֻמּוֹת בַּשָּׂדֶה הַזּוֹהֶרֶת
נוֹשֵׂא אֶת חַיָּיו לְעַמּוֹ אֲלֻמָּה.

אָכֵן פָּרָשָׁה יְחִידָה עֲלֵי דֶרֶךְ
שֶׁאֵין לָהּ שֶׁאֵין פָּרָשַׁת הַדְּרָכִים,
הַיָּד הָאַחַת הַזּוֹרַעַת בְּפֶרֶךְ
תָּנִיף תְּרוּמָתָהּ עַל חֻדֵּי רְמָחִים.

לַלּוֹחֲמִים – קִינָה
עין טור-מלכא

רְאֵה אֶת פְּנֵי הַיְשֵׁנִים הָאֵלֶּה
וְהִמָּה פְּנֵי מִתְכַּנְּסִים
וְלֹא פְּנֵי נֶעְדָּרִים —
פִּיהֶם בְּחוֹתָם. עֵינָם בְּקֶשֶׁת נִרְחֶבֶת.
אָזְנָם כַּאֲפַרְכֶּסֶת קוֹנְכִית הַיַּמִּים.
בְּמוֹתָם הַסְתִּירוּ, הוֹ נָא, פְּנֵיהֶם!
כִּי אֵשׁ שְׁחֹרָה פִּיהֶם תִּצְרֹב
וְצֹהַב אֵשׁ תְּלַחֵךְ עֵינָם.
אָזְנָם בְּתוֹף הַמָּוֶת תִּתְיַשֵּׁב.

לִבָּם הַקָּדוֹשׁ עַד עוֹלָם יִשָּׁמֵר.

מְבַשְּׂרֵי יְרוּשָׁלַיִם הַחֲדָשָׁה
עין טור-מלכא

לשמה של אריאלה הפלאית מחטיבת לוחמי הי״ד

הֲהָיוּ מִבֵּינֵינוּ חֲתָנִים וְכַלּוֹת
לִ יְ ר וּ שָׁ לַ יִ ם הַ חֲ דָ שָׁ ה ?
הֲהָיִינוּ תַּחַת חֻפָּה בִּשְׁבוּעָה לִירוּשָׁלַיִם?
הֲזָרְחוּ כוֹכָבִים בְּלֵב אַדְמַת-יְרוּשָׁלַיִם?
הֲרֻצְּפוּ מַזָּלוֹת תַּחַת כַּפּוֹת-רַגְלֵיהֶם
שֶׁל מְקַדְּשֵׁי יְרוּשָׁלַיִם בְּחַיֵּיהֶם וּבְמוֹתָם?

Did a light which is not of this world shine
From the walls of their waning hearts?

    — Pray for the peace of Jerusalem:
    See the all-encompassing canopy
    Over the ancient oath to Jerusalem:
    Take note in Heaven, in that Holy Place: We will be vouched for there!
And our sons and daughters, the bridegrooms and brides,
We will garland with wedding wreaths of myrtle
Scented with incense of moonlight!— !   ဆ

Mirror Of The Battle
Ayin Tur-Malka

In her youth she was muffled in a veil of longing
Because of woman's nature;
In her love she had deep softening,
Abundant in beauty.
She learned the patience rules
Of pregnancy
And her son was like one bending his head
Down, because of a flow of yearnings over it—

When her son was in his youth—
She sent him to the battlefield.
And the agitation as of birds at eventide
In her too was without cessation.

The moon lingers late in the morning,
When the sun rises, good it is for her!
The round mirror-moon in the west
Facing the sun of the east in Gibeon,
As in the day of Joshua in the valley of Ayalon
When the LORD God of Hosts prevailed!

She has no fear of the day in which the image of the sun
Is like the moon.

הֶאָיר אוֹר שֶׁלֹּא מֵעָלְמָא-הָדֵין
מִתּוֹךְ קִירוֹת לִבָּם הַנָּמוֹג!

— שַׁאֲלוּ שְׁלוֹם יְרוּשָׁלַיִם:
רְאוּ אֶת הַחֻפָּה הַשְּׁלֵמָה
עַל הַשְּׁבוּעָה עַתִּיקַת-הַיּוֹמִין לִירוּשָׁלַיִם:
בִּינוּ בָּרָקִיעַ בַּמָּקוֹם: יְסַהֲדוּנוּ שָׁם!
וּלְבָנֵינוּ וְלִבְנוֹתֵינוּ, הַחֲתָנִים וְהַכַּלּוֹת,
עֲטָרָה כְּלִילֵי כְלוּלוֹת הַדַּסִּיִּים
בְּקָטֹרֶת יְרֵחִית מְקַטְּרִים! — !

אַסְפַּקְלַר הַקְּרָב
עֵין טוּר-מַלְכָּא

מְצֻלֶּפֶת הָיְתָה בַּגַּעֲגוּעִים בִּנְעוּרֶיהָ
מִשּׁוּם טֶבַע הָאִשָּׁה;
בְּאַהֲבָתָהּ הָיְתָה בָּהּ הִתְרַכְּכוּת עֲמֻקָּה,
רְוַת יֹפִי.
לָמְדָה אֶת תּוֹרַת הַסַּבְלָנוּת
שֶׁל הֵהֵרָיוֹן
וְהָיָה בְּנָהּ כְּאֶחָד-מַרְכִּין-רֹאשׁוֹ
מַטָּה, מִשּׁוּם שֶׁטֵּף כְּסוּפִים עֲלֵי רֹאשׁ —

— לְעֵת בְּנָהּ בַּעֲלוּמָיו —
אֶל שְׂדֵה הַקְּרָב שְׁלָחַתְהוּ.
וְרִגְשַׁת הָעוֹף טֶרֶם עֶרֶב,
גַּם בָּהּ לְלֹא הֶרֶף.

יָרֵחַ מְאַחֵר בַּבֹּקֶר,
בְּתַמֶּר הַשֶּׁמֶשׁ, טוֹב הוּא לָהּ!
אַסְפַּקְלַר-הַיָּרֵחַ הָעֲגֻלִי בְּמַעֲרָב
לְנֹכַח הַשֶּׁמֶשׁ בְּמִזְרָח בְּגִבְעוֹן,
כְּבַיּוֹם יְהוֹשֻׁעַ בְּעֵמֶק אַיָּלוֹן
בִּגְבֹר צְבָאוֹת!

לֹא תָגוּר מִפְּנֵי הַיּוֹם בּוֹ תַּדְמִית שֶׁמֶשׁ
כַּלְּבָנָה הִיא.

On such a day, may it not come,
Dread arises: The light shimmers— —
Woe to a sun which stands aloof
When the armies of Israel fall!　ഔ

MEMORIAL SERVICE
Ayin Tur-Malka

Crags stand in the mountains before us
In the likeness of bereaved mothers
Who had altered since aforetime their image:
Dew does not quench them
Nor the sun gild them
— How portentous is their muteness.
And whither shall we flee?—
A memorial service: belated prayer for mercy.
The sons lie supine
Throughout the earth
And the mothers are upright:
In a line of rain they permeate
With weeping the depths of the graves— —　ഔ

THE TIME AND THE RESPONSE
Nathan Alterman

> The twenty-year-old soldier, Uri Ilan, who took his own life in a Syrian prison, was buried in Gan Shmuel, the kibbutz in which he was born and brought up. In his eulogy, Chief of Staff Moshe Dayan related that when the body was returned to the IDF at the border, a note was found with it containing the words "I did not betray" and the name of his mother, Feiga Ilanit. (1955)

Just like that— suddenly, in a single movement!— a barrier falls and disappears
And our Time rises with uncovered face as sudden-brilliance lights it.
And from this shore, for only a moment, with opened eyes,
We perceive its pith, its meaning, its essence.

Revealed is the face of a boy-soldier, of a man, of a promising girl,
For whom Time had suddenly transformed an outspread net.

בְּיוֹם כָּזֶה, אַל יָבוֹא,
הָאֵימָה מְעֻצֶּבֶת: הָאוֹר מִתְלַהְלֵהַּ — —
וַי יְהֵא לַשֶּׁמֶשׁ הַנּוֹכֵחַ לְגַרְמֵהּ
בִּנְפֹל צִבְאוֹת יִשְׂרָאֵל!

אַזְכָּרָה
עין טור-מלכא

כֵּפִים בֶּהָרִים לְפָנֵינוּ
בִּדְמוּת אִמָּהוֹת שַׁכּוּלוֹת
שֶׁהֶמִירוּ מִקֶּדֶם דְּמוּתָן:
טְלָלִים לֹא יְרַווּן,
הַשֶּׁמֶשׁ לֹא תְּפַגֵּן.
— מַה נּוֹרָא הָאֵלֶם
וְאָנָה נִבְרַח? —
אַזְכָּרָה: תְּפִלָּה מְאַחֶרֶת לָרַחֲמִים.
הַבָּנִים מֻטָּלִים פַּרְקְדָּן
לְרֹחַב הָאֲדָמָה
וְהָאִמָּהוֹת נִצָּבוֹת:
בָּקוּ הַגֶּשֶׁם הֵן מְחַלְחָלוֹת
לְעָמְקֵי הַקְּבָרִים בַּבֶּכִי — — —

הַזְּמָן וְהַתְּגוּבָה
נתן אלתרמן

החיל אורי אילן בן העשרים, שהתאבד בכלא דמשק, הובא לקבורות
באדמת גן-שמואל, המשק שבו נולד וגדל. בהספדו סיפר הרמטכ"ל,
משה דיין, כי כשהוחזרה גופתו של אורי אילן לידי צה"ל, על הגבול,
נמצא עמדו פתק ובו המלים "לא בגדתי" ושם אמו פיגה אילנית.
(1955)

וְכָכָה — בְּפִתְאֹם, בְּמַחִי! — נוֹפֵל וְנֶעֱלָם הַחַיִץ
וְקָם זְמַנֵּנוּ גְּלוּי-פָּנִים וְנִנְעַה-פֶּתַע מְאִירוֹ.
וּמֵרְצוּעַת הַחוֹף הַזֹּאת, לְרֶגַע קָט, פְּקוּחֵי עֵינַיִם,
רוֹאִים אֲנַחְנוּ אֶת תּוֹכוֹ, אֶת מַשְׁמָעוֹ, אֶת עִקָּרוֹ.

נִגְלִים פְּנֵי נַעַר-וְחַיָּל, פְּנֵי אִישׁ, פְּנֵי צְעִירָה נוֹדֶרֶת,
אֲשֶׁר פִּתְאֹם נֶהְפָּךְ לָהֶם הַזְּמָן כְּרֶשֶׁת מְזוֹרָה.

Revealed is the face of this nation, upon which fate and an area of land
Forced such a demanding and terrible game.

Even the high-style words, which have more than once been scorned,
Lofty words like "renaissance," "homeland," or "era"
Are suddenly real and weighty. In them looms a prison night
And a young body on its floor so foreign and bare.

Such words do have deep significance. At the time that we, without realizing,
Had learned to pass over them because they were held in doubt
That very same time, a young soldier, still but a lad,
Because of them climbed to tie the end of a rope onto the prison bars.

Because of them, in that hour he whispered to himself "This is the end"
And because of them, after his falling, no one can raise him.
Because of them, before that ending came, he scratched on a page "I did not
    betray"
And letter to letter he added to write a farewell, and the name of his mother.

Perhaps it is not yet the time to sing of him in this way... but perhaps
Today is not the time to sing or tell of any other matter, either ...
This is reality, this is our way of life. This is the everyday. And the soul-of-Time
Breathes in it— not in some buzzing and gyrating cacophony.

When demands for recompense and retribution be heard, let us take this to
    heart:
Such a reaction is not the sum and substance. Not in it are fair trial and full
    utilization of the resources of Law.
For, an echo is not an echo if it does not send its waves within, deep within ...
Into our very core, into the nation at whose doorstep its own agents die.

Retribution by fire? Such may, at times, relieve the public
From making other responses— ones which ARE the essence of his testament.
Perhaps we need— how can one say it briefly?— to live differently—
To live the time, the daily life, the hour, differently.

This nation needs to remember that *it* sends the ones who go,
It needs to avenge their blood— and not from enemies alone.
Over time many poems with morals will turn into transient dust
But there are crumpled slips of paper that shall be set as a seal upon the very
    heart of Time.   ဆ

נִגְלִים פָּנָיו שֶׁל זֶה הָעָם, אֲשֶׁר גּוֹרָל וְכִבְרַת-אֶרֶץ
כָּפוּ עָלָיו אֶת הַמִּשְׂחָק הַתַּבְעֵנִי וְהַנּוֹרָא.

אַף הַמִּלִּים הַנִּמְלָצוֹת שֶׁלֹּא אַחַת הָיוּ לְקֶלֶס,
מִלִּים רָמוֹת כְּגוֹן תְּחִיָּה מוֹלֶדֶת אוֹ תְּקוּפָה
פִּתְאֹם מִלִּים אֲמִתִּיּוֹת הֵן וּכְבֵדוֹת.　בָּהֵן לֵיל כֶּלֶא
וְגוּף צָעִיר עַל רִצְפָּתוֹ הַנָּכְרִיָּה וַחֲשׂוּפָה.

מִלִּים שֶׁיֵּשׁ בָּהֵן מַהוּת.　שָׁעָה שֶׁאָנוּ בִּבְלִי-דַעַת
לָמַדְנוּ פֶּסַח עֲלֵיהֶן שֶׁכֵּן טִיבָן כֻּלּוֹ סָפֵק
הֲלֹא אוֹתָהּ שָׁעָה מַמָּשׁ, חַיָּל צָעִיר, עוֹדֶנּוּ נַעַר,
בְּשָׁלְהֶן טִפֵּס לִקְשֹׁר אֶת קְצֵה הַחֶבֶל לַסּוֹרֵג.

בְּשָׁלְהֶן אוֹתָהּ שָׁעָה לָחַשׁ הוּא אֶל נַפְשׁוֹ "אָבַדְתִּי"
וּבְשָׁלְהֶן, אַחַר נָפְלוֹ, לֹא אִישׁ יוּכַל לַהֲקִימוֹ.
בְּשָׁלְהֶן, בְּטֶרֶם קֵץ, עַל דַּף שָׂרַט הוּא "לֹא בָּגַדְתִּי"
וְאוֹת אֶל אוֹת חִבֵּר לִרְשֹׁם בִּרְכַּת שָׁלוֹם וְשֵׁם אִמּוֹ.

אֶפְשָׁר שֶׁעוֹד לֹא עֵת לָשִׁיר עָלָיו בְּדֶרֶךְ זוֹ ... אַךְ שֶׁמָּא
לֹא עֵת לָשִׁיר אוֹ לְסַפֵּר כַּיּוֹם עַל כָּל עִנְיָן אַחֵר ...
זוֹ הַמְּצִיאוּת.　זֶה הַהֹוֶה.　זֶה יוֹם הַחֹל.　וּבוֹ נוֹשֶׁמֶת
נִשְׁמַת הַזְּמַן וְלֹא בָּרַעַשׁ הַמְּהֻמֶּה וְהַסּוֹחֵר.

בְּהִשָּׁמַע תְּבִיעוֹת הַגְּמוּל וְהַתִּגוּבָה, אֶל לֵב נָשִׂימָה:
לֹא הַתִּגוּבָה הַזֹּאת עִקָּר.　לֹא בָּהּ מִשְׁפָּט וּמִצּוּי דִּין.
הַהֵד לֹא הֵד אִם אֵין אֶת גַּלָּיו אֵינוֹ מַכֶּה הוּא פְּנִימָה, פְּנִימָה ...
אֶל תּוֹךְ תּוֹכֵנוּ, אֶל הָעָם שֶׁעַל סִפּוֹ שְׁלוּחָיו מֵתִים.

תְּגוּבָה שֶׁל אֵשׁ?　הִיא לִפְעָמִים אֶת הַצִּבּוּר כְּמוֹ פוֹטֶרֶת
מִן הַתִּגוּבוֹת הָאֲחֵרוֹת, שֶׁ הֵ ן עִקַּר הַצַּוָּאָה.
אוּלַי צָרִיךְ — כֵּיצַד לוֹמַר זֹאת בְּקִצְרָה?.. — לִחְיוֹת אַחֶרֶת —
לִחְיוֹת אַחֶרֶת אֶת הַזְּמַן, אֶת הַיּוֹמְיוֹם, אֶת הַשָּׁעָה.

הָעָם הַזֶּה חַיָּב לִזְכֹּר כִּי ה ו א אֶת הַהוֹלְכִים שׁוֹלֵחַ,
וְלֹא רַק מֵאוֹיֵב בִּלְבָד חַיָּב לִגְאֹל הוּא אֶת דָּמָם.
הַרְבֵּה שִׁירֵי-מוּסָר יַהְפֹּךְ הַזְּמַן לְמוֹ אָבָק פּוֹרֵחַ
אַךְ יֵשׁ פִּתְקֵי-נְיָר קְמוּטִים שֶׁעַל לִבּוֹ יִהְיוּ חוֹתָם.

The Dust Of Poems
Nathan Yonathan

Meanwhile a great deal of time has passed
What shall we erect in his memory on this ground?

The sand in the golden canyon
Will not tell the story of his life to the winds
The willow will not relate
How the lad struggled not to die.

Meanwhile a great deal of time has passed
What shall we erect in his memory on this ground?

The gray dust of poems
Whose destiny there is none who knows
But at times, when a man is wearied by walking,
He will press his body down against such dust.

The bundle of poems' dust which drifts down
Like powder from the chariot of Time
And is brought in a bag and is buried
At the heads of the dead and the era.

Then on some forgotten evening
A girl with sad arms will come
To embrace his memory like light
From that gray dust of poems.   ℘

Without The Boy
Nathan Yonathan

In memory of Reuven Yaron

It will probably not be our lot to return to the pellucid Straits of Tiran
To the pristine, melancholy translucency visible from the rocks of Sinafir
But the heart has its Via Maris and a parade of endless memories
From the darkness of the splendid Wadi Kid to the shores of the brilliant Gulf.

אֶת עֲפַר הַשִּׁירִים

נתן יונתן

בֵּינְתַיִם הַרְבֵּה זְמַן עָבַר
מַה נָּקִים לְזִכְרוֹ עַל עָפָר?

בַּעֲרוֹץ הַזָּהָב לֹא הַחוֹל
יְסַפֵּר אֶת חַיָּיו לָרוּחוֹת
לֹא תָּשִׂיחַ עַרְבַת-הַבָּכוֹת
אֵיךְ מֵאֵן הַנַּעַר לָמוּת.

בֵּינְתַיִם הַרְבֵּה זְמַן עָבַר
מַה נָּקִים לְזִכְרוֹ עַל עָפָר?

אֶת עֲפַר הַשִּׁירִים הָאָפֹר
שֶׁאֵין אִישׁ הַיּוֹדֵעַ סוֹפוֹ
אַךְ עִתִּים בְּלֶכְתּוֹ וּבְעָיְפוֹ
הוּא כּוֹבֵשׁ בֶּעָפָר אֶת גּוּפוֹ.

צְרוֹר עֲפַר הַשִּׁירִים הַשּׁוֹמֵט
כָּאָבָק מִמֶּרְכֶּבֶת הָעֵת
וּמוּבָא בְּשַׁקִּית וְנִטְמָן
לִמְרַאֲשׁוֹת הַמֵּתִים וְהַזְּמַן.

אָז בְּעֶרֶב שָׁכוּחַ תָּבוֹא
נַעֲרָה בִּזְרוֹעוֹת עֲצוּבוֹת
לְהַקִּיף אֶת זִכְרוֹ כְּמוֹ אוֹר
מֵעֲפַר הַשִּׁירִים הָאָפֹר.

בְּלִי הַנַּעַר

נתן יונתן

לְזֵכֶר רְאוּבֵן יָרוֹן

לֹא אֲנַחְנוּ נָשׁוּב כַּנִּרְאֶה לַמִּפְרָץ שֶׁל טִירָן הַצָּלוּל
אֶל הַבְּדֹלַח הַזַּךְ-הֶעָצוּב הַנִּשְׁקָף מְצוּקֵי סִינַאפִיר
אַךְ לֵלֵב וְיָה מַאֲרִיס שֶׁלוֹ וּמַסָּע זִכְרוֹנוֹת לְאֵין גְּבוּל
מַחֲשַׁכַת וַאדִי קִיד הַנּוֹרָא עַד חוֹפֵי הַמִּפְרָץ הַמֵּאִיר.

We will never say to the children that this was a glorious trek
This was a damnable war with dust and P.O.W.'s and smoke
How good that we are still alive to turn on the lamp at our house
And write the new poem in the sadness of the old style.

To tell of a friend. Someone who was in that infantry unit
His short life summed up by one quick piece of lead
With his fallen brothers he lay on the shores of the golden canyon
While on that night the battalions continued streaming towards southern Sinai.

They did not weep for him in the shade of the granite. Leaning on their rifles'
    butts
They spoke of how he was a poet and had left behind a girl and melodies
Only later, when the battles ebbed, and, weary, we went up north,
Did we hum in light-hearted melancholy one of his beautiful songs.

It will probably not be our lot to return to the pellucid Straits of Tiran
And the pristine translucency will darken as we go far off to who-knows-where
Without that boy
                    Without his comrades
                                    Amidst a straight column of stones
Thereon we will lay our pale hands and a gray notebook of poems.   ಎ

Into a Dead Zone
Mati Katz

I crawled.
My clothes clinging from sweat and blood.
There were shots and a grenade which died away.
My muscles weary from the warring
Of a thousand eyes and a burning sun.

I gave up,
I left everything to them.
I crawled at the border of the great noise
Wounded and bleeding—
I crawled to a dead zone.   ಎ

לַיְלָדִים לֹא נַגִּיד לְעוֹלָם שֶׁהָיָה זֶה מַסָּע תִּפְאָרָה
זֹאת הָיְתָה מִלְחָמָה אֲרוּרָה עִם אָבָק וּשְׁבוּיִים וְעָשָׁן
כַּמָּה טוֹב שֶׁעוֹדֶנּוּ חַיִּים לְהַדְלִיק בְּבֵיתֵנוּ מְנוֹרָה
וְלִכְתּוֹב אֶת הַשִּׁיר הֶחָדָשׁ בְּעָגְמַת הַסִּגְנוֹן הַיָּשָׁן.

לְסַפֵּר עַל יָדִיד. מִישֶׁהוּ שֶׁהָיָה בְּסַיֶּרֶת הַקְּרָב
וְצָרַר אֶת חַיָּיו הַקְּצָרִים בְּעוֹפֶרֶת אַחַת פִּתְאוֹמִית
עִם אֶחָיו הַנּוֹפְלִים הוּא שָׁכַב עַל חוֹפוֹ שֶׁל עֲרוּץ הַזָּהָב
וּבַלַּיְלָה הַהוּא נָהֲרוּ הַגְּדוּדִים אֶל סִינַי הַדְּרוֹמִי.

לֹא בָּכוּ לוֹ בְּצֵל הַגְּרָנִיט. נִשְׁעָנִים עַל קַתּוֹת הָרוֹבִים
הֵם סִפְּרוּ שֶׁהָיָה מְשׁוֹרֵר וְהִשְׁאִיר נַעֲרָה וְתָוִים
רַק אַחַר־כָּךְ כְּשֶׁךְ הַקְּרָבוֹת כְּשֶׁעָלֵינוּ צָפוֹן עֲיֵפִים
פִּזַּמְנוּ בְּעֶצֶב עָלָיו אֲחָדִים מִשִּׁירָיו הַיָּפִים.

לֹא אֲנַחְנוּ נָשׁוּב כַּנִּרְאֶה לַמִּפְרָץ הַצָּלוּל שֶׁל טִירָן
וְהַבְּדֹּלַח הַזַּךְ יֵעָתֵם וְנִרְחִיק מִי־יוֹדֵעַ־לְאָן
בְּלִי הַנַּעַר הַהוּא
בְּלִי רֵעָיו
בִּשְׂדֵרַת אֲבָנִים יְשָׁרָה
שָׁם נָנִיחַ יָדַיִם חִוְּרוֹת וּמַחְבֶּרֶת שִׁירִים אֲפֹרָה.

לְשֶׁטַח מֵת
מתי כץ

זָחַלְתִּי,
בְּגָדַי דְּבוּקִים בְּזֵעָה וָדָם.
יְרִיּוֹת וְרִמּוֹן שֶׁנָּדַם.
שְׁרִירֵי עֲיֵפִים מִמִּלְחֶמֶת
אַלְפֵי עֵינַיִם וְשֶׁמֶשׁ יוֹקֶדֶת.

הִפְקַרְתִּי,
הִשְׁאַרְתִּי לָהֶם הַכֹּל.
זָחַלְתִּי עַל גְּבוּל הָרַעַשׁ הַגָּדוֹל
פָּצוּעַ וְשׁוֹתֵת —
זָחַלְתִּי לְשֶׁטַח מֵת.

ON SILVER WINGS
Naomi Shemer

Riding on silver wings are
The knights of the wind in the clouds
The strong and the good
Like sparks that fly upward

And within clear skies
The seven heavens sparkle
And we take off
From Golan to the Red Sea.

The sea fled and was driven back
And the river became dry
My brother flies, his face towards the light,
And his banner over me is love.

The ladder has its feet on the earth
But its top is in the skies of war
My brother is flying towards the sun
Like sparks that fly upward

He passes like the blade of the scythe
He is like a luminous arrow in flight
He inscribes a letter of fire
From Golan to the Red Sea

The sea fled and was driven back
And the river became dry
My brother flies, his face towards the light,
And his banner over me is love.

On silver wings are riding
The knights of the wind in the clouds
The strong and the good
Like sparks
That fly
Upward   ∞

עַל כַּנְפֵי הַכֶּסֶף
נעמי שמר

עַל כַּנְפֵי הַכֶּסֶף רְכוּבִים
אַבִּירֵי הָרוּחַ בֶּעָבִים
הָעַזִּים וְהַטּוֹבִים
כִּבְנֵי-רֶשֶׁף יַגְבִּיהוּ עוּף

וּבְתוֹךְ שָׁמַיִם נְקִיִּים
זוֹהֲרִים שִׁבְעַת הָרְקִיעִים
וַאֲנַחְנוּ מַמְרִיאִים
מִגּוֹלָן וְעַד יַם-סוּף

נָס הַיָּם וַיִּסֹּב אָחוֹר
וְהַנָּהָר — חֳרָבָה
טָס אָחִי וּפָנָיו לָאוֹר
וְדִגְלוֹ עָלַי אַהֲבָה

הַסֻּלָּם רַגְלָיו בָּאֲדָמָה
אַךְ רֹאשׁוֹ בִּשְׁמֵי הַמִּלְחָמָה
טָס אָחִי אֶל מוּל חַמָּה
כִּבְנֵי-רֶשֶׁף יַגְבִּיהוּ עוּף

הוּא חוֹלֵף כַּלַהַב-הַחֶרְמֵשׁ
הוּא כַּחֵץ שָׁלוּחַ וְלוֹחֵשׁ
הוּא כּוֹתֵב מִכְתָּב שֶׁל אֵשׁ
מִגּוֹלָן וְעַד יַם-סוּף

נָס הַיָּם וַיִּסֹּב אָחוֹר
וְהַנָּהָר — חֳרָבָה
טָס אָחִי וּפָנָיו לָאוֹר
וְדִגְלוֹ עָלַי אַהֲבָה

עַל כַּנְפֵי הַכֶּסֶף רְכוּבִים
אַבִּירֵי הָרוּחַ בֶּעָבִים
הָעַזִּים וְהַטּוֹבִים
כִּבְנֵי-רֶשֶׁף
יַגְבִּיהוּ
עוּף

PARADE OF THE FALLEN
Haiim Hefer

They come from the mountains, from the lowlands, from the desert\ They come
—names, faces, eyes— and present themselves for the parade\ They come with
manly stride, strong and tanned\ They come out of the crashed planes and from
the burnt tanks\ They rise from behind rocks, beyond the dunes, and in the
trenches\ Brave as lions, strong as leopards, and swift as an eagle\ And they pass
one by one between two rows of angels\ Who feed them sweets and drape gar-
lands around their necks\ I look at them and they are all happy\ These are my
brothers, these are my brothers.

And they meet each other, brown eyes and blue and black\ And they speak to
each other of names and weapons and places\ And they pour each other cups of
coffee and tea\ And suddenly break out in shouts of "Hurrah!"\ And they meet in
the great crowd comrades and friends\ Officers slap the backs of the privates and
privates shake officers' hands\ And they start singing and clapping\ And all those
dwelling in heaven listen to them with amazement\ And the reunion goes on day
and night, night and day\ Because such a group has never been up there before\
Then suddenly they hear familiar voices weeping\ And they look towards home at
mother and father, at the women and children and brothers\ And their faces
slacken and they stand in confusion\ And then someone whispers: Forgive us,
but we just had to\ We won the battles and now we are at rest\ These are my
brothers, these are my brothers.

And thus they stand with their faces in the light\ And only God himself walks
among them\ And with tears in his eyes he kisses their wounds\ And he says with
throbbing voice to his white angels:\ These are my sons, these are the sons.   ℘

THE PARATROOPERS ARE WEEPING
Haiim Hefer

This Wall has heard many prayers\ This Wall has seen many walls tumbling
down\ This Wall has felt the hands of mourning women and notes that are
slipped between its stones\ This Wall has seen Rabbi Judah Halevi trampled in
front of it\ This Wall has seen emperors rising and overthrown\ But this Wall has
not yet seen paratroopers weeping.

This Wall has seen them weary and exhausted\ This Wall has seen them wounded
and gashed\ Running to it with swift beating of hearts, with shouts, and with
silence\ And forward-leaping, like madmen, in the alleys of the Old City\ And they
are covered with dirt and their lips are parched\ And they whisper: "If I forget

מִסְדַּר הַנּוֹפְלִים
חיים חפר

הֵם בָּאִים מִן הֶהָרִים, מִן הַשְּׁפֵלָה, מִן הַמִּדְבָּר ∞ הֵם בָּאִים - שֵׁמוֹת, פָּנִים, עֵינַיִם — וּמִתְיַצְּבִים אֶל הַמִּסְדָּר ∞ הֵם בָּאִים בְּצַעַד גַּבְרִי, חֲזָקִים וּשְׂזוּפִים ∞ הֵם יוֹצְאִים מִתּוֹךְ הַמְּטוֹסִים הַמְרֻסָּקִים וּמִן הַטַּנְקִים הַשְּׂרוּפִים ∞ הֵם קָמִים מֵאֲחוֹרֵי הַסְּלָעִים, מֵעֵבֶר לַדִּיּוּנוֹת וּמִתּוֹךְ תְּעָלוֹת הַקֶּשֶׁר ∞ גִּבּוֹרִים כַּאֲרָיוֹת, עַזִּים כִּנְמֵרִים וְקַלִּים כַּנֶּשֶׁר ∞ וְהֵם עוֹבְרִים אֶחָד אֶחָד בֵּין שְׁתֵּי שׁוּרוֹת שֶׁל מַלְאָכִים ∞ הַמַּאֲכִילִים אוֹתָם סֻכָּרִיּוֹת וְעוֹנְדִים עַל צַנָּארָם פְּרָחִים ∞ וַאֲנִי מַבִּיט בָּהֶם וְהֵם כֻּלָּם שְׂמֵחִים ∞ אֵלֶּה הָאַחִים שֶׁלִּי, אֵלֶּה הָאַחִים.

וְהֵם פּוֹגְשִׁים זֶה אֶת זֶה, עֵינַיִם שְׁחוֹרוֹת וּכְחֻלּוֹת וְחוּמוֹת ∞ וְהֵם מַזְכִּירִים זֶה לָזֶה שֵׁמוֹת וּכְלֵי נֶשֶׁק וּמְקוֹמוֹת ∞ וּמוֹזְגִים זֶה לָזֶה סְפָלֵי קָפֶה וְתֵה ∞ וּמִתְפָּרְצִים פִּתְאֹם יַחַד בִּקְרִיאוֹת: כֵּיפַאק הַיי! ∞ וְהֵם פּוֹגְשִׁים בַּקָּהָל הָרָב רֵעִים וִידִידִים ∞ וְהַמְּפַקְּדִים טוֹפְחִים עַל שֶׁכֶם הַטּוּרָאִים וְטוּרָאִים לוֹחֲצִים יָד לַמְּפַקְּדִים ∞ וְהֵם פּוֹרְצִים בְּשִׁירָה וּמוֹחֲאִים כַּפַּיִם ∞ וּמַקְשִׁיבִים לָהֶם בְּהִתְפַּעֲלוּת כָּל יוֹשְׁבֵי הַשָּׁמַיִם ∞ וְהַפְּגִישָׁה נִמְשֶׁכֶת יוֹם וָלַיְלָה יוֹם וָלַיְלָה ∞ כִּי חֲבוּרָה שֶׁכַּזֹּאת לֹא הָיְתָה עוֹד לְמַעְלָה ∞ וְאָז פִּתְאֹם הֵם שׁוֹמְעִים קוֹלוֹת מֵכָרִים בּוֹכִים ∞ וְהֵם מַבִּיטִים הַבַּיְתָה אֶל אַבָּא וְאִמָּא, אֶל הַנָּשִׁים וְהַיְלָדִים וְהָאַחִים ∞ וּפְנֵיהֶם דּוֹמְמוֹת וְהֵם עוֹמְדִים נְבוֹכִים ∞ וְאָז מִישֶׁהוּ מָהֵר מָהֵר לוֹחֵשׁ: סְלִיחָה, אֲבָל הָיִינוּ מֻכְרָחִים ∞ נִצַּחְנוּ בַּקְּרָבוֹת וְכָעֵת אָנוּ נָחִים ∞ אֵלֶּה הָאַחִים שֶׁלִּי ∞ אֵלֶּה הָאַחִים.

וְכָכָה הֵם עוֹמְדִים וְהָאוֹר עַל פְּנֵיהֶם ∞ וְרַק אֱלֹהִים לְבַדּוֹ עוֹבֵר בֵּינֵיהֶם ∞ וּכְשֶׁדִּמְעוֹת בְּעֵינָיו הוּא מְנַשֵּׁק אֶת פִּצְעֵיהֶם ∞ וְהוּא אוֹמֵר בְּקוֹל רוֹטֵט לַמַּלְאָכִים הַלְּבָנִים: ∞ אֵלֶּה הַבָּנִים שֶׁלִּי, אֵלֶּה הַבָּנִים.

הַצַּנְחָנִים בּוֹכִים
חיים חפר

הַכֹּתֶל הַזֶּה שָׁמַע הַרְבֵּה תְּפִלּוֹת ∞ הַכֹּתֶל הַזֶּה רָאָה הַרְבֵּה חוֹמוֹת נוֹפְלוֹת ∞ הַכֹּתֶל הַזֶּה חָשׁ יְדֵי נָשִׁים מְקוֹנְנוֹת וּפִתְקָאוֹת הַנִּתְחָבוֹת בֵּין אֲבָנָיו ∞ הַכֹּתֶל הַזֶּה רָאָה אֶת רַבִּי יְהוּדָה הַלֵּוִי נִרְמָס לְפָנָיו ∞ הַכֹּתֶל הַזֶּה רָאָה קֵיסָרִים קָמִים וְנִמְחִים ∞ אַךְ הַכֹּתֶל לֹא רָאָה עוֹד צַנְחָנִים בּוֹכִים.

הַכֹּתֶל הַזֶּה רָאָה אוֹתָם עֲיֵפִים וּסְחוּטִים ∞ הַכֹּתֶל הַזֶּה רָאָה אוֹתָם פְּצוּעִים וְשָׂרוּטִים ∞ רָצִים אֵלָיו בְּהַלְמוּת לֵב, בִּשְׁאָגוֹת וּבִשְׁתִיקָה ∞ וּמְזֻנָּקִים כְּמֶטְרָפִים בְּסִמְטָאוֹת הָעִיר הָעַתִּיקָה ∞ וְהֵם שְׁטוּפֵי אָבָק וְצָרוּבֵי שְׂפָתַיִם ∞

thee, if I forget thee, O Jerusalem…"\ And they are as agile as eagles and fiercely strong as lions\ And their tanks— the chariot of fire of Elijah the prophet\ Passing by like thunder\ Passing by in fury\ And they remember all the woeful years\ In which we hadn't even had a Wall before which to shed tears.

And behold, they are here standing before it, breathing deeply\ And behold, they are here gazing upon it in such sweet pain\ And the tears are running and they look at each other, embarrassed\ How is it that paratroopers are weeping\ How is it that they are touching, exultant, the wall\ How is it that from weeping they change to song\ Perhaps it is that nineteen-year-olds who were born with the founding of the nation\ Carry upon their backs— two thousand years.   ∞

(June 1967)

In The Night
Karmela Lakhish

You did not open the door
And you did not come in your gray military tunic
From the dirt of the field
I heard your voice tonight
I heard the rifle.
But you did not pass by in your dusty military tunic
And you did not come up in your army boots
In the night
And it was not the rifle that bumped against the wall
For you did not open the door in the night
And your breathing you did not quicken
You did not whisper
I did not cry out
Your head is not sleeping on my heart.   ∞

Missing Out
Eli Alon

Foliage of years, autumn of life
They lie layer upon layer,
The casualties of war.

וְהֵם לוֹחֲשִׁים: אִם אֶשְׁכָּחֵךְ, אִם אֶשְׁכָּחֵךְ, יְרוּשָׁלַיִם ◈ וְהֵם קַלִּים כַּנֶּשֶׁר וְעַזִּים
כַּלָּבִיא ◈ וְהַטַּנְקִים שֶׁלָּהֶם – מֶרְכֶּבֶת הָאֵשׁ שֶׁל אֵלִיָּהוּ הַנָּבִיא ◈ וְהֵם
עוֹבְרִים כָּרַעַם ◈ וְהֵם עוֹבְרִים בְּזַעַם ◈ וְהֵם זוֹכְרִים אֶת כָּל הַשָּׁנִים הַנּוֹרָאוֹת
◈ שֶׁבָּהֶן לֹא הָיָה לָנוּ אֲפִלּוּ כֹּתֶל כְּדֵי לִשְׁפּוֹךְ לְפָנָיו דְּמָעוֹת.

וְהִנֵּה הֵם כָּאן עוֹמְדִים לְפָנָיו וְנוֹשְׁמִים עָמֹק ◈ וְהִנֵּה הֵם כָּאן מַבִּיטִים עָלָיו
בִּכְאֵב הַמָּתוּק ◈ וְהַדְּמָעוֹת יוֹרְדוֹת וְהֵם מַבִּיטִים זֶה בָּזֶה נְבוֹכִים ◈ אֵיךְ זֶה
קוֹרֶה, אֵיךְ זֶה קוֹרֶה שֶׁצַּנְחָנִים בּוֹכִים ◈ אֵיךְ זֶה קוֹרֶה שֶׁהֵם נוֹגְעִים נִרְגָּשִׁים
בַּקִּיר ◈ אֵיךְ זֶה קוֹרֶה שֶׁמָּן הַבֶּכִי הֵם עוֹבְרִים לְשִׁיר ◈ אוּלַי מִפְּנֵי שֶׁבָּחוּרִים
בְּנֵי י"ט שֶׁנּוֹלְדוּ עִם קוֹם הַמְּדִינָה ◈ נוֹשְׂאִים עַל גַּבָּם – אַלְפַּיִם שָׁנָה.

יוני 67

בַּלַּיְלָה
כרמלה לכיש

אֶת הַדֶּלֶת אַתָּה לֹא פָּתַחְתָּ
וְלֹא בָּאתָ בִּמְעִיל הַחַיָּלִים הָאָפֹר
מֵעֲפַר הַשָּׂדֶה
שָׁמַעְתִּי קוֹלְךָ הַלַּיְלָה
שָׁמַעְתִּי אֶת הָרוֹבֶה.
וְלֹא עָבַרְתָּ בִּמְעִיל הַחַיָּלִים הֶעָפֹר
וְלֹא עָלִיתָ בְּמִנְעֲלֵי הַחַיָּלִים
בַּלַּיְלָה
וְלֹא הָרוֹבֶה נֶחְבַּט אֶל הַקִּיר
וְלֹא פָּתַחְתָּ אֶת הַדֶּלֶת בַּלַּיְלָה
וּנְשִׁימָתְךָ לֹא הֶחֱשָׁתְ
לֹא לָחַשְׁתָּ
לֹא צָעַקְתִּי
לֹא רֹאשְׁךָ הַיָּשֵׁן עִם לִבִּי.

הַחֲמָצָה
א. עלי

עֲלוֹת שָׁנִים, שַׁלֶּכֶת חַיִּים
הֵם שׁוֹכְבִים שָׁם שִׁכְבָה עַל שִׁכְבָה,
הֲרוּגֵי הַמִּלְחָמוֹת,

And just as one cannot distinguish the separate bodies—
Their integrity too has melted and commingled
And naught is left but suffocation in the darkness;

And the thirsty, pallid earth of the dead clings
Onto the arrivals from the latest war
Leaching-out life—

And David from '48 (who was hit in the back by a bullet)
Sighs without words: Had I lived
And had I taken myself a wife
I would have had a son now,
A soldier…

And the dirt nods without a head in understanding,
And falls into thoughts of yearnings,
Long long thoughts of the dead,
Endless calculations,

And the earth daydreams agony.   ൚

If There Is A God
Eli Alon

If there is a god in war
He comes down as an army doctor
In the company of his angel-medics
Lacerated by the volume of work

With his khaki wings he leans over the dying there among the bullets
Blocking their open arteries with soft hopes

Injecting them with a last joke
In preparation for the terrible excursion
He cannot prevent wars
He can not win in them either

He always loses
To the Angel of Death   ൚

וּכְשֵׁם שֶׁאֵין לְהַבְחִין בַּגּוּפוֹת —
גַּם צִדְקוֹתֵיהֶם נָמַסּוּ וְהִתְעַרְבְּבוּ
וְלֹא נוֹתַר אֶלָּא מַחֲנָק בָּאֲפֵלָה;

וּצְמֵאָה נִצְמֶדֶת אַדְמַת הַמֵּתִים הַחוֹזֶרֶת
לְבָאֵי הַמִּלְחָמָה הָאַחֲרוֹנָה
נוֹטְפֵי הַחַיִּים —

וְדָוִד מֵ-48 (שֶׁקִּבֵּל כַּדּוּר בְּגַבּוֹ)
נֶאֱנַח בְּלִי פֶּה: אִלּוּ חָיִיתִי
וְהָיִיתִי נוֹשֵׂא לִי אִשָּׁה
הָיָה לִי בֵּן עַכְשָׁו,
חַיָּל ...

וְהֶעָפָר מְנַעֲנֵעַ בַּהֲבָנָה לְלֹא רָאשִׁים,
וְשׁוֹקֵעַ בְּהִרְהוּרֵי גַּעְגּוּעִים,
הִרְהוּרֵי מֵתִים אֲרֻכִּים,
חֲשׁוּבִים לְלֹא סוֹף,

וְהָאֲדָמָה הוֹזָה יָגוֹן.

אִם יֵשׁ אֱלֹהִים
א. עֵלִי

אִם יֵשׁ אֱלֹהִים בַּמִּלְחָמָה,
הוּא יוֹרֵד כְּרוֹפֵא קְרָבִי
עִם פְּלֻגַּת מַלְאָכָיו הַחוֹבְשִׁים
הַנִּקְרַעַת מֵרֹב עֲבוֹדָה

הוּא רוֹכֵן בְּכַנְפֵי הַחַאקִי אֶל הַגּוֹסְסִים בֵּין הַכַּדּוּרִים
חוֹסֵם אֶת עוֹרְקֵיהֶם הַפְּתוּחִים בְּתִקְוָות רַכּוֹת

מַזְרִיק לָהֶם בְּדִיחָה אַחֲרוֹנָה
לִקְרַאת הַמַּסָּע הַנּוֹרָא
אֵין הוּא יָכֹל לִמְנוֹעַ מִלְחָמוֹת
גַּם לְנַצֵּחַ בָּהֶן אֵינוֹ יָכֹל

הוּא מַפְקִיד אוֹתָן
לְמַלְאַךְ הַמָּוֶת.

Leave-Taking
Eli Alon

Death in a war
Is the most difficult leave-taking.
We go to die so that our loved ones will live
Yet we will see them no more.

We give them life in the places that we loved,
Under the cool trees,
In the whimsical wind—

Over there, on the green lawns—
There they will forget us
In their pleasures…

They will not accompany us to that land of exile
To which we descend
As an old lady would accompany her husband
To pat him and comfort him
And divert his thoughts
With her chitchat—

Alone we descend
Into the rooms without furniture
Where there is nothing at all
On which to hang our love.   &

In The Mount Of Final Repose
Eli Alon

    To Amnon and Hanan from Ein Shemer, who fell in Jerusalem

In The Mount of Final Repose there is no repose.
Rank by rank the burnt-offerings are lowered
    Into the narrow graves—
But the earth cannot accept them.

פְּרֵדָה

א. עלי

הַמָּוֶת בַּמִּלְחָמָה
הוּא הַפְּרֵדָה הַקָּשָׁה בְּיוֹתֵר.
הוֹלְכִים לָמוּת כְּדֵי שֶׁהָאֲהוּבִים יִחְיוּ
וְלֹא נִרְאֶה אוֹתָם עוֹד.

אָנוּ נוֹתְנִים לָהֶם חַיִּים בַּמָּקוֹם אֲשֶׁר אָהַבְנוּ,
תַּחַת הָעֵצִים הַקְּרִירִים,
בְּרוּחַ הַשּׁוֹבֵבָה —

שָׁם, עַל הַדְּשָׁאִים הַיְרֻקִּים —
שָׁם יִשְׁכְּחוּנוּ
בַּתַּעֲנוּגוֹת ...

הֵם לֹא יְלַוּוּנוּ לְאֶרֶץ הַגְּזֵרָה
אֲלֶיהָ אָנוּ יוֹרְדִים
כְּהַלָּוֹת הַזְּקֵנָה לְבַעֲלָה
לְלַטֵּף אוֹתוֹ וּלְנַחֲמוֹ
וּלְהַסִּיחַ אֶת דַּעְתּוֹ
בְּפִטְפּוּטֶיהָ —

בָּדָד אָנוּ יוֹרְדִים
אֶל הַחֲדָרִים חַסְרֵי הָרַהוּט
שֶׁאֵין בָּם גַּם חֵפֶץ אֶחָד
לִתְלוֹת עָלָיו אַהֲבָה.

בְּהַר-הַמְּנֻחוֹת

א. עלי

לאמנון וחנן, בני עין-שמר, שנפלו בירושלים

בְּהַר-הַמְּנֻחוֹת אֵין מְנֻחוֹת.
שׁוּרוֹת שׁוּרוֹת מֵנָחוֹת הָעוֹלוֹת
בַּקֶּבֶר הַצַּר —
וְהָאֲדָמָה אֵינָהּ יְכוֹלָה לְקַבְּלָן.

There is no repose in the Mount of Final Repose.
Desperate soldiers— rank upon rank
    Are struggling: digging in with their fingernails in the rock,
Spearing the darkness with their elbows,
Whispering to the Earth: Accept our offering, O Mother,
Accept us…

And the hard, faithful soil of Jerusalem
The loving soil of Jerusalem,
Cannot accept them:

They are not composed of death,
They are not hers—
Vigorous, young forever, they are laughing and boisterous
With their death upon them lightly like a mask
So how can she accept them, how incorporate them into her veins—
The decrepitude of pine, pallor of stone,
Stillness of mountains,
To place them as frozen pillars of memories
In the eternal walls of Jerusalem?

(Oh, the muteness of the ones left behind in the emptiness,
And the weeping of mothers and widows and children
Pleading for the dead)

And the hard, good soil of Jerusalem
The soil of Jerusalem who is drained of tears
The faithful soil of Jerusalem
Strains herself… and strains herself…
To naught but helplessness…

And in The Mount of Final Repose there is no repose.
Rank upon rank of burnt-offerings
Untrammeled, peerless,
Are crying in the narrow graves,
Are imploring the Earth: Accept us, O Mother—
Harbor us—
For we have been torn out of life
Yet unto death we cannot come.   &

אֵין מְנוּחוֹת בְּהַר-הַמְּנוּחוֹת.
חַיָּלִים נוֹאָשִׁים — שׁוּרוֹת שׁוּרוֹת
נֶאֱבָקִים: מִתְחַפְּרִים בְּצִפָּרְנֵיהֶם בַּסֶּלַע,
חוֹתְרִים בְּמַרְפְּקֵיהֶם בָּאֹפֶל,
לוֹחֲשִׁים לָאֲדָמָה קְחִי אֶת מְנָחָתֵנוּ, הוֹ אִמָּא,
קַבְּלִי אוֹתָנוּ ...

וְאַדְמַת יְרוּשָׁלַיִם הַקָּשָׁה וְהַנֶּאֱמָנָה,
אַדְמַת יְרוּשָׁלַיִם הָאוֹהֶבֶת,
אֵינָהּ יְכוֹלָה לְקַבְּלָם:

הֵם אֵינָם עֲשׂוּיִים מָוֶת,
הֵם אֵינָם שֶׁלָּהּ:
שׁוֹקְקִים, צְעִירִים לָעַד הֵם צוֹחֲקִים וְרוֹעֲשִׁים
וּמוֹתָם עֲלֵיהֶם כְּמַסֵּכָה
וְאֵיךְ תְּקַבְּלֵם, אֵיךְ תְּעָרֵם בְּמַחְזוֹר דָּמָהּ —
זִקְנַת-אֶרֶץ, חֶרְרוֹן-אֶבֶן,
דִּמְמַת-הָרִים,
לָשִׂימָם נְצִיבֵי זִכְרוֹנוֹת קוֹפְאִים
בְּחוֹמוֹת הַנֶּצַח שֶׁל יְרוּשָׁלַיִם?

(וּשְׁתִיקַת הַנּוֹתָרִים בַּחֲלָלִים
וּבְכִי אִמָּהוֹת וְאַלְמָנוֹת וִילָדִים
מְבַקְּשִׁים עַל הַחֲלָלִים)

וְאַדְמַת יְרוּשָׁלַיִם הַקָּשָׁה וְהַטּוֹבָה,
אַדְמַת יְרוּשָׁלַיִם שֶׁיָּבְשָׁה מִדֶּמַע,
אַדְמַת יְרוּשָׁלַיִם הָאֲמוּנָה
מִתְאַמֶּצֶת וּמִתְאַמֶּצֶת —
וְאֵינֶנָּה עוֹצֶרֶת כֹּחַ ...

וּבְהַר-הַמְּנוּחוֹת אֵין מְנוּחוֹת.
שׁוּרוֹת שׁוּרוֹת שֶׁל עוֹלוֹת
טְהוֹרוֹת, מֵבְחָרוֹת
בּוֹכוֹת בַּקֶּבֶר הַצַּר,
מִתְחַנְּנוֹת לָאֲדָמָה קַבְּלִי אוֹתָנוּ, הוֹ אִמָּא,
אִסְפִי אוֹתָנוּ,
כִּי קְרַעֲנוּ מִתּוֹךְ הַחַיִּים
וְאֶל הַמָּוֶת אֵינֶנּוּ יְכוֹלִים לָבוֹא.

Always In Anguish
Eli Alon

Always in anguish.
Always in blood.
For us, spring does not come without cost.

Under each cyclamen, every new-life, every poppy
Some man goes to lie
In the fullness of his strength, in the fullness of his warmth,
In the fullness of his love—
To render his life into them.

Down, to the caverns of death, to the dungeons of torment
Go the brave, the loyal
For who can withstand
This death— and not betray?

Who shall go down into the mouth of Avernus, to the Gehenna of anguish,
To the fiery pit of the world
To fuel life with one's body
And utter no word?

Only dark forces flow from the abyss
Recrudescent in all their intensity—

So this is spring.
And in all the land there is not one flower that is not
A man.   &

[I sat upon the ground]
Abba Kovner

I sat upon the ground, and the ground was fire.
I got up from the ground, and the ground was fire.
I ran
Oceans in front of my face, my face on my hands
And my hands were fire.

תָּמִיד בְּיִסּוּרִים
א. עלי

תָּמִיד בְּיִסּוּרִים.
תָּמִיד בְּדָם.
אֵין לָנוּ אָבִיב חִנָּם.

מִתַּחַת כָּל רַקֶּפֶת, כָּל תִּינוֹק, כָּל פֶּרַג
הוֹלֵךְ אָדָם לִשְׁכַּב
בִּמְלֹא אוֹנוֹ, בִּמְלֹא חֵמוֹ,
בִּמְלֹא אַהֲבָתוֹ —
לָתֵת בָּהֶם אֶת חַיָּיו.

לְמַטָּה, לְמִכְרוֹת הַמָּוֶת, לְמַרְתְּפֵי הָעִנּוּיִים
הוֹלְכִים הָאַמִּיצִים, הַנֶּאֱמָנִים
כִּי מִי עוֹד יוּכַל לַעֲמֹד
בַּמָּוֶת הַזֶּה — וְלֹא יִבְגֹּד?

לָרֶדֶת אֶל לַעַ תַּחְתִּיּוֹת, אֶל שְׁאוֹל הַיִּסּוּרִים,
אֶל תַּנּוּר הָעוֹלָם
לְהַסִּיק בְּגוּפָם אֶת הַחַיִּים
וְלֹא לְהוֹצִיא מִלָּה? ...

רַק כֹּחוֹת אֲפֵלִים זוֹרְמִים מִמַּעֲמַקִּים
פּוֹרְחִים בְּכָל מְאֹדָם —

וְזֶה הָאָבִיב.
וְאֵין בָּאָרֶץ פֶּרַח שֶׁאֵינֶנּוּ
אָדָם.

[יָשַׁבְתִּי עַל הָאָרֶץ]
אבא קובנר

יָשַׁבְתִּי עַל הָאָרֶץ, וְהָאָרֶץ אֵשׁ.
קַמְתִּי מֵהָאָרֶץ. הָאָרֶץ אֵשׁ.
רַצְתִּי
יַמִּים לְפָנַי פָּנַי עַל יָדִי
וְיָדִי אֵשׁ.

There must be a land
Which is of us
Behold— land passed through fire!   ∞

[My comrades]
Abba Kovner

My comrades
Inasmuch as they are comrades do not need to study the map
By the light of a candle. All they need is a simple marker,
Like a stone that sometimes one turns over, like
A tree blossoming reluctantly in the bare sand.
A desert

This is not a waste howling wilderness
In the eyes of the comrades, but simply
A desert. And the name is spelled out
On the pocket map. Because my comrades
And the desert

They are a multiple who became one. And one is
The place, perhaps the only place in all the world
Where a man does not die alone.   ∞

MY CHILD SMELLS OF PEACE
Yehudah Amichai

My child smells of peace.
When I lean over him,
It is not merely the scent of soap.

All men were once children who smelled of peace.
(And in all the land was heard no more
The sound of the mill.)

Oh, land torn like clothing
That cannot be mended.

יְשָׁנָה וַדַּאי אֶרֶץ
וְהִיא מִשֶּׁלָּנוּ
אֵיךְ בָּאָה אֶרֶץ בָּאֵשׁ!

[רֵעִי]

אבא קובנר

רֵעִי
בַּאֲשֶׁר הֵם רֵעִים אֵינָם צְרִיכִים עִיּוּן בַּמַּפָּה
לְאוֹר הַנֵּר. דַּיָּם בִּנְקֻדַּת צִיּוּן פְּשׁוּטָה
כְּמוֹ אֶבֶן שַׁיִשׁ וְהוֹפְכִים כְּגוֹן
עֵץ מְלַבְלֵב עַל כָּרְחוֹ בְּקָרַחַת הַחוֹל.
מִדְבָּר

לֹא תְּהוּ יְלֵל יְשִׁימוֹן הוּא
בְּעֵינֵי הָרֵעִים אֶלָּא מִדְבָּר
כִּפְשׁוּטוֹ. וְהַשֵּׁם מְפֹרָשׁ
בְּמַפַּת הַכִּיס. כִּי רֵעִי
וּמִדְבָּר

הֵם אֲחָדִים שֶׁהָיוּ לְאֶחָד. וְאֶחָד
הַמָּקוֹם וְאוּלַי הַיָּחִיד בָּעוֹלָם
לֹא יָמוּת בּוֹ הָאָדָם לְבַדּוֹ.

יַלְדֵי נוֹדֵף שָׁלוֹם

יהודה עמיחי

יַלְדֵּי נוֹדֵף שָׁלוֹם.
כְּשֶׁאֲנִי רָכוּן מֵעָלָיו,
זֶה לֹא רַק רֵיחַ הַסַּבּוֹן.

כָּל הָאֲנָשִׁים הָיוּ יְלָדִים שֶׁנָּדְפוּ שָׁלוֹם.
(וּבְכָל הָאָרֶץ לֹא נִשְׁאַר
אַף גַּלְגַּל טַחֲנָה אַחַת שֶׁיִּסְתּוֹבֵב.)

הוֹ, הָאָרֶץ הַקְּרוּעָה כִּבְגָדִים
שֶׁאֵין לָהֶם תִּקּוּן.

Harsh and lonely ancestors in the caves of Machpelah.
Barren silence.

My child smells of peace.
His mother's womb promised him
What God cannot
Promise us.   ℘

We Have No Unknown Soldiers
Yehudah Amichai

In memory of Yonathan Yahil

We have no unknown soldiers,
Nor a Tomb of The Unknown Soldier,
Whoever wants to lay a wreath
Would have to take his wreath apart
Into many flowers and separate them
Into petals and scatter them.
And all the dead come home
And all of them have names,
You too, Yonathan
My student, whose name on the class roster
Is now in the list of the dead.
My student that you were,
One-of-a-name that you were,
The one of your name.
Just a while back I sat with you
In the cabin of a truck on the dirt road
Near Ein Gedi. Dust
Rose behind us
So we did not see the mountains.
Dust concealed what was destined
To happen three years
Later: Now.
Please, even those of you who did not know him,
Love him after his death, too,
Love him: now one of the fallen,

אָבוֹת קָשִׁים וּבוֹדְדִים גַּם בִּמְעָרוֹת הַמַּכְפֵּלָה.
דְּמָמָה חֲשׂוּכַת בָּנִים.

יַלְדֵי נוֹדֵף שָׁלוֹם.
רֶחֶם אִמּוֹ הִבְטִיחָה לוֹ
מַה שֶׁאֱלֹהִים אֵינוֹ יָכוֹל
לְהַבְטִיחַ לָנוּ.

אֵין לָנוּ חַיָּלִים אַלְמוֹנִים
יהודה עמיחי

לְזֵכֶר יוֹנָתָן יְחִיל

אֵין לָנוּ חַיָּלִים אַלְמוֹנִים.
אֵין לָנוּ קֶבֶר הַחַיָּל הָאַלְמוֹנִי,
מִי שֶׁרוֹצֶה לְהָנִיחַ זֵרוֹ
צָרִיךְ לְפָרֵק אֶת זֵרוֹ
לְהַרְבֵּה פְּרָחִים וּלְחַלְּקָם
לְעָלִים וּלְפַזְּרָם.
וְכָל הַמֵּתִים שָׁבִים הַבַּיְתָה
וּלְכֻלָּם שֵׁמוֹת,
גַּם לְךָ, יוֹנָתָן
תַּלְמִידִי, אֲשֶׁר שִׁמְךָ בְּיוֹמַן הַכִּתָּה
כְּשִׁמְךָ בִּרְשִׁימַת הַמֵּתִים.
תַּלְמִידִי שֶׁהָיִיתָ,
בַּעַל שֵׁם שֶׁהָיִיתָ,
בַּעַל שִׁמְךָ.
בָּאַחֲרוֹנָה יָשַׁבְתִּי אִתְּךָ
בְּאַרְגַּז מְכוֹנִית בְּדֶרֶךְ הֶעָפָר
לְיַד עֵין גֶּדִי. אָבָק
הִתְרוֹמֵם מֵאֲחוֹרֵינוּ
וְלֹא רָאִינוּ אֶת הֶהָרִים.
אָבָק הִסְתִּיר אֶת מַה שֶׁצָּרִיךְ
הָיָה לִקְרוֹת שָׁלֹשׁ שָׁנִים
לְאַחַר מִכֵּן: עַכְשָׁו.
אָנָּא, גַּם אֵלֶּה שֶׁלֹּא הִכִּירוּ אוֹתוֹ,
אֶהֱבוּ אוֹתוֹ גַּם אַחַר מוֹתוֹ,
אֶהֱבוּ אוֹתוֹ: עַכְשָׁו חָלָל,

An empty space whose shape— his shape
Whose name— his name.   ഌ

WILDLING PEACE
Yehudah Amichai

Not that of a truce,
Nor yet that of the vision of wolf with lamb,
But,
As in the heart after fierce excitement:
Speaking only of great exhaustion.
I know that I know to slay,
Therefore I am grown up.
And my son plays with a toy gun which knows how
To open and close its eyes and say "Mama."
Peace
Without the clangor of beating swords into plowshares, without words, without
The heavy thumping of official seals; let it be frothy
All over, like some white and languid foam.
Simply respite for the wounds;
Not even healing.
(The crying of orphans is passed from one generation
To another as in a relay: never a baton falls.)

Let it be
Like wildflowers,
Sudden, from the field's own need:
Wildling peace.   ഌ

A PLACE OF FIRE
Zelda

Mountain air Living air
Beloved blowing
Beg mercy for our sakes
From the One Who Is Above All.
A place of fire,

מָקוֹם רֵיק שֶׁצּוּרָתוֹ — צוּרָתוֹ
וּשְׁמוֹ — שְׁמוֹ.

שָׁלוֹם בַּר
יהודה עמיחי

לֹא זֶה שֶׁל שְׁבִיתַת נֶשֶׁק,
אֲפִלּוּ לֹא שֶׁל חָזוֹן זְאֵב עִם גְּדִי,
אֶלָּא,
כְּמוֹ בַּלֵּב אַחַר הַהִתְרַגְּשׁוּת:
לְדַבֵּר רַק עַל עֲיֵפוּת גְּדוֹלָה.
אֲנִי יוֹדֵעַ שֶׁאֲנִי יוֹדֵעַ לְהָמִית,
לָכֵן אֲנִי מְבֻגָּר.
וּבְנִי מְשַׂחֵק בְּרוֹבֶה צַעֲצוּעִים שֶׁיּוֹדֵעַ
לִפְתֹּחַ וְלַעֲצֹם עֵינַיִם וּלְהַגִּיד, אִמָּא.
שָׁלוֹם
בְּלִי רַעַשׁ כְּתוּת חֲרָבוֹת לְאִתִּים, בְּלִי מִלִּים, בְּלִי
קוֹל חוֹתָמוֹת כְּבֵדוֹת; שֶׁיִּהְיֶה קַל
מֵעַל, כְּקֶצֶף לָבָן וְעָצֵל.
מְנוּחָה לַפְּצָעִים;
אֲפִלּוּ לֹא אֲרוּכָה.
(וְזַעֲקַת יְתוֹמִים נִמְסֶרֶת מִדּוֹר
לְדוֹר, כְּמוֹ בְּמֵרוֹץ שְׁלִיחִים: מַקֵּל לֹא נוֹפֵל.)

שֶׁיִּהְיֶה
כְּמוֹ פִּרְחֵי בַּר,
פִּתְאֹם בְּכֹרַח הַשָּׂדֶה:
שָׁלוֹם בַּר.

מָקוֹם שֶׁל אֵשׁ
זלדה

אֲוִיר הָרִים אֲוִיר חַי
אָהוּב נוֹשֵׁב
בַּקֵּשׁ לְמַעֲנֵנוּ רַחֲמִים
מִן הָעֶלְיוֹן עַל כֹּל.
מָקוֹם שֶׁל אֵשׁ,

A place of crying,
A place of madness—
A bride and a bridegroom both
Entreat the mercy of Heaven
That the horizon may not crumble.
Dogs and cats are fearful.
Only in plants are nectars
Not befouled
One step from the abyss,
Only in flowers does sweetness not retreat
One step from death.
For plants are a race different
From us,
Except for the olive trees
Who are sad and wise like people.
And when a king foreign and inimical
Besmirches our relation to the city
On whose neck
A loving prophet hung
Sapphires, turquoise, and rubies—
The silvery tree tops quiver like my heart,
And when a king foreign and inimical
Besmirches our awesome love
For the City of David—
The roots of the olive tree
Hear how the blood
Of some little soldier whispers
Within the ground:
The city beds down on my life.   ೞ

How Much A Word Could Help
Zelda

        Weary silence bends
        Your body. Your look searches for an answering look
    As the branches move in bewilderment.
You suddenly think

מָקוֹם שֶׁל בֶּכִי,
מָקוֹם שֶׁל טֵרוּף —
גַּם חָתָן וְכַלָּה
רַחֲמֵי שָׁמַיִם מְבַקְשִׁים
שֶׁלֹּא יִתְפּוֹרֵר הָאֹפֶק.
כְּלָבִים וַחֲתוּלִים נִבְהָלִים.
רַק בַּצְּמָחִים לֹא נִדְלָחִים
עֲסִיסִים
פְּסִיעָה מִן הַתְּהוֹם,
רַק בַּפְּרָחִים הַמְּתִיקוּת לֹא נָסוֹגָה
פְּסִיעָה מִן הַמָּוֶת.
כִּי הַצְּמָחִים עַם אַחֵר
מֵאִתָּנוּ,
חוּץ מֵעֲצֵי הַזַּיִת
שֶׁהֵם עֲצוּבִים וַחֲכָמִים כַּאֲנָשִׁים.
וְכַאֲשֶׁר מֶלֶךְ זָר וְאוֹיֵב
מַכְפִּישׁ שַׁיָּכוּתֵנוּ לָעִיר
שֶׁנָּבִיא אוֹהֵב
תָּלָה עַל צַוָּארָהּ
סַפִּירִים נֹפֶךְ וְכַדְכֹּד —
נִרְעָדוֹת כְּמוֹ לִבִּי צַמְרוֹת הַכֶּסֶף,
וְכַאֲשֶׁר מֶלֶךְ זָר וְאוֹיֵב
מַכְפִּישׁ אַהֲבָתֵנוּ הַנּוֹרָאָה
לְעִיר דָּוִד —
שׁוֹמְעִים הַשָּׁרָשִׁים
שֶׁל עֵץ הַזַּיִת אֵיךְ לוֹחֵשׁ דָּמוֹ
שֶׁל הַחַיָּל הַקָּטָן
בְּתוֹךְ הֶעָפָר:
הָעִיר רוֹבֶצֶת עַל חַיַּי.

כַּמָּה יָכְלָה הַמִּלָּה לַעֲזֹר
זלדה

שְׁתִיקָה עֲיֵפָה כּוֹפֶפֶת
אֶת גּוּפְךָ. מַבָּטְךָ תָּר מַבָּט
וּתְנוּעַת הָעֲנָפִים נְבוֹכָה.
אַתָּה חוֹשֵׁב לְפֶתַע

How much a word could help.
Quivering enfolds her shoulders.
She is longing for his body which perished.
Silence is painful on your lips
You understand
How much a word could help.
Now she is exposed
                    Solitary next to him
                        In front of our eyes
If only there was a word which would cover the quivering
Which covers the weeping
                    Which hangs like dew upon her face
Above the stone. Carrying his name.
A grove like a caress of mercy.
Distraught birds. Their voice which drips
On my ears
Is as a loudspeaker to a silence.   ಹಿ

On A Stone Pillow
Haiim Gouri

Now this happened on one of the nights of utter exhaustion
I was there. Completely relaxed on a stone pillow,
Basalt under my filthy head,
A crowned capital at my smelly wanderers.
Lying and metamorphosed into rock and metals and pitch-darkness
And over yonder the war which fell asleep.
Resembling Jacob without a ladder, Jacob without a multitude of angels
On a rocky ridge, on a ridge like an altar
Lying and smoking into my bitter black fist:
And over there charred vehicles and iron cooling along with the diminishing
Hot southern wind
And yonder the war which fell asleep between the dead and the heroes.
Not far from the LORD God of Hosts, war went to fall asleep
And I am there among all this:
Reclining on a stone and smoking into my bitter fist,
Leaning upon perfect peace

כַּמָּה יָכְלָה הַמִּלָּה לַעֲזֹר.
רַעַד כְּתֵפֶיהָ מְכֻסֶּה.
נִכְסֶפֶת אֶל גּוּפוֹ שֶׁכָּלָה.
הַשְּׁתִיקָה מַכְאִיבָה לִשְׂפָתֶיךָ
אַתָּה מֵבִין
כַּמָּה יָכְלָה הַמִּלָּה לַעֲזֹר
עַתָּה הִיא חֲשׂוּפָה
יְחִידָה לְיָדוֹ
לְעֵינֵינוּ
לוּ נִתְּנָה מִלָּה לְכַסּוֹת עַל הָרַעַד
הַמְכַסֶּה עַל הַבֶּכִי
הַתָּלוּי כְּטַל עַל פָּנֶיהָ
מֵעַל לָאֶבֶן. נוֹשֵׂאת אֶת שְׁמוֹ.
חֲרֵשָׁה כִּלְטִיפָה שֶׁל רַחֲמִים.
צִפֳּרִים נִרְעָשׁוֹת. קוֹלָם הַנּוֹטֵף
עַל אָזְנִי
כְּרַמְקוֹל לִשְׁתִיקָה.

עַל אֶבֶן מְרַאֲשׁוֹת
חיים גורי

וְזֶה קָרָה בְּלַיְלָה אֶחָד מֵלֵילוֹת הָעֲיֵפוּת
וַאֲנִי שָׁם. נִרְגָּע כָּלִיל עַל אֶבֶן מְרַאֲשׁוֹת,
בַּזֶּלֶת לְרָאשֵׁי הַמִּזְהָם,
בִּירָה מַעֲטִירָה לְצַלְעֹנֵי הַמַּסְרִיחִים.
שׁוֹכֵב וּמְתֻרְגָּם לִסְלָעִים וּמַתְּכוֹת וְחֹשֶׁךְ מִצְרָיִם
וְשָׁם הַמִּלְחָמָה שֶׁנִּרְדְּמָה.
דּוֹמֶה לְיַעֲקֹב אֵין סֻלָּם, לְיַעֲקֹב אֵין מַלְאָכִים לָרֹב
עַל רֶכֶס מֵאֶבֶן, עַל רֶכֶס מִזְבְּחִי —
שׁוֹכֵב וּמְעַשֵּׁן אֶל אֶגְרוֹפֵי הַמַּר וְהַשָּׁחֹר:
וְשָׁם כְּלֵי-רֶכֶב שְׁחוֹרִים וּבַרְזֶל מִצְטַגֵּן בַּאֲפִיסַת כֹּחוֹת
שֶׁל רוּחַ דְּרוֹמִית חַמָּה
וְשָׁם הַמִּלְחָמָה שֶׁנִּרְדְּמָה בֵּין הַמֵּתִים וּבֵין הַגִּבּוֹרִים.
לֹא הָרְחֵק מֵאַדְנֵי צְבָאוֹת, הָלְכָה לְהֵרָדֵם הַמִּלְחָמָה
וַאֲנִי שָׁם בֵּינֵיהֶם:
יוֹשֵׁב עַל אֶבֶן וּמְעַשֵּׁן אֶל אֶגְרוֹפֵי הַמַּר,
נִשְׁעָן אֶל הַמְּנוּחָה הַנְּכוֹנָה

Thinking slowly and sorting out one thing from another like someone who came
    in late after
Like a man who was thrust
Into another time.   ຄ

SETTING-UP CAMP
Yonathan Gefen

We found a place for the mess tent and a place
                                For the quartermaster's store,
We made a campfire, with twigs of terebinth and blackberry,
We pitched tents and called for inspection
And we drank-up whole canteens and water bottles.
We replenished our provisions and fixed-up our battle packs
And set guards to scare away dread.
Near the North Star, without praise or psalm
We discerned many ordinary stars.
We analyzed the battle, counted casualties,
Encouraged two who were wounded (they were
                                Very lightly wounded)
We had found a place for the mess tent and a place
                                For the quartermaster's store,
We had made a campfire, with twigs of terebinth and blackberry,
We had found a place for the medical tent, a place
                                For stretchers,
                    But not a place where officers
                                Can cry.   ຄ

(Kuneitra, in June)

SETTLEMENT
David Avidan

From the top of MountSinai
Captured by our forces
Captured by our forces
Without casualties

חוֹשֵׁב לְאַט וּמֵבִין דָּבָר מִתּוֹךְ דָּבָר כְּמוֹ כְּמוֹ מְאַחֵר
כְּמוֹ אִישׁ אֲשֶׁר נִקְלַע
אֶל תַּאֲרִיךְ אַחֵר.

הַתְאַרְגְּנוּת

יהונתן גפן

מָצָאנוּ מָקוֹם לְמִטְבָּח וּמָקוֹם
לְאַפְסְנָאוּת
הִבְעַרְנוּ מְדוּרָה, זָרְדֵי אֵלָה וָתוּת,
הֵקַמְנוּ מַאֲהָל וְעָרַכְנוּ מִפְקָד
וְשָׁתִינוּ כְּבָר מְלֹא מֵימִיָּה וָכַד.
הִשְׁלַמְנוּ צִיּוּד וְתִקַּנּוּ חֲגוֹר
וְהִצַּבְנוּ שׁוֹמְרִים לְהַבְרִיחַ מָגוֹר.
לְיַד כּוֹכַב הַצָּפוֹן, בְּלִי הַלֵּל וּמִכְתָּם,
גִּלִּינוּ הֲמוֹן כּוֹכָבִים שֶׁל סְתָם.
נִתַּחְנוּ אֶת הַקְּרָב, סָפַרְנוּ אֲבֵדוֹת,
עוֹדְדְנוּ שְׁנֵי פְּצוּעִים (פְּצוּעִים הֵם
קַל מְאֹד).
מָצָאנוּ מָקוֹם לְמִטְבָּח וּמָקוֹם
לְאַפְסְנָאוּת
הִבְעַרְנוּ מְדוּרָה, זָרְדֵי אֵלָה וָתוּת,
מָצָאנוּ מָקוֹם לְמִרְפָּאָה, מָקוֹם
לַאֲלֻנְקוֹת,
אַךְ לֹא מָקוֹם שֶׁהַקְצִינִים
יוּכְלוּ שָׁמָּה לִבְכּוֹת.

קוניטרה, ביוני.

הַתְנַחֲלוּת

דוד אבידן

מֵרֹאשׁ הַרְסִינִי
בִּידֵי כּוֹחוֹתֵינוּ
בִּידֵי כּוֹחוֹתֵינוּ
בְּלִי אֲבֵדוֹת

I saw a cloud
Lying on its back
Drinking coffee
In a Bedouin tent
I want to die on a cloud
To die on a cloud lying on its back
On the top of MountSinai captured by our forces
By our forces one casualty
To die on my back partly cloudy
Have Dayan himself close my eye
And the other one be open and in shrouds by "Maskit."   ❧

Twenty Years In The Wadi
Dan Pagis

And afterwards? I do not know.
Each one of us fell
Into his own oblivion

The road has widened tremendously. Still left on its shoulder
My armored car, upturned.
At noon I sometimes look from within
Its burnt eyes: I do not remember
These cypresses.
Fresh travelers pass us by
To forget yet another war,
Other casualties, faster than us.

But at times a wind comes down onto us,
Softly whistling through a wreath
That rolled into the wadi,
Pulling off petal after petal, guessing:

They love. Yes. No. Yes.
A little bit. No.
A lot.
No.
Too much.   ❧

(1968)

רָאִיתִי עָנָן
מֻטָּל עַל גַּבּוֹ
וְלוֹגֵם קָפֶה
בְּאֹהֶל בֶּדוּאִי
אֲנִי רוֹצֶה לָמוּת עַל עָנָן
לָמוּת עַל עָנָן מֻטָּל עַל גַּבּוֹ
בְּרֹאשׁ הַרְסִינִי בִּידֵי כּוֹחוֹתֵינוּ
בִּידֵי כּוֹחוֹתֵינוּ נִפְגַּע אֶחָד
לָמוּת עַל גַּבִּי מֵעֲנַן חֶלְקִית
שֶׁדַּיָּן אִישִׁית יַעֲצֹם לִי עַיִן
וְהַשְּׁנִיָּה פְּקוּחָה וּבְתַכְרִיכֵי 'מַשְׂכִּית'

עֶשְׂרִים שָׁנָה בַּגַּיְא

דן פגיס

וְאַחֲרֵי כֵן? אֵינֶנִּי יוֹדֵעַ.
כָּל אֶחָד מֵאִתָּנוּ נָפַל
לְתוֹךְ שִׁכְחָה מִשֶּׁלּוֹ.

הַכְּבִישׁ הִתְרַחֵב מְאֹד.   נִשְׁאַר בְּשׁוּלָיו
הַמִּשְׁרָיָן שֶׁלִּי, הָפוּךְ.
בַּצָּהֳרַיִם אֲנִי מַבִּיט לִפְעָמִים מִתּוֹךְ
עֵינָיו הַשְּׂרוּפוֹת: אֵינֶנִּי זוֹכֵר
אֶת הַבְּרוֹשִׁים הָאֵלֶּה.
נוֹסְעִים חֲדָשִׁים חוֹלְפִים עַל פָּנֵינוּ
לִשְׁכֹּחַ מִלְחָמָה אַחֶרֶת,
הֲרוּגִים אֲחֵרִים, מְהִירִים מֵאִתָּנוּ.

אֲבָל לִפְעָמִים יוֹרֶדֶת אֵלֵינוּ רוּחַ,
מְרַשְׁרֶשֶׁת בְּזֵר
שֶׁנִּתְגַּלְגֵּל לַגַּיְא,
תּוֹלֶשֶׁת עָלֶה עָלֶה, מְנַחֶשֶׁת:

הֵם אוֹהֲבִים. כֵּן. לֹא. כֵּן.
מְעַט. לֹא.
הַרְבֵּה.
לֹא.
יוֹתֵר מִדַּי.

(1968)

WHEN YOU GROW UP
Anadad Eldan

My son, trenches dug deep by my hands
Rose up to become a barrier.
Unavailingly you are trying to find help in our history.
When you grow up, and something becomes incrusted,
They will remain wide open.
Before you knew anything
You had already seen
From a nearby lawn, while leaning against a white apron,
How I injured and hewed
Those open areas
Breaking through and disappearing
Out of these depths cry

❦❧

Surround him in his years by walls
To close him off from his abyss.
Let him climb upon them.
What do you see—
                An echo of voices in the path of the storm. Very close.
                Leave to him his years
            Which grew tall, empowered by doubts.
What do you see——
I see his eyes flashing
When he imagines that the ways of love
Were opened for him
                In the dirt of the trenches which have been covered   ظ

DEAD IN A BEREFT HORAH
Yehiel Hazak

Tomorrow autumn will come
And again birds will fly between my eyes,
And this road which reigns in a dream
Will continue to constrict all the horizons within me.
Like a tank slagged and capsized

כְּשֶׁתִּגְדַּל

אנדד אלדן

בְּנִי, תְּעָלוֹת קֶשֶׁר שֶׁהֶעֱמִיקוּ
יָדַי קָמוּ לְחַיִץ.
לַשָּׁוְא אַתָּה מְנַסֶּה לְהֵעָזֵר בְּקוֹרוֹתֵינוּ.
כְּשֶׁתִּגְדַּל וּמַשֶּׁהוּ יַגְלִיד
פְּעוּרוֹת תִּשָּׁאַרְנָה.
בְּטֶרֶם יָדַעְתָּ דָּבָר
כְּבָר רָאִיתָ
מֵדֶשֶׁא סָמוּךְ, נִשְׁעָן לְסִנָּר לְבַנְבַּן,
אֵיךְ אֲנִי פּוֹצֵעַ וּמְשַׁסֵּף
אֶת שִׁטְחֵי הַמַּעֲבָר
וּמַבְקִיעַ וְאוֹבֵד
מִן הַמַּעֲמַקִּים הָאֵלֶּה קָרָא

*

הַקֵּף אוֹתוֹ בִּשְׁנוֹתָיו חוֹמוֹת
לְסָגְרוֹ מִתְּהוֹמוֹ.
תֵּן לוֹ לַעֲלוֹת עֲלֵיהֶן.
מָה אַתָּה רוֹאֶה —
הֵד קוֹלוֹת בְּדֶרֶךְ הַסּוּפָה. קָרוֹב.
הָנַח לוֹ אֶת שְׁנוֹתָיו
שֶׁגָּבְהוּ מִכֹּחָם שֶׁל הַסְּפֵקוֹת.
מָה אַתָּה רוֹאֶה — —
אֲנִי רוֹאֶה אֶת עֵינָיו לוֹהֲבוֹת
בִּדְמוּתוֹ כִּי נִפְתְּחוּ
לוֹ דַּרְכֵי הָאַהֲבָה
בֶּעָפָר תְּעָלוֹת הַקֶּשֶׁר שֶׁכֻּסּוּ

מֵתִים בְּהוֹרָה עֲזוּבָה

יחיאל חזק

מָחָר יָבוֹא הַסְּתָו
וְשׁוּב הַצִּפֳּרִים תִּפְרַחְנָה בֵּין עֵינַי,
וְהַדֶּרֶךְ הַזֹּאת הַמּוֹלֶכֶת בַּחֲלוֹם
תּוֹסִיף לִסְחֹט אֶת כָּל הָאֲפָקִים שֶׁבִּי.
כְּטַנְק שָׂרוּף עַל גַּבּוֹ

And in the dance into which I stepped—
A bereft horah—
All my dead will come to dance with me.
And in our hands the heads of an iron flower
Which arouses with the arrival of autumn
From the heart of a desert, and chill night,
Footprints of ants on the sands
We will leave behind us
Now that stars are no longer with us—
Only traces of a lost way
And death breaking out from the dream.   ༄

WAKE
Yehiel Hazak

> To Hagai Ronen of blessed memory
>   The pilot from Afiqim,
>   Who parachuted into the gulf of Suez—
>   Where his secret remains…

Has death indeed cut off his breath
We all walked weeping during his wake
You loved him
Even before his birth ripened
In the approaching spring
The offerings were brought to the gate, our heavy tributes
When the prayer engulfed the silk of his curls.
Suffocatingly the dawn advances, directly from the east
With a southern wind
Supporting   ༄

MILITARY CALL-UP
Meir Wieseltier

Then they will call-up the Little Prince
And give him a submachine gun and say to him:
Indeed you have come to us from a different planet,

וּבַמָּחוֹל אֲשֶׁר אָחַזְתִּי —
הוֹרָה עֲזוּבָה —
יָבוֹאוּ כָּל מֵתַי לָחוּל עִמִּי.
וּבְיָדֵינוּ כּוֹתָרוֹת שֶׁל פֶּרַח בַּרְזֶל
הַמִּתְעוֹרֵר עִם בּוֹא הַסְּתָו
מִלֵּב מִדְבָּר וְלַיְלָה קַר,
עֲקֵבוֹת שֶׁל נְמָלִים עַל הַחוֹלוֹת
נַשְׁאִיר מֵאֲחוֹרֵינוּ
בְּאֵין עוֹד כּוֹכָבִים עִמָּנוּ —
רַק סִימָנִים שֶׁל דֶּרֶךְ אֲבוּדָה
וּמָוֶת פּוֹרֵץ מִן הַחֲלוֹם.

מִשְׁתֶּה
יחיאל חזק

לחגי רונן ז״ל,
הטייס בן אפיקים,
שצנח למפרץ סואץ -
שם סודו ...

הַאָמְנָם חֲנָקַהוּ הַמָּוֶת
כֻּלָּנוּ הָלַכְנוּ בּוֹכִים בְּמִשְׁתֵּה הַפְּרֵדָה חֲנָקָהוּ הַמָּוֶת
אָהַבְתָּ אוֹתוֹ
עוֹד בְּטֶרֶם גָּמְלָה לֵדָתוֹ
בַּאֲבִיב הַקְּרָב
הַזְּבָחִים אֶל הַשַּׁעַר הֻגְּשׁוּ מִנְחוֹתֵינוּ כְּבֵדוֹת
בַּעֲטֹף הַתְּפִלָּה אֶת מְשִׁי תַּלְתַּלָּיו
וְהַשַּׁחַר הוֹלֵךְ וְחוֹנֵק חֲזִיתִית מִמִּזְרָח
וְרוּחַ דְּרוֹמִית
מְסַיַּעַת.

צַו-קְרִיאָה
מאיר ויזלטיר

אָז יִקְרְאוּ לַנָּסִיךְ הַקָּטָן
וְיִתְּנוּ בְּיָדוֹ תַּת-מִקְלָע וְיֹאמְרוּ לוֹ:
אָמְנָם בָּאתָ אֵלֵינוּ מִכּוֹכָב אַחֵר,

But you are here now,
And from under that drawing of a hat,
It won't be an elephant that comes out, but a tank,
And the lamplighter is a terrorist,
And if you don't do away with the sheep
We will do away with you instead;
That's the way things are, Little Prince.   &

(1969)

LOVE IS PROGRESSING
Meir Wieseltier

Love is progressing   one can see precisely
The progress of love   the army

The army with the enemy   Is in love with the enemy   stalking in the vineyards
Swooping by surprise   with great love
                        Destruction

Yes, love is progressing   it knows no stop
The people have no shortage   of love for their army

The people with their army   Where has my beloved turned aside   people ask the Press
The heart of the people palpitates   great palpitations
                        In the barracks

And love does not stop   do not covet
All that they have   the army paints its eye

The army with itself   A damsel or two   the army, braying with love
For itself   kisses its own mouth in the mirror
                        Aha   &

RETURN
Yoseph Sarig

Not thirsting for battle
Did we go to war—
Always, we had loved home…

אֲבָל עַכְשָׁו אַתָּה כָּאן,
וּמִתַּחַת לַכּוֹבַע הַמְּצֻיָּר
לֹא יֵצֵא פִיל אֶלָּא טָנְק,
וּמַדְלִיק-הַפָּנָסִים הוּא מְחַבֵּל,
וְאִם לֹא תְּחַסֵּל אֶת הַכְּבָשִׂים הָאֵלֶּה,
נִתֵּן אֶת רֹאשְׁךָ תַּחְתָּן;
כָּכָה זֶה, הַנָּסִיךְ הַקָּטָן.

1969

הָאַהֲבָה מִתְקַדֶּמֶת
מאיר ויזלטיר

	הָאַהֲבָה מִתְקַדֶּמֶת נִתָּן לִרְאוֹת עַיִן בְּעַיִן
	אֶת הִתְקַדְּמוּת הָאַהֲבָה הַצָּבָא
הַצָּבָא בָּאוֹיֵב	מְאֹהָב בָּאוֹיֵב אוֹרֵב בַּכְּרָמִים
	עָט כַּחֵתֶף בְּאַהֲבָה גְּדוֹלָה
	כָּלָה

	וְהָאַהֲבָה מִתְקַדֶּמֶת לֹא תֵּדַע מַעֲצוֹר
	לָעָם אֵין מַחְסוֹר בְּאַהֲבָה לִצְבָאוֹ
הָעָם בִּצְבָאוֹ	אָנָה פָּנָה דּוֹדִי שׁוֹאֵל הָעָם אֶת הָעִתּוֹנוּת
	לֵב הָעָם נִצְבָּט צְבִיטָה גְּדוֹלָה
	בַּגְּדוּד

	וְהָאַהֲבָה לֹא תַּעֲמֹד לֹא תַּחְמֹד
	אֶת כָּל אֲשֶׁר לוֹ הַצָּבָא שָׂם בַּפּוּךְ עֵינָיו
הַצָּבָא בְּעַצְמוֹ	רַחַם רַחֲמָתַיִם גּוֹעֶה מֵאַהֲבָה
	לְעַצְמוֹ הַצָּבָא מְנַשֵּׁק עַל פִּיו בָּרָאִי
	אֲהָהּ

שִׁיבָה
יוסף שריג

לֹא צְמֵאֵי מִלְחָמָה
אֶל הַקְּרָב הָלַכְנוּ
אָהַבְנוּ תָּמִיד אֶת הַבַּיִת,

The sun… a meadow opening in the soul…
And we are now returned to you
Artless as always
And breath not in us.

Can you, friends,
Sustain Mother
For our sake?   ೞ

(September 1969)

MEMORIAL DAY, 1969
T. Carmi

In memoriam Isaac Halevy-Levin

1
She orders vegetables over the telephone
And tidies-up, tidies-up the house.
It is difficult to think about her.
There are awful screams in her navel
But the line is disconnected.
It is difficult to think about her.
If she is connected—
It is only to the ground
An ear of flesh and blood to an ear of dirt
And hearing, hearing awful voices.
It is difficult to think about her.

2
He leaves for work in the morning,
His chin crying
And his sunglasses laughing.
I met him in the afternoon
The eulogy he uttered was short:
"Tomorrow it will be three months,
He made a 9.2 on the matriculation exams."
I was afraid to follow him with my eyes:
Laden with earth and rock,

הַשֶּׁמֶשׁ, שָׂדֶה הַנִּפְתָּח בַּנְּשָׁמָה
וְשָׁבְנוּ עַתָּה אֲלֵיכֶם
פְּשׁוּטִים כְּתָמִיד
וְרוּחַ אֵין בָּנוּ.

הֲתוּכְלוּ, רֵעִים,
לַחֲזֹק אֶת אִמָּא
בִּמְקוֹמֵנוּ?

9.1969

יוֹם הַזִּכָּרוֹן תשכ״ט
ט. כרמי

לְזֵכֶר י. ה.

1

הִיא מַזְמִינָה יְרָקוֹת בַּטֶּלֶפוֹן
וּמְסַדֶּרֶת, מְסַדֶּרֶת אֶת הַבַּיִת.
קָשֶׁה לַחְשֹׁב עָלֶיהָ.
יֵשׁ צְעָקוֹת נוֹרָאוֹת בַּטַּבּוּרָה
אֲבָל הַקַּו מְנֻתָּק.
קָשֶׁה לַחְשֹׁב עָלֶיהָ.
אִם הִיא מְחַבֶּרֶת—
רַק לָאֲדָמָה:
אֹזֶן בָּשָׂר וָדָם אֶל אֹזֶן עָפָר
וְשׁוֹמַעַת, שׁוֹמַעַת קוֹלוֹת נוֹרָאִים.
קָשֶׁה לַחְשֹׁב עָלֶיהָ.

2

הוּא יוֹצֵא לַעֲבוֹדָה בַּבֹּקֶר.
סַנְטֶרוֹ בּוֹכֶה
וּמִשְׁקְפֵי-הַשֶּׁמֶשׁ צוֹחֲקִים.
פָּגַשְׁתִּי אוֹתוֹ בַּצָּהֳרַיִם,
הַהֶסְפֵּד שֶׁלּוֹ הָיָה קָצָר:
"מָחָר זֶה יִהְיֶה שְׁלֹשָׁה חֳדָשִׁים,
הוּא קִבֵּל 9.2 בִּבְחִינוֹת הַבַּגְרוּת."
פָּחַדְתִּי לְהִסְתַּכֵּל אַחֲרָיו:
עָמוּס עָפָר וָסֶלַע,

A hod carrier of memories—
How will he manage to get across the street in time?
I was afraid to look in his face:
A man without features,
Without a now—
How is it possible to shake his hand?
He has a dimension missing
And he has no time.

3
We spoke about the measurements of the paper and the size of the page.
I, too, like precision
And many dates are entered in my diary.
On other pages there are
A shorthand transcription of night birds
And awful voices at midday;
Many syllables of horror
And a first draft of stillnesses.   ೫

THE OTHER DAYS
Haiim Hefer

We will yet see The Other Days\ Which are beyond the mountains of smoking
flames\ We will yet see The Other Days\ Coming up from the Jordan valley\ Com-
ing down toward us from the mountains\ Laughing spring, loves, youth\ And
things which we have already forgotten what they look like.

We will yet see The Other Days\ The Other Days

We will yet go out towards them from holed structures\ From the bomb-shelters
and the blackened fields\ We will go out on crutches, dazzled by their light\ Down
they come singing like a thousand birds from the top of antennas\ While we per-
ceive them with clear eyes\ And accompanying their singing are guitars of a
thousand boys.

We will yet see The Other Days\ The Other Days

We will yet see The Other Days\ Proud as chapters of the Bible, beautiful, as the
Song of Songs\ Flowing like a torrent in the desert, rosy like dawn on the moun-
tains\ Days of grace and tranquillity, quiet and happy days\ And on Memorial
Day only, in the moments of reflection\ We will again speak of everything and

סַבָּל שֶׁל זִכְרוֹנוֹת —
אֵיךְ יַסְפִּיק לַחֲצוֹת אֶת הַכְּבִישׁ?
פָּחַדְתִּי לְהִסְתַּכֵּל בְּפָנָיו:
אִישׁ בְּלִי פְּרוֹפִיל,
בְּלִי עַכְשָׁו —
אֵיךְ אֶפְשָׁר לִלְחֹץ אֶת יָדוֹ?
חָסֵר לוֹ מֵמַד
וְאֵין לוֹ זְמָן.

3
דִּבַּרְנוּ עַל מִדּוֹת הַדַּף וְגֹדֶל הָעַמּוּד.
גַּם אֲנִי אוֹהֵב דִּיוּק
וְהַרְבֵּה תַּאֲרִיכִים רְשׁוּמִים בְּפִנְקָסִי.
בַּדַּפִּים הָאֲחֵרִים יֵשׁ
סְטֶנוֹגְרָמָה שֶׁל עוֹפוֹת לַיְלָה
וְקוֹלוֹת נוֹרָאִים בְּצָהֳרֵי הַיּוֹם;
הַרְבֵּה הֲבָרוֹת שֶׁל בְּעָתָה
וְטִיּוּטָה שֶׁל דּוּמִיּוֹת.

הַיָּמִים הָאֲחֵרִים
חיים חפר

אֲנַחְנוּ עוֹד נִרְאֶה אֶת הַיָּמִים הָאֲחֵרִים ∞ אֲשֶׁר מֵעֵבֶר לֶהָרִים הָעֲשֵׁנִים הַבּוֹעֲרִים
∞ אֲנַחְנוּ עוֹד נִרְאֶה אֶת הַיָּמִים הָאֲחֵרִים ∞ עוֹלִים בָּאִים מִן הַבִּקְעָה, יוֹרְדִים
אֵלֵינוּ מִן הֶהָרִים ∞ צוֹחֲקִים אֶת הָאָבִיב, הָאֲהָבוֹת, הַנְּעוּרִים, וְאֶת הַדְּבָרִים
אֲשֶׁר שָׁכַחְנוּ כְּבָר אֵיךְ הֵם נִרְאִים.

אֲנַחְנוּ עוֹד נִרְאֶה אֶת הַיָּמִים הָאֲחֵרִים ∞ אֶת הַיָּמִים הָאֲחֵרִים

נֵצֵא עוֹד לִקְרַאתָם מִתּוֹךְ מִבְנִים מְחוֹרָרִים ∞ מִתּוֹךְ הַמִּקְלָטִים וְהַשָּׂדוֹת
הַמַּשְׁחִירִים ∞ נֵצֵאָה עַל קַבַּיִם מְאוֹרָם מְסֻנְוָרִים ∞ מֵרֹאשׁ אַנְטֶנוֹת מִלְחָמָה
שָׁרִים כְּמוֹ אֶלֶף צִפֳּרִים ∞ וְנַבִּיט בָּהֶם קָרוֹב בַּמַּבָּטִים הַבְּהִירִים ∞ וּמְלַוּוֹת
אֶת זִמְרָתָם גִּיטָרוֹת שֶׁל אֶלֶף נְעָרִים.

אֲנַחְנוּ עוֹד נִרְאֶה אֶת הַיָּמִים הָאֲחֵרִים ∞ אֶת הַיָּמִים הָאֲחֵרִים

אֲנַחְנוּ עוֹד נִרְאֶה אֶת הַיָּמִים הָאֲחֵרִים ∞ גֵּאִים כְּמוֹ פִּרְקֵי תָּנָ"ךְ, יָפִים, כְּמוֹ שִׁיר
הַשִּׁירִים ∞ שׁוֹטְפִים כְּמוֹ אֶשֶׁד בַּמִּדְבָּר, וְרָדִים כְּמוֹ שַׁחַר בֶּהָרִים ∞ יָמִים שֶׁל
חֶסֶד וְשַׁלְוָה, יָמִים שְׁקֵטִים וּמְאֻשָּׁרִים ∞ וְרַק בְּיוֹם הַזִּכָּרוֹן, בְּרִגְעֵי הַהִרְהוּרִים

eulogize the young men\ And we will hear the sound of shooting and the salvos of bullets\ And the wars that had taken place before with such mighty momentum.

We will yet see The Other Days\ The Other Days

We will yet see The Other Days\ We will see them sooner than we expect\ And when calm comes to rule within the gates of the cities\ And all this history of our times is engraved in the books\ We will stare at each other with strange expressions\ And we will remember then how we went together toward The Other Days.

We will yet see The Other Days\ The Other Days   ၏

(June 9 1970)

THE YOUNG DEAD SOLDIERS
Haiim Hefer

> *"The young dead soldiers do not speak. Nevertheless, they are heard…"*
> *(Archibald MacLeish)*

The young dead soldiers do not speak, nevertheless they are heard\ And their voice is strong and firm and it pertains to me and to you— to everyone\ And it screams of the wounds, of their pain, and the dazing of senses— and their utter depletion of blood\ And it screams of the books that they will not read, the movies that they will not see, and the love that they will never ever know again\ And it screams of their brothers and their sons and their mothers with whom they will never be again\ And those smells and colors and tastes which they had not experienced\ And this is the voice that gives the answers to things-as-they-are\ And it is a voice that knows better than we what a homeland and a country and a nation are\ And what liberty is and independence and freedom and many phrases whose meaning has suddenly become clear\ Because these are the things that the soldiers gave us at the moment of the fading away of their breath.

In the temporary cemeteries we walk among the mounds of earth\ Among the wreathes and the tears, amid the eulogies and salvos\ And family embraces family— and the men are as brothers and the women as sisters\ And they all know that the deaths of their sons are not temporary\ And they gaze around them— a whole nation again become a family\ Wearing expressions of silence and shock, wearing expressions of pain and bafflement\ And they leave with a last mourning look the graves of men who live no more\ And they ask themselves: What was, and ask themselves: What will be.

נַחֲזֹר וּנְסַפֵּר הַכֹּל וְנִסְפֹּד לַבַּחוּרִים ∞ וְנִשְׁמַע אֶת קוֹל הָאֵשׁ וְאֶת מַטַּח
הַכַּדּוּרִים ∞ וְאֶת הַקְּרָב שֶׁהִתְחוֹלֵל אָז בִּתְנוּפַת הָאַדִּירִים.

אֲנַחְנוּ עוֹד נִרְאֶה אֶת הַיָּמִים הָאֲחֵרִים ∞ אֶת הַיָּמִים הָאֲחֵרִים

אֲנַחְנוּ עוֹד נִרְאֶה אֶת הַיָּמִים הָאֲחֵרִים ∞ נִרְאֶה אוֹתָם יוֹתֵר מַהֵר מֵאֲשֶׁר
מְשַׁעֲרִים ∞ וּכְשֶׁיָּבוֹא הַשֶּׁקֶט וְיִמְשֹׁל בַּשְּׁעָרִים ∞ וְכָל דִּבְרֵי יָמֵינוּ אֵלֶּה יֵחָרְטוּ
בְּתוֹךְ הַסְּפָרִים ∞ נַבִּיט אָז זֶה בָּזֶה בַּמַּבָּטִים מוּזָרִים ∞ וְנִזְכֹּר אָז כִּי הָלַכְנוּ
יַחַד לַיָּמִים הָאֲחֵרִים.

אֲנַחְנוּ עוֹד נִרְאֶה אֶת הַיָּמִים הָאֲחֵרִים ∞ אֶת הַיָּמִים הָאֲחֵרִים

9.6.70

הַחַיָּלִים הַצְּעִירִים שָׁמְתוּ
חיים חפר

"החילים הצעירים שמתו לא ידברו ובכל זאת ישמע קולם" ...
(ארצ'יבלד מקליש)

הַחַיָּלִים הַצְּעִירִים שָׁמְתוּ לֹא יְדַבְּרוּ וּבְכָל זֹאת יִשָּׁמַע קוֹלָם ∞ וְהַקּוֹל הוּא חָזָק
וְקָשֶׁה וְהוּא פּוֹנֶה אֵלַי וְאֵלֶיךָ — אֶל כֻּלָּם ∞ וְהוּא זוֹעֵק אֶת פִּצְעֵי מַכְאוֹבָיו
וְאֶת עַרְפֶל הַחוּשִׁים — וְאֶת אֶפֶס הַדָּם ∞ וְהוּא זוֹעֵק אֶת הַסְּפָרִים שֶׁלֹּא יִקְרָא,
אֶת הַסְּרָטִים שֶׁלֹּא יִרְאֶה וְאֶת הָאַהֲבָה שֶׁלֹּא יֵדַע עוֹד לְעוֹלָם ∞ וְהוּא זוֹעֵק אֶת
אָחִיו וְאֶת בָּנָיו וְאֶת אִשְׁתּוֹ וְאֶת אִמּוֹ שֶׁלֹּא יָשׁוּב לִהְיוֹת עִמָּם ∞ וְאֶת הָרֵיחַ
הַהוּא וְאֶת הַצֶּבַע הַהוּא וְאֶת הַטַּעַם הַהוּא שֶׁלֹּא טָעַם ∞ וְהוּא הַקּוֹל הָעוֹנֶה
אֶת הַתְּשׁוּבוֹת לַדְּבָרִים כִּפְשׁוּטָם ∞ וְהוּא קוֹל הַיּוֹדֵעַ יוֹתֵר טוֹב מֵאִתָּנוּ מַה
זֹּאת מוֹלֶדֶת וְאֶרֶץ וְעָם ∞ וּמָה זֹאת חֵרוּת וְעַצְמָאוּת וְחֹפֶשׁ וּמִשְׁפָּטִים רַבִּים
שֶׁלְּפֶתַע הִתְבַּהֵר מוּבָנָם ∞ כִּי הֵם הַדְּבָרִים אֲשֶׁר הַחַיָּלִים נָתְנוּ לָנוּ לְעֵת סוֹף,
בְּהַמּוֹג נְשִׁימָתָם.

בְּבָתֵּי הַקְּבָרוֹת הָאַרְעַיִּים אֲנַחְנוּ מְהַלְּכִים בֵּין הַתְּלוּלִיּוֹת ∞ בֵּין הַזֵּרִים וְהַבֶּכִי,
בֵּין הַהֶסְפֵּד וְהַיְּרִיּוֹת ∞ וּמִשְׁפָּחָה נוֹפֶלֶת עַל צַוְּארֵי מִשְׁפָּחָה — וְהַגְּבָרִים
אַחִים וְהַנָּשִׁים — אֲחָיוֹת ∞ וְהֵם כֻּלָּם יוֹדְעִים כִּי הַמִּיתוֹת שֶׁל בְּנֵיהֶם אֵינָן
אַרְעִיּוֹת ∞ וְהֵם מַבִּיטִים סְבִיבָם — עִם שֶׁלֶם אֲשֶׁר חָזַר לִהְיוֹת שׁוּב
מִשְׁפָּחָה ∞ בְּמַבָּטֵי הָאֵלֶם וְהַהֵלֶם, בְּמַבָּטֵי הַכְּאֵב וְהַמְּבוּכָה ∞ וְהֵם נוֹטְשִׁים
בְּמַבָּט אֵבֶל אַחֲרוֹן אֶת קִבְרוֹ שֶׁל הָאִישׁ אֲשֶׁר לֹא יִחְיֶה ∞ וְשׁוֹאֲלִים אֶת עַצְמָם:
מַה הָיָה, וְשׁוֹאֲלִים אֶת עַצְמָם: מַה יִּהְיֶה.

And then the young dead soldiers say from within the ground:\ Shake the dirt from off your clothes, tear open the stillness\ Hang from the roofs of your houses the flag which became shreds\ Hoist the words for which we died over all the houses of the dead and the living\ Allow our last pictures to escape from their frames\ And fill with our faces the white spaces between the lines\ Open all windows to our stormy winter winds\ Because now we come to you with a command stronger than a thousand trumpets\ And we sing to you: Live as we died— with courage, with virtue, with sacrifice\ Live as we died— with devotion, with love\ Live as we died— with faith, with camaraderie, with integrity\ Live as we died— with youth that is more beautiful than any adjective\ Hope for the end of wars— be brave and strong\ And live, for us the dead— Live!

The young dead soldiers do not speak, nevertheless they are heard\ And we, facing their names and bidding their memory farewell\ Must swear to the truth of their final testament\ And that we will live the way we were commanded to live upon their death\ For the sake of these dead, for the sake of those who live\ For the sake of the beautiful dreams that will drive away the nightmares\ For the days of Tomorrow which are coming, clear and wonderful and clean\ So that there be a final name, on a final row, in the temporary cemeteries.   ∽

(November 9 1973)

ONLY 20 YEARS OLD
Gideon Rosenthal

I have not stood back to back with friends now fallen
And I have not heard the weeping of mothers
I have not smelled the odor of war casualties
And I have not yet seen severed arms
But I have lived twenty years
Upon this earth
It was good, and I want to keep on,
Simply keep on living

I lie down in bed and dream forbidden dreams
How wonderful
I walk in lighted streets among a multitude of people
How wonderful
I walk in darkened streets and sing songs to myself
How wonderful
And think— I am only 20, I am only 20 years old

וְאָז הַחַיָּלִים הַצְּעִירִים שֶׁמֵּתוּ אוֹמְרִים מִתּוֹךְ הָאֲדָמָה: ‏‏‏ נַעֲרוּ אֶת הָאָבֵל מֵעַל
בִּגְדֵיכֶם קִרְעוּ אֶת הַדְּמָמָה ‏‏‏ תְּלוּ עַל גַּגּוֹת בָּתֵּיכֶם אֶת הַדֶּגֶל שֶׁהֻפַּךְ קְרָעִים
‏‏‏ הָנִיפוּ אֶת הַמִּלִּים שֶׁמַּתְנוּ עֲבוּרָן עַל כָּל בָּתֵּי הַמֵּתִים וְהַחַיִּים ‏‏‏ תְּנוּ
לִתְמוּנוֹתֵינוּ הָאַחֲרוֹנוֹת לִפְרֹץ מִתּוֹךְ הַמִּסְגָּרוֹת ‏‏‏ וּלְמַלֵּא בְּפָנֵינוּ אֶת הַחֲלָלִים
הַלְּבָנִים בֵּין הַשּׁוּרוֹת ‏‏‏ פִּתְחוּ אֶת כָּל הַחַלּוֹנוֹת לְרוּחוֹת הַחֹרֶף שֶׁלָּנוּ הַסּוֹעֲרוֹת
‏‏‏ כִּי הִנֵּה אֲנַחְנוּ בָּאִים אֲלֵיכֶם בִּקְרִיאָה רָמָה מֵאֶלֶף חֲצוֹצְרוֹת ‏‏‏ וַאֲנַחְנוּ
שָׁרִים לָכֶם: חֲיוּ כְּפִי שֶׁמַּתְנוּ — בְּאֶמֶץ, בָּתֹם, בְּהַקְרָבָה ‏‏‏ חֲיוּ כְּפִי שֶׁמַּתְנוּ
בִּמְסִירוּת נֶפֶשׁ, בְּאַהֲבָה ‏‏‏ חֲיוּ כְּפִי שֶׁמַּתְנוּ — בֶּאֱמוּנָה, בְּרֵעוּת, בְּטֹהַר ‏‏‏ חֲיוּ
כְּפִי שֶׁמַּתְנוּ — בַּנְּעוּרִים הַיָּפִים מִכָּל שֵׁם תֹּאַר ‏‏‏ קְווּ אֶל קֵץ הַמִּלְחָמוֹת —
אַמִּיצִים וַחֲזָקִים הֱיוּ ‏‏‏ וִחְיוּ, לְמַעַנְנוּ הַמֵּתִים — חֲיוּ!

הַחַיָּלִים הַצְּעִירִים שֶׁמֵּתוּ לֹא יְדַבְּרוּ וּבְכָל זֹאת יִשָּׁמַע קוֹלָם ‏‏‏ וַאֲנַחְנוּ
הָעוֹמְדִים מוּל שְׁמוֹתֵיהֶם וְאוֹמְרִים שָׁלוֹם לָעַפְרָם ‏‏‏ מֻכְרָחִים לְהִשָּׁבַע כִּי יֵשׁ
אֱמֶת בְּצַוָּאָתָם ‏‏‏ וְכִי נִחְיֶה אֶת הַחַיִּים כַּאֲשֶׁר צֻוִּינוּ לִחְיוֹת בְּמוֹתָם ‏‏‏ לְמַעַן
הַמֵּתִים הָאֵלֶּה, לְמַעַן אֵלֶּה הַחַיִּים ‏‏‏ לְמַעַן הַחֲלוֹמוֹת הַיָּפִים שֶׁיְּגָרְשׁוּ אֶת
הַחֲלוֹמוֹת הָרָעִים ‏‏‏ לְמַעַן יְמֵי הַמָּחָר הַבָּאִים צְלוּלִים וּמֻפְלָאִים וּנְקִיִּים ‏‏‏
לְמַעַן הַשֵּׁם הַסּוֹפִי, בַּשּׁוּרָה הַסּוֹפִית בְּבָתֵּי הַקְּבָרוֹת הָאַרְעִיִּים.

9.11.73

רַק בֶּן 20
גדעון רוזנטל

לֹא תָּמַכְתִּי בַּחֲבֵרִים נוֹפְלִים
וְלֹא שָׁמַעְתִּי בְּכִי אִמָּהוֹת
לֹא הֵרַחְתִּי רֵיחַ חֲלָלִים
וְלֹא רָאִיתִי עוֹד זְרוֹעוֹת קְטוּעוֹת
אַךְ חָיִיתִי עֶשְׂרִים שָׁנִים
עַל הָאֲדָמָה הַזֹּאת
זֶה הָיָה טוֹב, וְרוֹצֶה לְהַמְשִׁיךְ
פָּשׁוּט לְהַמְשִׁיךְ לִחְיוֹת.

אֲנִי שׁוֹכֵב בַּמִּיטָה וְחוֹלֵם חֲלוֹמוֹת אֲסוּרִים
כַּמָּה נִפְלָא
אֲנִי הוֹלֵךְ בֵּין הֲמוֹן אֲנָשִׁים בִּרְחוֹבוֹת מוּאָרִים
כַּמָּה נִפְלָא
אֲנִי הוֹלֵךְ בִּרְחוֹבוֹת חֲשׁוּכִים וּמְזַמֵּר לִי שִׁירִים
כַּמָּה נִפְלָא
וְחוֹשֵׁב — אֲנִי רַק בֶּן 20, אֲנִי רַק בֶּן 20.

If I live until the age of eighty
I still have sixty years
One can engender twenty great-grandchildren
And build yet another state.

I am in love but she does not love me
How sad
I am absent-minded and forget everything
How sad
And what mostly distresses the depth of my soul
How sad
Look— I am already twenty, I am already twenty years old

But
If I live until the age of eighty
I still have sixty years
One can engender twenty great-grandchildren
And build yet another state.

There are people who fall in battle when they are still young
How stupid
Not in bed but of bullets' fire
How stupid
For the sake of parents whose life will be bitter
How stupid
Die when they are only 20, when they are only 20 years old

But I
Have not stood back to back with friends now fallen
And I have not heard the weeping of mothers
I have not smelled the odor of war casualties
And I have not yet seen severed arms

But I have lived for twenty years
Upon this earth
It was good, and I want to keep on,
Simply keep on living.   ଚ

אִם אֶחְיֶה עַד גִּיל שְׁמוֹנִים
יֵשׁ לִי עוֹד שִׁשִּׁים שָׁנָה
אֶפְשָׁר לַחֲנוֹךְ עֶשְׂרִים נִינִים
וְלִבְנוֹת עוֹד מְדִינָה.

אֲנִי מְאֹהָב אֲבָל הִיא לֹא אוֹהֶבֶת אוֹתִי
כַּמָּה עָצוּב
אֲנִי מְפֻזָּר וְשׁוֹכֵחַ אֶת כָּל הַדְּבָרִים
כַּמָּה עָצוּב
וּמַה שֶּׁמֵּעִיק בְּיוֹתֵר עַל עִמְקֵי נִשְׁמָתִי
כַּמָּה עָצוּב
תִּרְאוּ — אֲנִי כְּבָר בֶּן עֶשְׂרִים, אֲנִי כְּבָר בֶּן עֶשְׂרִים.

אֲבָל
אִם אֶחְיֶה עַד גִּיל שְׁמוֹנִים
יֵשׁ לִי עוֹד שִׁשִּׁים שָׁנָה
אֶפְשָׁר לַחֲנוֹךְ עֶשְׂרִים נִינִים
וְלִבְנוֹת עוֹד מְדִינָה.

יֵשׁ אֲנָשִׁים הַנּוֹפְלִים כְּשֶׁהֵם עוֹד צְעִירִים
כַּמָּה טִפְּשִׁי
לֹא בַּמִּטָּה אֶלָּא דַּוְקָא מֵאֵשׁ כַּדּוּרִים
כַּמָּה טִפְּשִׁי
לְמַעַן הוֹרִים שֶׁחַיֵּיהֶם יִהְיוּ מָרִים
כַּמָּה טִפְּשִׁי
מֵתִים כְּשֶׁהֵם רַק בְּנֵי 20, רַק בְּנֵי 20.

אֲבָל אֲנִי
לֹא תָּמַכְתִּי בַּחֲבֵרִים נוֹפְלִים
וְלֹא שָׁמַעְתִּי בְּכִי אִמָּהוֹת
לֹא הֵרַחְתִּי רֵיחַ חֲלָלִים
וְלֹא רָאִיתִי עוֹד זְרוֹעוֹת קְטוּעוֹת

אַךְ חָיִיתִי עֶשְׂרִים שָׁנִים
עַל הָאֲדָמָה הַזֹּאת
זֶה הָיָה טוֹב, וְרוֹצֶה לְהַמְשִׁיךְ
פָּשׁוּט לְהַמְשִׁיךְ לִחְיוֹת.

On The Readiness For Sacrifice
Reuven ben Yoseph

Greater than the readiness for sacrifice
Is the urgency for weeping, and you would not weep
When a thistle-filled field by the road
Ignites, burns in a susuration, then explodes
Because of the ammunition in it, fragments ricocheting, then a young man
From the fortified post runs to the reserve halftrack
Grabs a fire extinguisher and sprays
The field to no avail, it is still burning, and across
The road the dead, greater than the readiness for sacrifice is the need
For anger, and you will not scream, when a young man
Weeps over his dead comrade who clings to
His weapon and looks forever to the heavens
As if he knew that a helicopter
Rising from the direction of the Kineret will appear;
And from the head of the hill
They call out your halftrack upon the return of the enemy,
Two tanks against your proud, slender cannon,
And greater than the readiness to sacrifice

Is the eagerness to kill, and you have no compunction
When a tank swells in the gun-sight and your finger
Releases its diminutive shells to drive
The enemy from the land, but you have to stop,
For the tanks are fleeing and the halftrack is still and you
Are looking forever to the heavens and knowing there is naught
Greater than the readiness for sacrifice.   ෨

Around The Water Near The Birds
Yair Hurvitz

Around the water near the birds
The city Ararat is renewing her youth in the year of '73
Her situation seemed clear in the year of '48: the threat

עַל הַנְּכוֹנוּת לְהַקְרָבָה
ראובן בן-יוסף

גְּדוֹלָה מִן הַנְּכוֹנוּת לְהַקְרָבָה
הִיא דְּחִיפוּת הַבֶּכִי, וְלֹא תִּבְכֶּה
בְּשָׁעָה שֶׁשָּׂדֶה קוֹצִים לְיַד הַדֶּרֶךְ
מִתְלַקֵּחַ, בּוֹעֵר בְּרַחַשׁ וּמִתְפַּצֵּץ
כִּי תַחְמֹשֶׁת בּוֹ, נִתָּזִים רְסִיסִים, עַד שֶׁנַּעַר
מִן הַמַּצָּב רָץ אֶל זַחְלָם הַמְּלוּאִים
וְחוֹטֵף מַטָּף כִּבּוּי וּמַקְצִיף
עַל הַשָּׂדֶה לַשָּׁוְא, עוֹדוֹ בּוֹעֵר, וּמֵעֵבֶר
לַדֶּרֶךְ הַחֲלָלִים, גְּדוֹלָה מִן
הַנְּכוֹנוּת לְהַקְרָבָה הִיא נְחִיצוּת
הֶחָרוֹן, וְלֹא תִּזְעַק, בְּשָׁעָה שֶׁנַּעַר
בּוֹכֶה עַל פְּנֵי רֵעֵהוּ הַמֵּת, הַלּוֹפֵת
אֶת נִשְׁקוֹ וּמַבִּיט לָעַד הַשָּׁמַיְמָה
כְּאִלּוּ יָדַע שֶׁיּוֹפִיעַ הַמָּסוֹק
הָעוֹלֶה מִכִּוּוּן הַכִּנֶּרֶת, וּמֵרֹאשׁ הַתֵּל
מַזְעִיקִים אֶת זַחְלָמְךָ בְּשׁוּב הָאוֹיֵב,
שְׁנֵי טַנְקִים מוּל תּוֹתָחֲךָ הַדַּק וְהַגֵּא,
וּגְדוֹלָה מִן הַנְּכוֹנוּת לְהַקְרָבָה

הִיא לְהִיטוּת הַקֶּטֶל, וְלֹא תַּחְמֹל
בְּשָׁעָה שֶׁטַּנְק מִתְעַצֵּם בַּכַּוֶּנֶת וְאֶצְבָּעֲךָ
מְשַׁלַּחַת פְּגָזִים זְעִירִים לְגָרֵשׁ
אֶת הַצַּר מִן הָאָרֶץ, אַךְ עָלֶיךָ לַחְדֹּל,
כִּי הַטַּנְקִים בּוֹרְחִים וְהַזַּחְלָם דּוֹמֵם וְאַתָּה
מַבִּיט לָעַד הַשָּׁמַיְמָה וְיוֹדֵעַ שֶׁאֵין
גְּדוֹלָה מִן הַנְּכוֹנוּת לְהַקְרָבָה.

סְבִיב הַמַּיִם לְיַד הַצִּפֳּרִים
יאיר הורוביץ

סְבִיב הַמַּיִם לְיַד הַצִּפֳּרִים
מְחַדֶּשֶׁת הָעִיר אֲרַרְט נְעוּרֶיהָ שְׁנַת 73'.
עֲנָנָהּ נִרְאָה כְּמוֹ נָהִיר בִּשְׁנַת 48'. הָאִיּוּם

Became reality. Weapons of destruction bearing the appearance of men moved
   ponderously
Ponderously toward her body like darkening clouds in the dwelling places on
   high.
The drapery over her heart trembled. A flock of birds in the sky
And among the shutters rose in noisy commotion to set
The essence of the hour with clock-hands of wrinkles and danger.
What was referred to by people as the spirit of the city
Sounds now like a breath of retreat toward a posture of defense.
Thoughts of words, words, withdrew before thoughts of deeds, deeds.
Last will after last will was written as camouflage
To a climatic, meteorological movement. Death, they said,
Desecrates tombs but gives rise to life in the city of Ararat
Year of '48.

In the history of days the year of '48 is written-of very little, if at all,
Like the twitch of turning pages, but in the twitching of the body
And in the heart-drapery of the city of Ararat in the year of '73
This year is written like a knife,
The city of Ararat in the year of '73 writes the year as a masque
When her embarrassed nights go marching by drunk with emotions
And from the labyrinths in the night which stands within her like a cold and
   sharp wall
Riderless horses come and go with stamping of phosphorescence
For all the light like a wick is granting life
And it is the ruling whip and it is like a wisp for permanence
As if from love stroking flesh with the oil of its fragrance
And the storm has crimsoned garments
From the west of twilights it wields molten seas upon the city,
Moving by the pommels of her chapiters the wheels in her body and the wheels
Move rooms, halls, labyrinths,
A wall supports a wall, a wall stoops toward a wall like a grimace
And the storm from the radiance of the rainbow of the dwelling places on high
   like a knife
Cuts into her sorrow slice after slice
Like iron ruling iron
Until the knowledge of a salty, scattered tear dissipates.

The year of '48 is written in history like a wind through empty rooms,
A fleeting flow of water.

הַמֵּחַשׁ. כְּלֵי מַשְׁחִית דְּמוּיֵי אָדָם נָעוּ כָּבֵד
כָּבֵד אֶל גּוּפָהּ כַּעֲנָנִים מַקְדִּירִים בִּמְעוֹנַת מָרוֹם.
חַפַת לְבָבָהּ רָעֲדָה. סִיעַת צִפֳּרִים בַּשָּׁמַיִם
וּבַתְּרִיסִים קַמָּה לְכַוֵּן בְּשָׁאוֹן תְּכוּנָה
אֶת מַהוּת הַשָּׁעָה בְּמַחוֹגֵי קְמָטִים וְסַכָּנָה.
מַה שֶּׁכֵּנָה בְּפִי הַבְּרִיּוֹת נִשְׁמַת הָעִיר
נִשְׁמַע עַתָּה כִּנְשִׁימַת נְסִיגָה אֶל עֵבֶר הַגְּנָה.
מַחְשָׁבוֹת מִלִּים, מִלִּים, נָסוֹגוּ מִלִּפְנֵי מַחְשָׁבוֹת מַעֲשִׂים, מַעֲשִׂים.
צַוָּאָה אַחַר צַוָּאָה נִרְשְׁמָה כְּהַסְוָאָה לִתְזוּזָה
אַקְלִימִית, מִזְגִּית. הַמָּוֶת, אָמְרוּ,
מְחַלֵּל קְבָרִים וּמְחוֹלֵל חַיִּים בָּעִיר אֶרֶרֶט
שְׁנַת 48׳.

בְּדִבְרֵי הַיָּמִים רְשׁוּמָה, אִם בִּכְלָל, שְׁנַת 48׳ כְּשַׂעֲרָה,
כְּרַעַד דְּפָדוּף, אֲבָל בְּרַעַד הַגּוּף
וּוִילָאוֹת הַלֵּב שֶׁל הָעִיר אֶרֶרֶט שְׁנַת 73׳
רְשׁוּמָה הַשָּׁנָה כְּסַכִּין,
הָעִיר אֶרֶרֶט שְׁנַת 73׳ רוֹשֶׁמֶת אוֹתָהּ מַסֵּכָה
בַּעֲבֹר בַּסָּךְ לֵילוֹתֶיהָ הַנְּבוֹכִים סְבוּאֵי רִגְשָׁה
וּמִן הַמְּבוֹכִים בַּלַּיְלָה שֶׁעוֹמֵד בָּהּ כְּקִיר קַר נָחָד
סוּסִים רֵיקִים בָּאִים וְיוֹצְאִים בְּשַׁעֲטַת מִצְנְפוֹת הִלָּה
וְכָל הָאוֹר כִּפְתִיל נוֹתֵן חַיִּים
וְהוּא הַשּׁוֹט הָרוֹדֶה וְהוּא כְּשַׂעֲרָה לְהַשְׁאָרָה
כְּמוֹ מֵאַהֲבָה דּוֹחֶקֶת בָּשָׂר שֶׁמֶן בָּשְׁמָהּ
וְהַשַּׂעֲרָה חֲמוּצַת בְּגָדִים
מִמַּעֲרָב דְּמַדּוּמִים מְנִיפָה עַל הָעִיר יָמִים,
מְנִיעָה בְּגִלּוֹת רֹאשָׁהּ אוֹפָנִים בְּגוּפָהּ וְהָאוֹפַנִּים
מְנִיעִים חֲדָרִים, מִסְדְּרוֹנוֹת, מְבוֹכִים,
קִיר סוֹמֵךְ קִיר, קִיר כּוֹפֵף קִיר כְּעַוּוֹת פָּנִים
וְהַשַּׂעֲרָה מִזִּיו הַקֶּשֶׁת שֶׁלִּמְעוֹנַת מָרוֹם כְּסַכִּין
בּוֹצַעַת לְעָצְבָּהּ פְּרוּסָה פְּרוּסָה
כְּבַרְזֶל שׁוֹלֵט בַּרְזֶל
עַד מֶלַח דִּמְעָה שֶׁבוּרָה לְקָחָהּ אוֹזֵל.

שְׁנַת 48׳ רְשׁוּמָה בְּדִבְרֵי הַיָּמִים כְּרוּחַ חֲדָרִים,
מַבּוּעַ.

The year of '73 over the city of Ararat renews its youth nourishing a storm
After which, around the water near the birds, placation is like death.   ∞

Again A Drab Khaki Light Is Coming Down
Elegy
Meir Wieseltier

Again a drab khaki light is coming down
In a stifling, tainted cloud
Against the gaping balconies
Of our houses that stand canted on the sand

Against facial nerves longing
For relief by the touch of an autumn wind,
A slight shudder in a scorched cheek,
Again a drab khaki light is coming down:

Again a drab khaki light is coming down
Against the shattered thoughts
Of an elongated elliptical form
Which we wanted to outline again in the sand,

And upon our simple food
Which we set on a table in the shade of the tree
And joined together to eat in happiness,
Again a drab khaki light is coming down:

Again a drab khaki light is coming down
On the wine which we poured into the glasses
And plunged passionately to its living scarlet
And the memory of its taste last year,

And on the breasts of the girls like plums
Held cradled within open, loose wrappings
Absorbing the touch of a hungry wind,
Again a drab khaki light is coming down:

Again a drab khaki light is coming down
On our wounded love,

שְׁנַת 73' עַל הָעִיר אֲרֶרֶט מְחַדֶּשֶׁת נְעוּרֶיהָ סָבָה סְעָרָה,
שֶׁאַחֲרֶיהָ, סְבִיב הַמַּיִם לְיַד הַצִּפֳּרִים, הַשְׁכָבָה כַּמָּוֶת.

שׁוּב יוֹרֵד אוֹר חַקִּי אֲפַרְפּוֹרִי
אֶלֶגְיָה
מֵאִיר וִיזֶלְטִיר

שׁוּב יוֹרֵד אוֹר חַקִּי אֲפַרְפּוֹרִי
בְּעָנָן דָּחוּס וְלֹא טָהוֹר
מוּל הַמִּרְפָּסוֹת הַפְּעוּרוֹת
שֶׁל בָּתֵּינוּ הַנְּטוּיִים בַּחוֹל,

מוּל עַצְבֵי פָנִים מִתְגַּעְגְּעִים
לִרְוָחָה בִּנְגִיעָה שֶׁל רוּחַ סְתָו,
חֲלַחֲלָה קַלָּה בִּלְחִי חֲרוּכָה,
שׁוּב יוֹרֵד אוֹר חַקִּי אֲפַרְפּוֹרִי:

שׁוּב יוֹרֵד אוֹר חַקִּי אֲפַרְפּוֹרִי
מוּל הַמַּחְשָׁבוֹת הָרְסוּקוֹת
עַל צוּרָה אֶלְפָטִית מְתוּחָה
שֶׁבִּקַּשְׁנוּ לְהַתְווֹת שֵׁנִית בַּחוֹל,

וְעַל־פְּנֵי מַאֲכָלֵינוּ הַפְּשׁוּטִים
שֶׁעָרַכְנוּ עַל שֻׁלְחָן בְּצֵל הָעֵץ
וְחָבַרְנוּ לֶאֱכֹל מִתּוֹךְ שִׂמְחָה,
שׁוּב יוֹרֵד אוֹר חַקִּי אֲפַרְפּוֹרִי:

שׁוּב יוֹרֵד אוֹר חַקִּי אֲפַרְפּוֹרִי
עַל הַיַּיִן שֶׁמָּזַגְנוּ בַּכּוֹסוֹת
וְגָהַרְנוּ אֶל אַרְגְּמָנוֹ הַחַי
וְאֶל זֵכֶר טַעֲמוֹ מֵאֶשְׁתָּקַד,

וְעַל שְׁדֵי הַבַּחוּרוֹת כְּמוֹ שְׁזִיפִים
הַקְּלוּטִים בְּתוֹךְ כְּרִיכוֹת רָפוֹת פְּרוּמוֹת
וְסוֹפְגִים מַגָּע שֶׁל רוּחַ רְעֵבָה,
שׁוּב יוֹרֵד אוֹר חַקִּי אֲפַרְפּוֹרִי:

שׁוּב יוֹרֵד אוֹר חַקִּי אֲפַרְפּוֹרִי
עַל אַהֲבָתֵנוּ הַפְּגוּעָה,

On the melting memories
We thought to sort out in time,

On our flesh which conspires to collapse suddenly,
On our strength to maintain a human form
That it be an eagerly receptive, perceiving entity
Again a drab khaki light is coming down: ∞

MILITARY FUNERAL IN THE HEAT OF DAY
T. Carmi

In memoriam Joseph Ha'efrati

1
Kindled moons are moving on the road
A phosphorescent millipede
Creeping toward a final darkness.

At the head— a troop-carrier adorned with wreaths.
Young soldiers with closed faces;
Rifle barrels pointed upward.

2
A new military cemetery,
Full of scents.
The gardeners are coming and going,
A greenhouse for death.

Her face. Her sons. His parents. His sons—

The angel who made them forget
All of the wisdom of the womb
When they came forth into the world—
Strikes them for the second time.

Everything is erased, forgotten, worn away.

Another oblivion alters
The structure of the father's bones,

עַל הַזִּכְרוֹנוֹת הַנְּמַסִּים
שֶׁחָשַׁבְנוּ לְהַפְלוֹת אוֹתָם בַּזְּמַן,

עַל בְּשָׂרֵנוּ הַזּוֹמֵם לְקָרֵס פִּתְאֹם,
עַל כֹּחֵנוּ לְהַחֲזִיק צוּרַת אָדָם
שֶׁיִּהְיֶה מָהוּת גּוּמַעַת וְרוֹאָה,
שׁוּב יוֹרֵד אוֹר חֲקִי אֲפַרוּרִי:

לְוָיָה צְבָאִית כְּחֹם הַיּוֹם
ט. כרמי

לזכר י. ה.

1

יְרֵחִים דְּלוּקִים נָעִים בַּכְּבִישׁ.
מֻרְבֵּה-רַגְלַיִם זַרְחָנִי
מִזְדַּחֵל אֶל חֹשֶׁךְ אַחֲרוֹן.

בָּרֹאשׁ — קוֹמַנְדְּקַר עָטוּר זֵרִים.
חַיָּלִים צְעִירִים קְפוּצֵי-פָּנִים.
הַקָּנִים כְּלַפֵּי מַעְלָה.

2

בֵּית-קְבָרוֹת צְבָאִי חָדָשׁ,
מָלֵא נִיחוֹחִים.
הַגַּנָּנִים בָּאִים וְשָׁבִים,
חֲמָמָה שֶׁל מָוֶת.

פָּנֶיהָ. בָּנֶיהָ. הוֹרָיו. בָּנָיו —

הַמַּלְאָךְ שֶׁהִשְׁכִּיחַ מֵהֶם
אֶת כָּל חָכְמַת הָרֶחֶם
בְּצֵאתָם לַאֲוִיר הָעוֹלָם —
הוֹלֵם בָּהֶם בַּפַּעַם הַשְּׁנִיָּה.

הַכֹּל נִמְחַק, נִשְׁכַּח, נִשְׁחַק.

שִׁכְחָה אַחֶרֶת מְשַׁנָּה
אֶת מִבְנֵה עַצְמוֹתָיו שֶׁל הָאָב,

The route of his tendons
And the whiteness of his eyes.

Another oblivion changes
The composition of the mother's blood,
The color of her skin,
And the blackness of her eyes.

They will have to revise
All their documents.
Today they become strangers
In a strange land.

New immigrants in the land of the living.

3
Go
Go and figure their ages,
Your age and the ages of your sons.
Move
Among the rows of numbers.
Move
By the loose clods.
Each tombstone
A command post.
You are surrounded, entrapped, captured,
Alive— in a zone of the dead.
Go.

4
Snuffed-out moons move in a column
Back to the built-up area.

The troop-carrier has already returned,
According to instructions.

The millipede
Is breaking up into its segments.

Each man off to himself.
Each man to his house.

אֶת מַסְלוּל הַגִּידִים
וְלֹבֶן הָעֵינַיִם.

שָׁכְחָה אַחֶרֶת מִשָּׁנָה
אֶת הֶרְכֵּב דָּמָהּ שֶׁל הָאֵם,
אֶת צֶבַע עוֹרָהּ
וְהַשָּׁחֹר שֶׁבְּעֵינֶיהָ.

הֵם יִצְטָרְכוּ לְהַחֲלִיף
אֶת כָּל הַמִּסְמָכִים.
הַיּוֹם הֵם הוֹפְכִים לְזָרִים
בְּאֶרֶץ נָכְרִיָּה,

עוֹלִים חֲדָשִׁים בְּאַרְצוֹת הַחַיִּים.

3
צֵא
צֵא וְחַשֵּׁב אֶת גִּילָם,
אֶת גִּילְךָ וְגִיל בָּנֶיךָ.
נוּעַ
בֵּין טוּרֵי הַמִּסְפָּרִים
נוּעַ
בָּאֲדָמָה הַתְּחוּחָה.
כָּל מַצֵּבָה
מַצַּב פִּקּוּד.
אַתָּה מֻקָּף, מֻכְתָּר, שָׁבוּי,
חַי — בִּשְׁטַח הַמֵּת.
צֵא.

4
יְרֵחִים כְּבוּיִים נָעִים בִּשְׂדֵרָה
אֶל הַשֶּׁטַח הַבָּנוּי.

הַקּוֹמַנְדְּקַר כְּבָר חָזַר,
כָּפוּף לְהוֹרָאוֹת.

מַרְבֵּה-הָרַגְלַיִם
מִתְפַּקֵּק לַחֲלָיוֹתָיו.

אִישׁ לְנַפְשׁוֹ.
אִישׁ לְבֵיתוֹ.

Each man to his own mezuzah
And to his own mailbox.

5
The new military cemetery
Is full of scents.

Screams diluted in water,
Tears which have left a residue of salt
On the gravestones.

Weeping hangs in the hollow of the enclosure
Like stalactites in a dark cave.

Moons are kindled to move on the road
Faces are closing.
Rifle barrels are pointed upward. ဆ

(April 1974)

[I saw you]
Yehiel Hazak

I saw you.
You were like scarred stones scattered on the green
Hills
And the earth was hot and breathing the smell of bodies and even
The dew refused to cool it,
But only a few spots shone bald, bared
Of the burnet that had been uprooted by your anger
At it,
Igniting the scarlet anemones with the clatter of the caterpillar treads,
And their fiery scarlet was trampled into stripes,
Stripes which the treads gouged in the ground, captives,
Like stones
Flung in the anger of some unknown god,
You wanted to ignite into your own dreams in the sleeping bags,
And the noises from the burnt exploding dreams
Gathered in the open spaces,

אִישׁ לִמְזוּזָתוֹ
וּלְתֵבַת מִכְתָּבָיו.

5
בֵּית-הַקְּבָרוֹת הֶחָדָשׁ,
מָלֵא נִיחוֹחִים.

צְעָקוֹת שֶׁנִּמְהֲלוּ בַּפְּרָחִים,
דְּמָעוֹת שֶׁהִשְׁאִירוּ דַּק שֶׁל מֶלַח
עַל הַמַּצֵּבוֹת.

הַבֶּכִי תָּלוּי בַּחֲלַל הַחֶלְקָה
כְּמוֹ נְטִיפִים בִּמְעָרָה חֲשׁוּכָה.

יְרֵחִים נִדְלָקִים לָנוּעַ בַּכְּבִישׁ.
הַפָּנִים נִקְפָּצִים.
הַקָּנִים כְּלַפֵּי מַעְלָה.

אפריל 1974

[רָאִיתִי אֶתְכֶם]
יחיאל חזק

רָאִיתִי אֶתְכֶם
הֱיִיתֶם כַּאֲבָנִים פְּצוּעוֹת פְּזוּרִים עַל הַגְּבָעוֹת
הַיְרַקּוֹת,
וְהָאֲדָמָה חַמָּה וְנוֹשֶׁמֶת אֶת רֵיחַ הַגּוּפוֹת וַאֲפִלּוּ
הַטַּל מְסָרֵב לְצַנְּנָהּ,
וְרַק כַּמָּה כְּתָמִים בּוֹהֲקִים קָרַחוֹת, קָרַחוֹת
מִן הַסִּירָה הַקּוֹצָנִית שֶׁנֶּעְקְרָה בְּזַעֲמְכֶם
עָלֶיהָ,
מִצִּית אֶת הַכַּלָּנִיּוֹת הָאֲדֻמּוֹת בְּרַעַשׁ הַזְּחָלִים,
וְהָאֵשׁ הָאֲדָמָה נִרְמְסָה לְפַסִּים,
פַּסִּים שָׂרְטוּ הַשַּׁרְשָׁרָאוֹת אֶת הָאֲדָמָה שְׁבוּיִים
כַּאֲבָנִים
בְּזַעֲמוֹ שֶׁל אֵיזֶה אֵל לֹא יָדוּעַ,
בְּקַשְׁתֶּם לְהִדָּלֵק אֶל תּוֹךְ חֲלוֹמוֹתֵיכֶם בְּשַׁקֵּי הַשֵּׁנָה,
וְקוֹלוֹת הַנֶּפֶץ שֶׁל הַחֲלוֹמוֹת הַשְּׂרוּפִים
נֶאֶסְפוּ אֶל תּוֹךְ הַמֶּרְחָבִים,

And in the morning you awoke with amputated fingers—

Otherwise you would not know how the spirit will return,
How it will return—
And only the silent stumps give witness that you tried to catch it
In your palm and how
It will return   ∞

CURRENT ACCOUNT
Haiim Gouri

And again, as always in the Land of Israel, the stones are steaming,
The dust does not cover,
And my brothers are again crying out in their distress.

Clip-eared dogs howl in the night at the passing stranger
And their brethren howl in return.

And again, as always in the Land of Israel, stone pillows are dangerous.
Many of the sleeping see a ladder.

The moon is larger, moving
Chanting retributions and other sleepwalkers
And those lying in wait slumber by the road, as before.

And again, as always in the Land of Israel,
The gate of mercy is still locked
And gravestones are in the shadow of the wall.

And an Elul sun, and the mountains drip sweet wine
And the hills flow with it
And honey is oozing.

And again, as always in the Land of Israel,
God's-eyes are peeking from their palms
And the rims of stones are sooty from distant fires
And before dawn the valley is filled with mist
And in watermelon season the sea is rough.

— וּבַבֹּקֶר הֱקִיצוֹתֶם קְטוּעֵי-אֶצְבָּעוֹת

אַחֶרֶת לֹא יְדַעְתֶּם אֵיךְ תָּשׁוּב הָרוּחַ,
— אֵיךְ תָּשׁוּב
וְרַק הַגְּלָדִים הָאִלְּמִים יָעִידוּ שֶׁנִּסִּיתֶם לִתְפֹּס אוֹתָהּ
בְּכַף יֶדְכֶם וְאֵיךְ
תָּשׁוּב

חֶשְׁבּוֹן עוֹבֵר
חיים גורי

וְשׁוּב, כְּמוֹ תָּמִיד בְּאֶרֶץ-יִשְׂרָאֵל, הָאֲבָנִים רוֹתְחוֹת,
הָאֲדָמָה אֵינֶנָּה מְכֻסָּה.
וְשׁוּב קוֹרְאִים אַחַי מִן הַמֵּצַר.

כְּלָבִים קְצוּצֵי אָזְנַיִם צוֹעֲקִים בַּלַּיְלָה אֶל הַנָּכְרִי הַנָּע
וַאֲחֵיהֶם עוֹנִים לְעֻמָּתָם.

וְשׁוּב, כְּמוֹ תָּמִיד בְּאֶרֶץ-יִשְׂרָאֵל, אַבְנֵי הַמְּרַאֲשׁוֹת מְסֻכָּנוֹת.
רַבִּים מִן הַנָּמִים רוֹאִים סֶלַע.

הַלְּבָנָה גְּדוֹלָה יוֹתֵר וּמַנִּיעָה
גְּמוּלוֹת מְשׁוֹרְרוֹת וְעוֹד סַהֲרוּרִים
וְהָאוֹרְבִים נָמִים עַל אֵם הַדֶּרֶךְ, כְּמֵאָז.

וְשׁוּב, כְּמוֹ תָּמִיד בְּאֶרֶץ-יִשְׂרָאֵל,
שַׁעַר-הָרַחֲמִים נָעוּל עֲדַיִן
וְאַבְנֵי קְבָרִים בְּצֵל חוֹמָה.

וְשֶׁמֶשׁ אֱלוּלִית וְהֶהָרִים נוֹטְפִים עָסִיס
וְהַגְּבָעוֹת תִּתְמוֹגַגְנָה
וּדְבָשׁ נִגָּר.

וְשׁוּב, כְּמוֹ תָּמִיד בְּאֶרֶץ-יִשְׂרָאֵל,
עֵינַיִם מְצִיצוֹת מִכַּפּוֹת הַמַּזָּל
וְשׁוּלֵי הָאֲבָנִים פִּיחַ שְׂרֵפוֹת רְחוֹקוֹת
וְטֶרֶם שַׁחַר מָלְאָה הַבִּקְעָה עֲרָפֶל
וּבְעוֹנַת הָאֲבַטִּיחִים סוֹעֵר הַיָּם.

And again, as always in the Land of Israel,
Roads are aching from the footprints of pilgrims
And God makes himself at home
And my brothers are still crying in their distress.

And fire power
And night power
And not a needle can pass
Nor a feather in the mountains.

And again, as always in the Land of Israel,
The stones remember.
The dust does not cover.
Justice is certainly served.   ∞

SINCE THEN
Yehudah Amichai

I fell in the battle in Ashdod
In the War of Independence.
My mother said then, he is twenty-four years old,
And now she says, he is fifty-four,
And lights a memorial candle
Like birthday candles
Candles for a cake, to puff at and blow out

And since then my father has died of great pain and sorrow
And since then my sisters have married
And given their children my name,
And since then my home is my grave, and my grave— my home.
Because I fell in the pale sands
Of Ashdod.

And since then all the cypress trees and all the trees of the orange groves
Between Negbah and Yad Mordechai
Move in a slow procession of grief,
And since then all my children and all my ancestors
Are orphans and bereft

וְשׁוּב, כְּמוֹ תָּמִיד בְּאֶרֶץ-יִשְׂרָאֵל,
הַדְּרָכִים כְּאָבוֹת מְעֻקְּבוֹת עוֹלֵי רֶגֶל
וֵאלֹהִים מַרְגִּישׁ כְּמוֹ בַּבַּיִת
וְאַחַי עוֹדָם קוֹרְאִים מִן הַמֵּצַר.

וְכֹחַ אֵשׁ
וְכֹחַ לַיְלָה
וּמַחַט לֹא תַּעֲבֹר
וְנוֹצָה בֶּהָרִים.

וְשׁוּב, כְּמוֹ תָּמִיד בְּאֶרֶץ-יִשְׂרָאֵל,
הָאֲבָנִים זוֹכְרוֹת.
הָאֲדָמָה אֵינֶנָּה מְכַסָּה.
הַדִּין נוֹקֵב אֶת הֶהָרִים.

מֵאָז
יהודה עמיחי

נָפַלְתִּי בַּקְרָב בְּאַשְׁדּוֹד
בְּמִלְחֶמֶת הַשִּׁחְרוּר.
אִמִּי אָמְרָה אָז, הוּא בֶּן עֶשְׂרִים וְאַרְבַּע,
וְעַכְשָׁו הִיא אוֹמֶרֶת, הוּא בֶּן חֲמִשִּׁים וְאַרְבַּע,
וּמַדְלִיקָה נֵר זִכָּרוֹן
כְּמוֹ נֵרוֹת שֶׁל יוֹם הֻלֶּדֶת
נֵרוֹת עַל עֻגָּה לִנְשִׁיפָה וְכִבּוּי.

וּמֵאָז אָבִי מֵת מֵרֹב כְּאֵב וָצַעַר
וּמֵאָז אַחְיוֹתַי הִתְחַתְּנוּ
וְקָרְאוּ לְיַלְדֵיהֶם בִּשְׁמִי,
וּמֵאָז בֵּיתִי הוּא קִבְרִי, וְקִבְרִי — בֵּיתִי.
כִּי נָפַלְתִּי בַּחֹלוֹת הַחִוְּרִים
שֶׁל אַשְׁדּוֹד.

וּמֵאָז כָּל הַבְּרוֹשִׁים וְכָל עֲצֵי הַפַּרְדֵּסִים
בֵּין נֶגְבָּה וּבֵין יַד מָרְדְּכַי
הוֹלְכִים בְּמִצְעַד אָבֵל אִטִּי,
וּמֵאָז כָּל יְלָדַי וְכָל אֲבוֹתַי
הֵם יְתוֹמִים וּשְׁכוּלִים

And since then all my children and all my ancestors
March together hand in hand
In a rally against death.
Because I fell in the war
In the soft sands of Ashdod.

I carried my friend on my back.
And since then I feel always his dead body,
Like a heavy vault upon me.
And since then he feels my arched back beneath him,
Like a curved segment of the globe of earth.
Because I too fell in the terrible sands of Ashdod, and not only him.

And since then I make amends to myself for my death
With loves and a Cimmerian feast,
And since then I am of blessed memory,
And since then I do not desire that God avenge my blood.
Since then I do not wish that my mother cry over me
In her beautiful perfect face,
And since then I fight against pain,
And since then I march against my memories
Like a man against the wind,
And since then I mourn my memories
Like a man someone of his who has died,
And since then I snuff-out my memories
Like a man a fire,
And since then I am quiet.
Because I fell in Ashdod
In the War of Independence.

"Emotions were stirred!" so they said back then, "Hopes
Ran high," so they said but say no longer,
"The arts flourished," so said the history books,
"Science thrived," so they said,
"An evening breeze cooled their burning
Foreheads," so they said then,
"A morning wind billowed their forelocks,"
So they said.
But since then the winds do other things,

וּמֵאָז כָּל יְלָדַי וְכָל אֲבוֹתַי
הוֹלְכִים יַחְדָּו שְׁלוּבֵי יָדַיִם
בְּהַפְגָּנָה נֶגֶד הַמָּוֶת.
כִּי נָפַלְתִּי בַּמִּלְחָמָה
בַּחוֹלוֹת הָרַכִּים שֶׁל אַשְׁדּוֹד.

נָשָׂאתִי אֶת חֲבֵרִי עַל גַּבִּי.
וּמֵאָז אֲנִי חָשׁ אֶת גּוּפוֹ הַמֵּת תָּמִיד,
כְּמוֹ רָקִיעַ כָּבֵד עָלַי,
וּמֵאָז הוּא חָשׁ אֶת גַּבִּי הַמְקֻמָּר תַּחְתָּיו,
כְּמוֹ קֶטַע מְקֻמָּר שֶׁל כַּדּוּר הָאֲדָמָה.
כִּי נָפַלְתִּי בַּחוֹלוֹת הַנּוֹרָאִים שֶׁל אַשְׁדּוֹד, וְלֹא רַק הוּא.

וּמֵאָז אֲנִי מְפַצֶּה אֶת עַצְמִי עַל מוֹתִי
בַּאֲהָבוֹת וּבְמִשְׁתֶּה אָפֵל,
וּמֵאָז אֲנִי זִכְרוֹנִי לִבְרָכָה,
וּמֵאָז אֲנִי לֹא רוֹצֶה שֶׁאֲדֹנָי יִקֹּם אֶת דָּמִי.
מֵאָז אֲנִי לֹא רוֹצֶה שֶׁאִמִּי תִּבְכֶּה עָלַי
בְּפָנֶיהָ הַיָּפִים וְהַמְדֻיָּקִים,
וּמֵאָז אֲנִי נִלְחָם נֶגֶד הַכְּאֵב,
וּמֵאָז אֲנִי צוֹעֵד נֶגֶד זִכְרוֹנוֹתַי
כְּאָדָם נֶגֶד הָרוּחַ,
וּמֵאָז אֲנִי מְבַכֶּה אֶת זִכְרוֹנוֹתַי
כְּאָדָם אֶת מֵתוֹ,
וּמֵאָז אֲנִי מְכַבֶּה אֶת זִכְרוֹנוֹתַי
כְּאָדָם אֶת הָאֵשׁ,
וּמֵאָז אֲנִי שָׁקֵט.
כִּי נָפַלְתִּי בְּאַשְׁדּוֹד
בְּמִלְחֶמֶת הַשִּׁחְרוּר.

"הָרְגָשׁוֹת גָּעֲשׁוּ!", כָּךְ אָמְרוּ אָז, "הַתִּקְווֹת
גָּאוּ," כָּךְ אָמְרוּ וְלֹא אוֹמְרִים עוֹד,
"הָאֱמָנִיּוֹת פָּרְחוּ," כָּךְ אָמְרוּ סִפְרֵי הַהִיסְטוֹרְיָה,
"הַמַּדָּע שָׂגְשֵׂג," כָּךְ אָמְרוּ,
"רוּחַ עֶרֶב הֵצֵנָה לָהֶם אֶת הַמֵּצַח
הַלּוֹהֵט," כָּךְ אָמְרוּ אָז,
"רוּחַ בֹּקֶר בִּדְרָה לָהֶם אֶת בְּלוֹרִיתָם,"
כָּךְ אָמְרוּ.
וּמֵאָז הָרוּחוֹת עוֹשׂוֹת דְּבָרִים אֲחֵרִים,

And since then words say other things,
(Look not upon me because I am alive),
Because I fell in the soft and pale sands
Of Ashdod in the War of Independence.   ℅

FROM THE SONGS OF THE LAND OF ZION AND JERUSALEM
Yehudah Amichai

On the last words of Trumpeldor—
It is good to die for our country— they built the new homeland,
Like wild hornets in crazed swarms.
And even if these were not the words
Or he had not said them or they were and had faded away
Their place remained, arched as a cave. The mortar
More hardened than stones. This is my homeland
Where I can dream without falling
And do evil deeds without perishing,
Forsake my wife without being lonely,
Cry without shame and betray and lie
Without being abandoned to perdition.

This is the land which we have covered with field and forest
So we had no time to cover our faces
And they are exposed in the corruption of grief and in the abhorrence of
     happiness.

This is the land in whose ground are the dead
Instead of coal and gold and iron
And they are the fuel for the advent of messiahs.   ℅

(June 1982)

YOUR SOCKS
Raiah Harnik

Your socks are in the drawer
Your clothes are in the closet, folded
Your fatigues, too

וּמֵאָז הַמִּלִּים אוֹמְרוֹת דְּבָרִים אֲחֵרִים,
(אַל תִּרְאוּנִי שֶׁאֲנִי חַי),
כִּי נָפַלְתִּי בַּחוֹלוֹת הָרַכִּים וְהַחִוְּרִים
שֶׁל אַשְׁדּוֹד בְּמִלְחֶמֶת הַשִּׁחְרוּר.

מִשִּׁירֵי אֶרֶץ צִיּוֹן וִירוּשָׁלַיִם
יהודה עמיחי

עַל הַמִּלִּים הָאַחֲרוֹנוֹת שֶׁל טְרוּמְפֶּלְדּוֹר
טוֹב לָמוּת בְּעַד אַרְצֵנוּ, בָּנוּ אֶת הַמּוֹלֶדֶת
הַחֲדָשָׁה, כְּמוֹ דַּבּוּרֵי בָּר בְּפִקְעוֹת מְטֹרָפוֹת.
וַאֲפִלּוּ אִם אֵלֶּה לֹא הָיוּ הַמִּלִּים
אוֹ שֶׁלֹּא אָמַר אוֹתָן אוֹ שֶׁהָיוּ וְהִתְנַדְּפוּ,
מְקוֹמָן נִשְׁאַר מְקֻמָּר כִּמְעָרָה. הַמְּלָט
הִתְקַשָּׁה יוֹתֵר מֵאֲבָנִים. זוֹהִי מוֹלַדְתִּי
שֶׁבָּהּ אֲנִי יָכוֹל לַחֲלוֹם בְּלִי לִפֹּל
וְלַעֲשׂוֹת מַעֲשִׂים רָעִים בְּלִי לֶאֱבֹד,
לִזְנֹחַ אֶת אִשְׁתִּי בְּלִי לִהְיוֹת בּוֹדֵד,
לִבְכּוֹת בְּלִי בּוּשָׁה וְלִבְגּוֹד וּלְשַׁקֵּר
בְּלִי לִהְיוֹת מֻפְקָר לַאֲבַדּוֹן.

זוֹהִי הָאָרֶץ שֶׁכִּסִּינוּ אוֹתָהּ בְּשָׂדֶה וּבְיַעַר
וְלֹא הָיָה לָנוּ זְמַן לְכַסּוֹת אֶת פָּנֵינוּ
וְהֵן עֲרֻמּוֹת בְּעִוּוּת הַצַּעַר וּבְכִעוּר הַשִּׂמְחָה.

זוֹהִי הָאָרֶץ שֶׁמֵּתֶיהָ בָּאֲדָמָה
בִּמְקוֹם הַפֶּחָם וְהַזָּהָב וְהַבַּרְזֶל
וְהֵם הַדֶּלֶק לְבִיאוֹת מְשִׁיחִים.

נדפס — יוני 1982

הַגַּרְבַּיִם שֶׁלָּךְ
רעיה הרניק

הַגַּרְבַּיִם שֶׁלָּךְ בַּמְּגֵרָה
הַבְּגָדִים מְקֻפָּלִים בָּאָרוֹן
הַדֻּגְמָחִים שֶׁלָּךְ, גַּם

And your clock ticks next to me
Waking me every morning for nothing
At four-thirty sharp.

Where did you rush to at four-thirty
To which oblivion to what end
At four-thirty in the month of June
Why did you hurry what was so urgent again…

And your clothes are in the closet
Dress uniform, fatigues,
A parka with epaulets, next to the curtain.
And a clock which wakes me every night
At four-thirty sharp.   ᴔ

(January 1983)

And At Night
Raiah Harnik

And at night came to me
The child who was not born
And looked into my eyes
And asked:
Where is my father?

His eyes were   .
Your eyes, my son, and the angle
Of the brows was yours
And mine, and the child asked:
Where is my father?

Your father, my child, was carried off by the wind
Of the mountain. In a foreign land
Your father remained, my child.
Somebody made a mistake, my beautiful son
And now you will not be.

וּשְׁעוֹנְךָ מְתַקְתֵּק עַל יָדִי
מֵעִיר אוֹתִי כָּל בֹּקֶר בִּכְדִי
בְּאַרְבַּע וּשְׁלוֹשִׁים בְּדִיּוּק.

לְאָן רָצְתָּ בְּאַרְבַּע וּשְׁלֹשִׁים
לְאֵיזֶה חַדָּלוֹן לְאֵיזֶה סוֹף
בְּאַרְבַּע וּשְׁלֹשִׁים בְּחֹדֶשׁ יוּנִי
מַה מִּהַרְתָּ מַה שׁוּב בָּעַר ...

וְהַבְּגָדִים שֶׁלְּךָ בָּאָרוֹן
מַדֵּי אֶלֶף, דַּגְמָחִים,
דֻּבּוֹן עִם דַּרְגָּה עַל יַד הַוִּילוֹן.
וְשָׁעוֹן הַמֵּעִיר אוֹתִי מַדֵּי לַיְלָה
בְּאַרְבַּע וּשְׁלוֹשִׁים בְּדִיּוּק.

ינואר 1983

וּבַלַּיְלָה
רעיה הרניק

וּבַלַּיְלָה בָּא אֵלַי
הַיֶּלֶד שֶׁלֹּא נוֹלַד
וְהִבִּיט בְּעֵינַי
וְשָׁאַל:
אֵיפֹה אָבִי?

הָעֵינַיִם שֶׁלּוֹ הָיוּ
עֵינֶיךָ, בְּנִי. וְזָוִית
הַגַּבּוֹת שֶׁלְּךָ
וְשֶׁלִּי, וְהַיֶּלֶד שָׁאַל:
אֵיפֹה אָבִי?

אָבִיךָ, יַלְדִּי, נִשָּׂא בְּרוּחַ
הָהָר. בְּאֶרֶץ נֵכָר
נִשְׁאַר אָבִיךָ, יַלְדִּי.
מִישֶׁהוּ טָעָה בְּנֵי הַיָּפֶה
וְעַכְשָׁו אַתָּה לֹא תִּהְיֶה.

Where is my father asks the child
That was not born.
Where is my son asks the mother
That no longer lives.
Where am I asks the man
That remained on the top of the mountain.   ⬧

(December 1982)

COFFINS
Eli Alon

Coffins.
Coffins from Beirut
Coffins from Tyre, from Sidon
From 630
From 205
Coffins from Karoun
From Zhalta
Command cars with confused recruits
A little major from the military rabbinate
Conducting a funeral;
Coffins in every kibbutz
In every moshav
In every city;
Coffins from Halda
From Aley
From Bahmadoun
From Shtura
More dead
Many dead

Bereaved parents, widows, disabled
Our children will lie beneath the flowers
A long, long row...
Until we comprehend.   ⬧

(July 15 1982)

אֵיפֹה אָבִי שׁוֹאֵל הַיֶּלֶד
שֶׁלֹא נוֹלַד.
אֵיפֹה בְּנִי שׁוֹאֶלֶת הָאֵם
שֶׁכְּבָר לֹא חַיָּה.
אֵיפֹה אֲנִי שׁוֹאֵל הַגֶּבֶר
שֶׁנִּשְׁאַר עַל פִּסְגַּת הָהָר.

דצמבר 1982

אֲרוֹנוֹת
א. עלי

אֲרוֹנוֹת.
אֲרוֹנוֹת מִבֵּירוּת
אֲרוֹנוֹת מִצּוֹר, מִצִּידוֹן
מ-630
מ-205
אֲרוֹנוֹת מִקַּרְעוּן
מִזְּחַלְתָּא
קוֹמַנְדְּקָרִים עִם טִירוֹנִים מְבֻלְבָּלִים
רַסָ"ר קָטָן מֵהָרַבָּנוּת הַצְּבָאִית
מְנַהֵל לְוָיָה;
אֲרוֹנוֹת בְּכָל קִבּוּץ
בְּכָל מוֹשָׁב
בְּכָל עִיר;
אֲרוֹנוֹת מֵחַלְדֶּה
מֵעַלַּיי
מִבַּחַמְדוּן
מִשְּׁתוּרָה
עוֹד מֵתִים
הַרְבֵּה מֵתִים

הוֹרִים שַׁכּוּלִים, אַלְמָנוֹת, נָכִים
יְלָדֵינוּ יִשְׁכְּבוּ מִתַּחַת לַפְּרָחִים
שׁוּרָה אֲרֻכָּה אֲרֻכָּה ...
עַד שֶׁנָּבִין.

(15 יולי 1982)

EULOGY
Amichai Israeli

This should be a eulogy without words:

Statistically speaking one can say
Almost with certainty, that twenty percent
Of the fallen in the Sharon war in Lebanon
Died virgins.

What will the demonstrations for and against the war do for them now?
What matters to them the speech of the military rabbi, the rent in the garment?
What matters for them the tears of their mothers the great sorrow of the
        mourners?

You see, they are fallen.
You see, they are casualties.
You see, they are virgins.   &

FRIENDS
Nathan Yonathan

> *To Sephi*
> *Who fell in the Lebanon War*
> *" …In the place that once was our land*
> *The islands are sinking, rust and ashes …"*
>   *George Seferis*

Joseph is without doubt rent in pieces an evil beast hath devoured him
And what about the dreams and his Ayelet and Ofir
Without doubt rent in pieces and gone because God had taken him, too
And left a charred tank with
Torn phylacteries in the turret
If a place exists where friends meet
After the wars, search for him and to that handsome lad
Of ours say: My brother. My brother, for nine years
I followed you on the roads, armored, breathing
Dust and love. Now I am come to put
A tired head on the same shoulder. "We all

הֶסְפֵּד
עמיחי ישראלי

זֶה צָרִיךְ לִהְיוֹת הֶסְפֵּד לְלֹא מִלִּים:

בְּאֹפֶן סְטָטִיסְטִי נִתָּן לוֹמַר
כִּמְעַט בְּוַדָּאוּת, כִּי 20 אֲחוּזִים
מִן הַנּוֹפְלִים בְּמִלְחֶמֶת שָׁרוֹן בִּלְבָנוֹן
מֵתוּ בְּתוּלִים.

מַה יִּתְּנוּ לָהֶם עַכְשָׁו הַפְּגָנוֹת הַבְּעַד וְהַנֶּגֶד?
מַה לָהֶם נְאוּם הָרַב הַצְּבָאִי, הַקֶּרַע בְּדַשׁ הַבֶּגֶד?
מַה לָהֶם דִּמְעוֹת אִמָּם, הַצַּעַר הָרַב שֶׁל הָאֲבֵלִים?

וַהֲרֵי הֵם נוֹפְלִים.
וַהֲרֵי הֵם חֲלָלִים.
וַהֲרֵי הֵם בְּתוּלִים.

חֲבֵרִים
נתן יונתן

לספי
שנפל במלחמת לבנון
"— — —במקום שהיה פעם ארצנו
שוקעים האיים, חלודה ואפר— —"
ספריס

טָרֹף טֹרַף יוֹסֵף חַיָּה רָעָה אֲכָלָתְהוּ
וּמָה עִם הַחֲלוֹמוֹת וְאַיֶּלֶת שֶׁלּוֹ וְאוֹפִיר
טָרֹף טֹרַף וְאֵינֶנּוּ כִּי לָקַח גַּם אוֹתוֹ
הָאֱלֹהִים וְהִשְׁאִיר טַנְק שָׂרוּף עִם
תְּפִלִּין קְרוּעִים בַּצְּרִיחַ.
אִם יֵשׁ מָקוֹם שֶׁבּוֹ נִפְגָּשִׁים חֲבֵרִים
אַחֲרֵי הַקְּרָב חִפֵּשׂ אַחֲרָיו וְלַיְפָה
שֶׁלָּנוּ תֹּאמַר: אָחִי, אָחִי, תֵּשַׁע שָׁנִים
אַחֲרֶיךָ בַּדְּרָכִים, עוֹטֶה שִׁרְיוֹן, נוֹשֵׁם
אָבָק וְאַהֲבָה, עַכְשָׁו אֲנִי בָּא לָשִׂים
רֹאשׁ עָיֵף עַל אוֹתָהּ כָּתֵף.   יְכַלֵּנוּ

Used to lean on him," you used
To say after the war. So if
Such a place exists, tell him that here day by
Day someone waits. In the place that once was
Our land the islands are sinking. Rust
And ashes. Our strength diminishes
Ever more and more. Near the places
Which he had passed we wish
We were dead
And, like a tank
Time
Tramples and tramples   ∽

(November 1982)

My Hand Is Extended For The Peace Of The Galilee
Ramy Ditzanny

My mortar shell I remember well.
I remember well.
Every night on a forehead-screen, silvery, flickering,
I dream it as in my old movie projector— a small homely movie projector,
In a very slow motion, in slowmotion screening: slow.
Very slow.

I fly it like an arrow. Like a kite covered with shiny cellophane,
Or freeze it like a bird of prey floating in the air
Or reverse the operation of the machine (reverse projection)—
So that it stops for a moment and hesitates, and is sucked backwards,
Then again forward, and again backwards. Like a bright tennis ball
Like some ambassador flying throughout the area
I launch it like a person-to-person rocket back towards its personal launcher;
And there behind a rifle-sight and a mask of sweat/dust—
Rises a hard brown face with a wrinkled forehead.
There it again returns like a sperm and is pulled into the mouth of the barrel of
    an anti-tank launcher
And again again it returns to be ejaculated.
Another short moment— and it is already coming at me in full heat
Bangs against the wall splatters escapes

הָיִינוּ נִשְׁעָנִים עָלָיו הָיִיתָ נוֹהֵג
לוֹמַר אַחֲרֵי הַמִּלְחָמָה. אָז אִם יֶשְׁנוֹ
כָּזֶה מָקוֹם, סַפֵּר לוֹ שֶׁאֶצְלֵנוּ יוֹם
יוֹם מְחַכִּים. בַּמָּקוֹם שֶׁהָיָה פַּעַם
אַרְצֵנוּ שׁוֹקְעִים הַחַיִּים. חֶלְדָּה
וָאֵפֶר וְהַכֹּחוֹת הַהוֹלְכִים
וְכָלִים וּלְיַד הַמְּקוֹמוֹת
שֶׁעָבַר שׁוֹאֲלִים אֶת
נַפְשֵׁנוּ לָמוּת
וְהַזְּמַן כְּמוֹ
טַנְק
דּוֹרֵס וְדוֹרֵס

נובמבר 82

יָדִי לַשָּׁלוֹם הַגָּלִיל מוּשֶׁטֶת
רמי דיצני

אֶת הַפֶּגַז שֶׁלִּי אֲנִי זוֹכֵר הֵיטֵב,
אֲנִי זוֹכֵר הֵיטֵב.
לַיְלָה לַיְלָה עַל מָסַךְ-מֵצַח מַכְסִיף מְהַבְהֵב
אֲנִי חוֹלֵם אוֹתוֹ בַּמְּטוֹלְנוֹעַ הַיָּשָׁן שֶׁלִּי — מְכוֹנַת קוֹלְנוֹעַ קְטַנָּה וּבֵיתִית,
בָּ-very slow motion — בְּהַקְרָנָה אִטְנוֹעִית; אִטִּית.
מְאֹד אִטִּית.

אֲנִי מֵטִיס אוֹתוֹ כְּחֵץ. כַּעֲפִיפוֹן מְצֻפֶּה צְלוֹפָן נוֹצֵץ.
אוֹ מַקְפִּיאוֹ כְּעוֹף-דּוֹרֵס צַף בָּאֲוִיר
אוֹ מַחֲזִיר אֶת פְּעוּלַת הַמַּכְשִׁיר (reverse projection)
וְהוּא נֶעֱצָר לְרֶגַע מְהַסֵּס, וְשָׁב נִינָק לְאָחוֹר,
וְשׁוּב הָלוֹךְ, וְשׁוּב חָזוֹר, כְּמוֹ כַּדּוּר טֶנִיס בָּהִיר
כְּמִין שַׁגְרִיר מְעוֹפֵף בָּאֵזוֹר
אֲנִי מְשַׁגְּרוֹ כָּטִיל בֵּין אֱנוֹשִׁי אֶל מְשַׁגְּרוֹ הָאִישִׁי;
— וְשָׁם מֵאֲחוֹרֵי כַּוֶּנֶת וּמַסֵּכַת זֵעָה/אָבָק —
קָמוֹת פָּנִים חוֹמוֹת קָשׁוֹת וּמֵצַח מְקֻמָּט,
שָׁם הוּא שָׁב חוֹזֵר כַּזֶּרַע וְנִקְלָט בְּלַעַ קָנֶה מָטוֹל נ"ט
וְשׁוּב שׁוּב-שָׁב נִפְלָט.
עוֹד רֶגַע קָט — וּכְבָר וּבָא אֵלַי מָלֵא לַהַט
נֶחְבָּט בַּדֹּפֶן נִתָּז נִמְלָט

And instantaneously in the air it breaks up
(The movie is silent so the blast was not recorded)
Into a myriad molecules splinters into a flash of molten copper coins
Fireworks of coruscating incandescence
A torrent of shavings frolicking in space
A cloud of splinters silver scales
Tiny flies curls of pure gold
Butterflies of molten iron preening flying upwards.
Butterflies.

Butterflies for people of khaki
Butterflies for young scouts on metal hillocks
Butterflies for crouching shadows against the background of welded steel—
Butterflies for young men in tanks
Butterflies for the horsemen in the chariots of Israel!

Come to me O lovely butterfly
Sit with me here on my palm!

It is coming! My dizzying butterfly. A dancing butterfly.
Slowly quickly
Slowly quickly
Slowly.
My butterfly has an address
My butterfly is locked-on-target.

Perhaps I covered my face with my arms horrified—
In a slow motion the hand goes up in the curling of an arched gesture
And my fluttering butterfly, a cruising mini-spaceship,
Takes my hand extended for peace
Plucks my hand ricochet my hand ricochet my hand ricochet my...　　∞

LEGGING BEHIND
Ramy Ditzanny

A stork has one leg.
A ladder two.
A tripod has tri pods.

וּבְבַת אַחַת בָּאֲוִיר נִפְרָד
(הַסֶּרֶט אִלֵּם הַמַּפָּץ לֹא הֻקְלַט)
לְאַלְפֵי פְּרוּדוֹת נִפְרָט לְרֶשֶׁף פְּרוּטוֹת נְחֹשֶׁת רוֹחֶשֶׁת
זִקּוּקִים שֶׁל אֵשׁ לוֹחֶשֶׁת
שִׁבֹּלֶת שְׁבָבִים מִשְׁתּוֹבְבִים בֶּחָלָל
עָנָן רְסִיסִים קַשְׁקַשִּׁים מַכְסָפִים
זְבוּבוֹנִים זָהָב שָׁחוּט מִתְלַתָּל
פַּרְפְּרֵי בַּרְזֶל יָצוּק מִתְיַפְיְפִים מְעוֹפְפִים אֶל עַל.
פַּרְפָּרִים.

פַּרְפָּרִים לָאֲנָשִׁים מֶחָאקִי
פַּרְפָּרִים לִנְעָרִים-צוֹפִים עַל תְּלוּלִיּוֹת מַתֶּכֶת
פַּרְפָּרִים לְצָלְיוֹת נְמוּכוֹת עַל רֶקַע רָקִיעַ פְּלָדָה מְרֻתֶּכֶת —
פַּרְפָּרִים לְבַחוּרִים בְּמֶרְכָּבוֹת בַּרְזֶל
פַּרְפָּרִים לְפָרָשִׁים בְּרֶכֶב יִשְׂרָאֵלִי

בּוֹא אֵלַי פַּרְפָּר נֶחְמָד
שֵׁב אֶצְלִי עַל כַּף הַיָּד!

הוּא בָּא! פַּרְפָּר מְסַחְרֵר שֶׁלִּי. פַּרְפָּר מְכַרְכֵּר.
לְאַט מַהֵר
לְאַט מַהֵר
לְאַט.
לַפַּרְפָּר שֶׁלִּי יֵשׁ כְּתֹבֶת
הַפַּרְפָּר שֶׁלִּי מְבַיָּת.

אוּלַי כִּסִּיתִי פָּנַי בִּזְרוֹעֵי מִבַּעַד —
בְּהָלוֹךְ אֲטִנּוֹעֵי הַיָּד מִתְעַלָּה בְּסִלְסוּל מְחֻנָּה מְקֻשֶּׁטֶת
וּפַרְפְּרֵי הַמְרַפְרֵף, חֲלָלִית-כִּיס מְשַׁיֶּטֶת,
נוֹטֵל אֶת יָדִי לְשָׁלוֹם מוֹשֵׁטֶת
קוֹטֵף אֶת יָדִי רֵיקוֹשֶׁט אֶת יָדִי רֵיקוֹשֶׁט אֶת יָדִי רֵיקוֹשֶׁט אֶת ...

לְמַרְבֵּה צַעַר
רמי דיצני

לַחֲסִידָה — רֶגֶל אַחַת.
לַסֻּלָּם — שְׁתֵּי רַגְלַיִם.
לְשֻׁלְחָן תְּלַת-רֶגֶל — תְּלַת-רֶגֶל.

A fly has four (says Aristotle).
A stud bull— has five.
A dung beetle— six.
A millipede may stampede over mille pede without missing a pede!

And I, a leg and a half.
A wooden calf.
A walking stick with a knob of ivory beautifully carved.

A few girls up the street
Have let me know my limp is elegant,
And I am grateful for that;
Indeed I am quite particular about my attire,
And I also have a degree— I am an electronics engineer!

Yet I have to say, that despite the prime of my years,
My great effort, my robust thighs,
And my splendid stick— it gets very hard for me
To overtake them   ∞

                            (Translation: Ramy Ditzanny)

A BRAND PLUCKED FROM THE ANTI-TANK FIRE
Ramy Ditzanny

Plastic surgery, Rambam Hospital

A chance-passing nurse grumbling about some visitor— He ought to stop smoking!
In the room a stark white bed. A blackened form with crumpled shape. Asleep. A smell of charred roast: a bad smell.
Next to it stands bobbing for hours a black hat-coat-vest.
In its hand a page of Gemara (or perhaps a Siddur, perhaps a Torah).

Suddenly the lump of burnt flesh wakes with a start
Opens lashless lids, two metal shards in the left brow, a pair of slits for eyes,
Smoky dull but so sharp (no wonder, against the background of such a black face)
And its torn lips discharging, crusting
Spreading like a vulva—
Uttering slowly, releasing burnt letters: w-a-t-e-r.

לַזְּבוּב — אַרְבַּע רַגְלַיִם (אֲרִיסְטוֹ).
לְפַר הָרְבָעָה — חָמֵשׁ רַגְלַיִם.
לְחִפּוּשִׁית-זֶבֶל — שֵׁשׁ רַגְלַיִם.
לְמַרְבֵּה-רַגְלַיִם — הַרְבֵּה רַגְלַיִם.

וְלִי — רֶגֶל וָחֵצִי.
תּוֹתָב.
מַקֵּל הֲלִיכָה מְחֻטָּב.
בַּשְּׁנָהָב.

בַּחוּרוֹת, אֲחָדוֹת בְּמַעֲלֵה הָרְחוֹב הוֹדִיעוּנִי שֶׁצְּלִיעָתִי אֶלֶגַנְטִית,
וַהֲרֵינִי מַכִּיר לָהֶן תּוֹדָה עַל כָּךְ,
כִּי אָכֵן אֲנִי מַקְפִּיד בִּלְבוּשִׁי, וְלִי גַּם דִּיפְּלוֹמָה — מְהַנְדֵּס חַשְׁמָל.

אֶפֶס, חַיָּב לוֹמַר, שֶׁלַּמְרוֹת טוּב שְׁנוֹתַי וְרֹב הֶעָמָל,
יַרְכֵּי הַחֲסָנוֹת וּמַטֵּי הַמְּהַדֵּר מִתְקַשֶּׁה
אָנֹכִי לַהֲשִׂיגָן.

אוּד מֻצָּל מֵאֵשׁ נ"ט
רמי דיצני

מחלקת פלסטיקה, בי"ח רמב"ם

אָחוֹת מִזְדַּמֶּנֶת נִרְגֶּנֶת בְּגִין מְבַקֵּר מִזְדַּמֵּן שֶׁיִּפְסִיק לְעַשֵּׁן!
בַּחֶדֶר מִטָּה צְחוֹרָה. צֶלֶם מְפֻחָם מְעוּךְ צוּרָה. יָשֵׁן. רֵיחַ צְלִי מְעֻשָּׁן. רֵיחַ רָע.
עַל יָדָהּ נִצֶּבֶת שָׁעוֹת מִתְנוֹעַעַת מִגִּבְעַת-קָפּוֹטָה-חֲזִיָּה-שְׁחוֹרָה.
בְּיָדָהּ דַּף גְּמָרָא (אוֹ אוּלַי סִדּוּר, אוּלַי סֵפֶר תּוֹרָה).

פִּתְאוֹם גּוּשׁ בָּשָׂר שָׂרוּף נֶחֱרַד מִשְּׁנָתוֹ
פּוֹקֵחַ אֵין-רִיסִים-עֵינַיִם, שְׁנֵי רְסִיסִים בַּגֻּבָּה הַשְּׂמָאלִית, שְׁנֵי חֲרִיצִים עֵינַיִם.
עֲשֵׁנוֹת-עֲכוּרוֹת אַךְ כָּל כָּךְ בְּהִירוֹת (כַּמּוּבָן עַל רֶקַע פָּנִים כֹּה שְׁחוֹרוֹת)
וּשְׂפָתָיו הַקְּרוּעוֹת זָבוֹת מַקְרִישׁוֹת
מִתְפַּשְׁקוֹת כְּפֹת —
רוֹחֲשׁוֹת לוֹאֲטוֹת מְמַלְטוֹת אוֹתִיּוֹת שְׂרוּפוֹת: מ-י-ם.

Immediately his father, Here I am, my son; startled away from his studying,
From atop the dresser he gets it, extends his hand to the boy, places a glass to the
   lips,
And off of the chin and of the chest, with utmost compassion, wipes with his
   handkerchief the dribbling water.

And afterwards he carefully removes the glass, hugs it with both palms,
Turns its rim to exactly the place where the sweetness of those lips had clung—
And presses his own to it kissing the mark they left.

Soundlessly he makes a Kiddush and takes a sip of water,
Puts the glass down
Covertly wipes his eyes
And with devotion goes back to holy study.   ഔ

COMPLICATED AND INNOVATIVE ORTHOPEDIC SURGERY
Ramy Ditzanny

Diagnosis:
On the one side— a leg thin and short
But on the other— one which is long.
Slight consolation.

The operation:
The shriveled shin bone you cut at the ankle
(And you discard the foot).
You saw off a length from the shriveled thigh
(Equal to the length of the shin bone stump minus the vertical distance between
   the knee caps).
You turn the knee and the two stumps a hundred and eighty degrees.
You stitch the end of the chopped shin to the end of a chopped thigh.
Now, on the operating table, the two knees are in equal distance from the groin;
What had been a thigh stump remains, in a new rôle— a shin stump
Swinging from the joint of a rotated knee ˙
Dazing tears of blood.
Immediately you cramp its end
And fit it with a high-quality prosthesis.
Now, on the operating table lies a normal leg aside a kind of a shriveled chopped
   one

מִיָּד אָבִיו, הִנְנִי בְנִי, נֶחֱרַד מִמִּשְׁנָתוֹ,
מֵעַל הָאָרוֹנִית לוֹקֵחַ, שׁוֹלֵחַ יָדוֹ אֶל הַנַּעַר, כּוֹס מַדְבִּיק לַשְּׂפָתַיִם,
וּמְסַנְטְרוֹ וּמְחַזְּהוּ, בְּרַחֲמִים שְׁפוּכִים, מוֹחֶה בְּמִטְפַּחְתּוֹ מוֹתַר הַמַּיִם.

וְהַכּוֹס אַחַר-כָּךְ בִּזְהִירוּת מְנַתְּקָה, מְחַבְּקָהּ בִּשְׁתֵּי כַּפּוֹת יָדַיִם,
מְסוֹבֵב שְׂפָתָהּ בְּדִיּוּק מוּל מָקוֹם בּוֹ דָּבַק מֶתֶק הַשְּׂפָתַיִם —
וּמְדַבֵּק בָּהּ שְׂפָתָיו מְנַשֵּׁק חֲתִימַת הַשְּׂפָתַיִם.

בְּלֹא קוֹל מְקַדֵּשׁ וְלוֹגֵם לְגִימַת מַיִם,
מַנִּיחַ הַכּוֹס
בִּגְנֵבָה מוֹחֶה עֵינַיִם,
וְשָׁב דָּבֵק לִמְלֶאכֶת שָׁמַיִם.

נִתּוּחַ אוֹרְתּוֹפֵּדִי מְסֻבָּךְ וְחַדְשָׁנִי
רמי דיצני

אַבְחָנָה:
מַצַּד אֶחָד — רֶגֶל אַחַת קְצָרָה וּכְחוּשָׁה
אֲבָל מִצַּד הַשֵּׁנִי — הַשְּׁנִיָּה אֲרֻכָּה.
נֶחָמָה פּוּרְתָּא.

מַעֲשֵׂה הַנִּתּוּחַ:
בַּשּׁוֹק הַצְּמוּקָה קוֹצְצִין בַּקַּרְסֹל
(וְכַף הָרֶגֶל מַשְׁלִיכִין).
מְנַסְּרִין בַּיָּרֵךְ הַצְּמוּקָה אֹרֶךְ
(כְּאֹרֶךְ גֶּדֶם הַשּׁוֹק פָּחוֹת מֶרְחָק אֲנָכִי בֵּין פְּקוֹת הַבִּרְכַּיִם).
מְסוֹבְבִין הַבֶּרֶךְ וּשְׁנֵי הַגְּדָמִים בְּמֵאָה שְׁמוֹנִים מַעֲלוֹת.
מְאַחִין קְצֵה שׁוֹק קְצוּצָה לִקְצֵה יָרֵךְ קְצוּצָה.
עַתָּה, עַל דַּרְגָּשׁ הַנִּתּוּחַ, שְׁתֵּי הַבִּרְכַּיִם בְּמֶרְחָק שָׁוֶה מִן הַמִּפְסָעַת;
נוֹתָר גֶּדֶם יָרֵךְ לְשֶׁעָבַר, בְּתַפְקִיד חָדָשׁ — גֶּדֶם שׁוֹק
מִתְנַדְנֵד לוֹ מִמִּפְרָק בֶּרֶךְ מְהֻפֶּכֶת
מְדַמְדֵּם דְּמָעוֹת דָּם.
מִיָּד סוֹכְרִין קָצֵהוּ
וּמַתְאִימִין לוֹ תּוֹתָב מְשֻׁבָּח.
עַתָּה, עַל דַּרְגָּשׁ הַנִּתּוּחַ — רֶגֶל. וְעוֹד מֵעֵין רֶגֶל מְצֻמֶּקֶת וּקְצוּצָה

With a prosthesis at its end.
And the bottom line— all in all, its length is like the length of its mate.

End of operation.

Conclusion:
The doctors are happy
The parents are happy
The brothers and sisters are happy
The young man is happy
A skullcap on his head—
The All Merciful is happy too:
In long green linoleum corridors
No more will our boy hurtle in a wheelchair
Run wild in his chariot
Startle nurses and orderlies—
Like one of the lame he will walk,
Like one of the lame.   ೫

PIGGY-BACK
Ramy Ditzanny

Levenstein House

And with the explosion a rag slapped my face
And a mighty light went out
Then came the smell of the earth
And long silence year after year
And perhaps the voice of Mother
Floating like debris of a ship and again sinking westward
And again silence
Red phlegm
And kind of a hard pleasant sleep
Tubes like a bridle-and-bit in my face
Sometimes a gnarled hand straightens my pajamas
Rubs my feet
Puts a warm cloth between my thighs
Then again sinking in the ground

וְתוֹתָב בְּקֵצָהּ.
וְעֻקַּר דָּבָר — בִּכְלָלוּתָהּ, אֲרֻכָּה כְּאֶרֶךְ אֲחוֹתָהּ.

תַּם מַעֲשֵׂה הַנִּתּוּחַ.

סוֹף דָּבָר:
שְׂמֵחִים הָרוֹפְאִים
שְׂמֵחִים הַהוֹרִים
שְׂמֵחִים הָאֲחָיוֹת וְהָאַחִים
שָׂמַח הַנַּעַר
כֻּפָּה לְרֹאשׁוֹ —
שְׂמֵחִים הָאֱלֹהִים:
בְּמִסְדְּרוֹנוֹת לִינוֹלֵיאוּם אֲרֻכִּים יְרֻקִּים
לֹא עוֹד יִשְׁעַט יַלְדֵּנוּ בְּרֶכֶב נָכִים
לֹא יִשְׁתּוֹלֵל בְּעֶגְלָתוֹ
לֹא יַחֲרִיד מִמְּקוֹמָם אֲחָיוֹת וְאַחִים —
כְּאַחַד הַפִּסְחִים יְהַלֵּךְ,
כְּאַחַד הַפִּסְחִים.

שַׂק קֶמַח
רמי דיצני

בית לוינשטיין

וְעִם הַהִתְפּוֹצְצוּת הַצְּלִיף סְמַרְטוּט בַּפָּנִים
וְאוֹר אַדִּיר כָּבָה
וּבָא רֵיחַ הָאֲדָמָה
וְשֶׁקֶט אָרֹךְ שָׁנִים עַל שָׁנִים
וְאוּלַי קוֹלָהּ שֶׁל אִמָּא
צָף כְּמוֹ שִׁבְרֵי אֳנִיָּה וְשׁוּב שׁוֹקֵעַ יָמָּה
וְשׁוּב דְּמָמָה
לֶחָה אֲדָמָה
וּמִין תְּנוּמָה קָשָׁה נְעִימָה
צְנוּרוֹת בַּפָּנִים כְּמוֹ רִתְמָה
לְעִתִּים יַד עֲקֻמָה מֵיטִיבָה אֶת הַנַּמְנֶמָה
שׁוֹרֶטֶת בְּכַפּוֹת הָרַגְלַיִם
שָׂמָה בֵּין הַיְרֵכַיִם מַטְלִית חָמָה
וְשׁוּב שׁוֹקֵעַ בָּאֲדָמָה

Year after year
Dry inside my face
And silence....
....
....
....

....
....
....
... And there are these that look like Father and Mother.
He is all gray
And Mother is pure silver. Mother.

Mother wipes a tear.
What befell us? And why!?—
Mother is quiet, stooped
Father bends over me slightly;
Oh, Papa
Carry me like before in your arms
Papa, give me a piggy-back ride on your shoulders
Papa
Oh, Papa, I am two legs lighter!   ❧

YOU DON'T KILL BABIES TWICE
Dahlia Ravikovitch

There among puddles of sewage in Sabra and Shatilah
You removed a substantial number
Of people
From the land of the living to the hereafter.

Night after night.
First they shot
Then they hanged
And finally slaughtered with knives.

שָׁנִים עַל שָׁנִים
יָבֵשׁ בִּפְנִים הַפָּנִים
וּדְמָמָה ....
....
....
....

....
....
....

... וְהִנֵּה כְּאִלּוּ אַבָּא אִמָּא.
כֻּלּוֹ אָפֹר
וְאִמָּא כֶּסֶף טָהוֹר, אִמָּא.

אִמָּא מוֹחָה דִּמְעָה.
מַה זֶּה הָיָה לָנוּ? וְלָמָּה?! —
אִמָּא שׁוֹתֶקֶת שְׁחוּחַת קוֹמָה
אַבָּא נִרְכָּן אֵלַי קִמְעָא;
הוֹי אַבָּא
שֶׁאֲנִי כְּמוֹ אָז בַּיָּדַיִם
אַבָּא, קָחֵנִי "שֲק-קֶמַח" עַל הַכְּתֵפַיִם
אַבָּא
הוֹי אַבָּא, אֲנִי קַל בִּשְׁתֵּי רַגְלַיִם!

תִּינוֹק לֹא הוֹרְגִים פַּעֲמַיִם
דַּלְיָה רַבִּיקוֹבִיץ

עַל שְׁלוּלִיּוֹת שׁוֹפְכִין בְּסַבְּרָה וְשַׁתִּילָה
שָׁם הֶעֱבַרְתֶּם כַּמִּיּוֹת שֶׁל בְּנֵי אָדָם
הָרְאוּיוֹת לְהִתְכַּבֵּד
מֵעוֹלָם הַחַי לְעוֹלָם הָאֱמֶת.

לַיְלָה אַחֲרֵי לַיְלָה.
קֹדֶם יָרוּ
אַחַר כָּךְ תָּלוּ
לְבָסוֹף שָׁחֲטוּ בְּסַכִּינִים.

Distraught women frantically appeared
From over heaps of dirt:
"They are slaughtering us there,
In Shatilah!"

A thin slice of the new moon was hanging
Over the camps.
Our soldiers lit up the area with flares
Like daylight
"Return to camp— march!" the soldier snapped
To the screaming women from Sabra and Shatilah.
He had his orders to obey.

And the children lay in the scummy puddles,
Their mouths open
Tranquil.
No one will hurt them
You don't kill babies twice.

And the slice of the moon slowly filled up
Till it turned into a full round loaf of gold.

Such sweet soldiers of ours
They did not seek anything for themselves
So strong was their desire
To return home safely.   ဆ

At A Time Like This
Alex L.

At a time like this
The scent of the sea in the arbors of Amalfi
Its yards enchanted with odors of indulgence
Is this poetry
The sea has no aroma Amalfi is not the city
And the poet hidden in his room fabricating
What
The pungency of blood in the alleys of Sidon

נָשִׁים מְבֹהָלוֹת הוֹפִיעוּ בִּדְחִיפוּת
מֵעַל תְּלוּלִית עָפָר:
"שָׁם שׁוֹחֲטִים אוֹתָנוּ
בִּשְׁתִּילָה."

זָנָב דַּק שֶׁל יָרֵחַ בֶּן רֵאשִׁית הַחֹדֶשׁ הָיָה תָּלוּי
מֵעַל לַמַּחֲנוֹת.
חַיָּלֵינוּ שֶׁלָּנוּ הֵאִירוּ אֶת הַמָּקוֹם בְּנוּרִים
כְּאוֹר יוֹם.
"לַחֲזֹר לַמַּחֲנֶה, מַארְשׁ!" צִוָּה הַחַיָּל
לַנָּשִׁים הַצּוֹרְחוֹת מִסַּבְּרָה וְשַׁתִּילָה.
הָיוּ לוֹ פְּקוּדוֹת לְמַלֵּא.

וְהַיְלָדִים הָיוּ מֻנָּחִים בִּשְׁלוּלִיּוֹת הַסְּחִי
פִּיהֶם פָּעוּר
שְׁלֵוִים.
אִישׁ לֹא יִגַּע בָּהֶם לְרָעָה.
תִּינוֹק לֹא הוֹרְגִים פַּעֲמַיִם.

וּזְנַב הַיָּרֵחַ הָלַךְ וְהִתְמַלֵּא
עַד שֶׁהָפַךְ כִּכַּר זָהָב מְלֵאָה.

חַיָּלִים מְתוּקִים שֶׁלָּנוּ
דָּבָר לֹא בִּקְשׁוּ לְעַצְמָם
מָה עַזָּה הָיְתָה תְּשׁוּקָתָם
לַחֲזֹר הַבַּיְתָה בְּשָׁלוֹם.

בְּעֵת כָּזוֹ

אלכס ל.

בְּעֵת כָּזוֹ
רֵיחַ הַיָּם בְּחַצְרוֹת אָמַלְפִי
הַחֲצֵרוֹת הַקְּסוּמוֹת רֵיחוֹת תַּפּוּנִקִים
הַאִם זוֹ שִׁירָה
לַיָּם אֵין רֵיחַ אָמַלְפִי אֵינָהּ הָעִיר
וְהַמְשׁוֹרֵר סָפוּן בְּחַדְרוֹ בּוֹדֶה
מָה
אֶת רֵיחַ הַיָּם בְּסִמְטָאוֹת צִידוֹן

The alleys are narrow the fumes are glutinous
And the blood is blood and the eyes in the alley are dark
The poet sheds a helmet and weeps
What
Is poetry.   ℘

(Rosh Hanikrah, 5 July 1982)

ON THE DESIRE TO BE PRECISE
Natan Zach

And then there was a major exaggeration in the body count:
There were some who counted about a hundred, and some counted several
    hundreds
And this one said, I counted thirty-six burnt women
And his friend said, You are wrong, because it was only eleven
And the error is deliberate and political, not accidental
And since I am started, I will also say
That only eight women were slaughtered, because two were shot
And there is one that is questionable, and it is not clear
If she was slaughtered, raped, or merely slashed in the belly
And also in the matter of the children the last word has not yet been said
Everybody admits that six were crucified and one was tortured
Before his head was crushed but who will assure us
That all those who had disappeared with nobody knowing their whereabouts
Were indeed thrown— all of them or some of them— into the sea
Because if that is so, how can we account for the blood-stains?
With things like these one should not lend oneself to exaggerations
And one should recognize and beware: this is a matter of life and death
And one might— God forbid— err in the reports
For such has, my learned friend, happened before.
And all of that day great disputation was in that place
And if it had not been for the terrible stench that rose there
They would have come to complete precision— or to blows
Since the desire to be precise is no less human
Than the desire to kill, to rape, to crush, and to exterminate

הַסִּמְטָאוֹת צָרוֹת הָרֵיחוֹת דְּבִיקִים
וְהַדָּם הוּא דָּם וְעֵינֵי הַסִּמְטָה חֲשׁוּכוֹת
הַמְשׁוֹרֵר מַשִּׁיל הַקַּסְדָּה וּבוֹכֶה
מָה
הִיא שִׁירָה.

(רֹאשׁ הַנִּקְרָה) 5.7.1982

עַל הָרָצוֹן לְדַיֵּק
נתן זך

וְאָז הָיְתָה הַגְזָמָה גְדוֹלָה בְּמִנְיַן הַגּוּיוֹת:
הָיוּ שֶׁמָּנוּ כְּמֵאָה וְהָיוּ שֶׁמָּנוּ כְּמֵאוֹת
וְזֶה אָמַר סָפַרְתִּי 36 נָשִׁים שְׂרוּפוֹת
וַחֲבֵרוֹ אָמַר לֹא צָדַקְתָּ, כִּי רַק אַחַת-עֶשְׂרֵה
וְהַמִּשְׁגֶּה מְכֻוָּן הוּא וּפוֹלִיטִי, לֹא יַד הַמִּקְרֶה
וְאִם כְּבָר פָּתַחְתִּי, אָמַר גַּם זֶה
שָׁרַק שְׁמוֹנֶה נָשִׁים נִשְׁחֲטוּ, כִּי שְׁתַּיִם נוֹרוּ
וְיֵשׁ אַחַת מְפַקְפֶּקֶת וְלֹא בָּרוּר
אִם נִשְׁחֲטָה, נֶאֶנְסָה אוֹ רַק שֶׁסָּפָה בַּטַּבּוּר
וְגַם בְּעִנְיַן הַיְלָדִים עוֹד לֹא נֶאֶמְרָה הַמִּלָּה הָאַחֲרוֹנָה
הַכֹּל מוֹדִים כִּי שִׁשָּׁה נִצְלְבוּ וְאֶחָד עָנָה
לִפְנֵי שֶׁרֹאשׁוֹ רֻצַּץ אֲבָל מִי לְיָדֵינוּ יִתְקַע
כִּי כָּל אֵלֶּה שֶׁנֶּעֶלְמוּ וְאֵין יוֹדֵעַ אֶת עִקְּבוֹתָם
אָמְנָם הֻשְׁלְכוּ כֻּלָּם אוֹ חֶלְקָם אֶל הַיָּם
שֶׁאִם כָּךְ, כֵּיצַד נַסְבִּיר אֶת כִּתְמֵי הַדָּם?
בִּדְבָרִים מִמִּין זֶה אָסוּר לְהִתָּפֵס לְהַגְזָמוֹת
וְיֵשׁ לְהַבְחִין וּלְהִזָּהֵר: הַמְדַבֵּר בְּדִינֵי נְפָשׁוֹת
שֶׁהֲרֵי עֲלוּלִים חָלִילָה לִטְעוֹת בְּדֻוְחוֹת
וּכְבָר הָיוּ, יְדִידֵי הַמְלֻמָּד, דְּבָרִים מֵעוֹלָם.
וַתְּהִי שָׁם מַחֲלֹקֶת רַבָּה כָּל אוֹתוֹ הַיּוֹם
וְלוּלֵא הַסִּרְחוֹן הַנּוֹרָא שֶׁעָלָה בַּמָּקוֹם
הָיוּ מַגִּיעִים לְדִיּוּק גָּמוּר — אוֹ לְמַכּוֹת
שֶׁהֲרֵי הָרָצוֹן לְדַיֵּק אֱנוֹשִׁי לֹא-פָחוֹת
מִן הָרָצוֹן לַהֲרֹג, לֶאֱנֹס, לִרְצֹחַ וּלְאַבֵּד מִן הָעוֹלָם

Your enemy, your opponent, your next door neighbor, the suspicious stranger,
   or just
Every man, woman, or child in the world.   ଚ୨

(November 1982)

To Live In The Land Of Israel
Aryeh Sivan

   In memory of Zvi Horwitz
   Pioneer, commander, and bereaved father

To be cocked like a rifle, the hand
Grasping a gun, to walk
In a closed, stern rank, even after
The cheeks are ingrained with dust
And flesh is progressively wasting away, and the eyes have difficulty
Cleaving to the target.

There is a saying: A loaded gun
Will eventually be fired. Wrong.
In the Land of Israel anything can happen:
Broken firing-pin, rusty spring,

Or an unexpected cancellation command

As happened to Abraham on Mount Moriah.   ଚ୨

(Fall, 1982)

Unpleasantness During A Memorial Service
Aryeh Sivan

An acquaintance of mine, an old-timer veteran
(Of all our wars, if I am not mistaken)
Told me how he had been invited to speak
About his fallen friends before a crowd
Including the bereaved parents

אֶת אוֹיִבְךָ, יְרִיבְךָ, שְׁכֵנְךָ שֶׁמִּמּוּל, אֶת הַזָּר הֶחָשׁוּד, אוֹ כָּךְ סְתָם
כָּל גֶּבֶר, אִשָּׁה וָיֶלֶד אֲשֶׁר בָּעוֹלָם.

נובמבר 82

לִחְיוֹת בְּאֶרֶץ-יִשְׂרָאֵל
אריה סיון

לזכר צבי הורביץ
חלוץ, מפקד ואב שכול

לִהְיוֹת דָּרוּךְ כְּמוֹ רוֹבֶה, הַיָּד
אוֹחֶזֶת בָּאֶקְדָּח, לָלֶכֶת
בְּשׁוּרָה סְגוּרָה וַחֲמוּרָה, גַּם לְאַחַר
שֶׁהַלְּחָיַיִם נִמְלְאוּ אָבָק
וְהַבָּשָׂר הוֹלֵךְ וָסָר, וְהָעֵינַיִם מִתְקַשּׁוֹת
לִדְבֹּק בַּמַּטָּרָה.

יֶשְׁנָהּ אִמְרָה: אֶקְדָּח טָעוּן
סוֹפוֹ לִירוֹת. טָעוּת.
בְּאֶרֶץ-יִשְׂרָאֵל הַכֹּל יָכוֹל לִקְרוֹת:
נוֹקֵר שָׁבוּר, קְפִיץ חָלוּד

אוֹ הוֹרָאַת בִּטּוּל בִּלְתִּי-צְפוּיָה

כְּפִי שֶׁאֵרַע לְאַבְרָהָם בְּהַר הַמּוֹרִיָּה.

(סתיו 1982)

אִי-נְעִימוֹת בְּאַזְכָּרָה
אריה סיון

מוֹדָע שֶׁלִּי, לוֹחֵם וָתִיק מְאֹד
(אִם אֵינִי טוֹעֶה — בְּכָל הַמִּלְחָמוֹת)
סִפֵּר לִי כִּי הַזְּמַן לָשֵׂאת דְּבָרִים
עַל חֲבֵרָיו מִן הַנּוֹפְלִים בִּפְנֵי קָהָל
וּבִכְלָלוֹ גַּם הַהוֹרִים הַשַּׁכּוּלִים

(Those who were still alive)
And had no words in his mouth.

"I experienced a great unpleasantness there:
There I was, standing on the podium, in front of everybody,
Like some Hamlet, that for some reason wasn't stabbed,
And none of them stood up to say,
Your time, dear fighter, is past.

"I felt my blood
Flowing in sluggish motion away from all the places
Where it was supposed to flow during the battles
And collect in the area of my face, while the parents
Sat quietly waiting
For my words and for me— and so were those friends."   &

To Wither Like Weeds In An Easterly Wind
Aryeh Sivan

> *(About the men of Gahal who fell in battle in
> the fields of Latroun during Operation Ben Nun)*

They gave them a rifle of the Mauzer model
With fifty bullets per man, a bayonet
And a small ration of water; and they were a moon-struck
Troop, until the sun of Ayalon
Stood motionless over their heads.
But they could not suck
A little water out of the ground,
Because "government issue" roots had not been supplied them.

Is it not strange… that those same young men, who had done so
Well in recognizing in every command
Whether someone was trying to get them to the asphyxiating chambers or to the
    furnace,
Or, to the stone quarry where laboring would keep one free
And living; who had done so well in garnering
Crusts of bread and peels of potatoes and leaves of turnips—

(אֵלֶּה שֶׁעֲדַיִן לֹא הָלְכוּ לְעוֹלָמָם)
וְלֹא הָיוּ בְּפִיו מִלִּים.

"הָיְתָה לִי שָׁם אִי-נְעִימוּת גְּדוֹלָה:
אֲנִי עוֹמֵד עַל הַבִּימָה, לִפְנֵי כֻלָּם,
כְּמוֹ אֵיזֶה הַמֶּלֶךְ, שֶׁמִּשׁוּם-מָה לֹא נִדְקַר,
וְאַף אֶחָד מֵהֶם לֹא קָם וְלֹא אָמַר,
עָבַר זְמַנְּךָ, לוֹחֵם יָקָר.

הִרְגַּשְׁתִּי שֶׁהַדָּם שֶׁלִּי
עוֹזֵב בַּהֲלִיכָה אִטִּית אֶת כָּל הַמְּקוֹמוֹת
שֶׁמֵּהֶם הָיָה אָמוּר לָזוּב בַּמִּלְחָמוֹת
וּמִתְכַּנֵּס בִּשְׁטַח הַפָּנִים, וְהַהוֹרִים
יוֹשְׁבִים בְּשֶׁקֶט בַּמְּקוֹמוֹת וּמַמְתִּינִים
לַדְּבָרִים שֶׁלִּי וְלִי, וְגַם הַחֲבֵרִים."

לְהִתְיַבֵּשׁ כְּמוֹ עֲשָׂבִים שׁוֹטִים בְּרוּחַ מִזְרָחִית
אריה סיוון

(על אנשי גח"ל שנפלו בשדות לטרון במהלך מבצע בן-נון)

נָתְנוּ לָהֶם רוֹבֶה דְּגַם מָאוּזֶר
וַחֲמִשִּׁים כַּדּוּר לְאִישׁ, כִּידוֹן
וּמַיִם בִּמְשׂוּרָה, וְהֵם הָיוּ שׁוּרָה
סַהֲרוּרִית, עַד שֶׁשֶּׁמֶשׁ אַיָּלוֹן
עָבְרָה עַל רָאשֵׁיהֶם לְדָם.
וְלֹא עָלָה בְּחַיֵּיהֶם לָמֹץ
קְצָת מַיִם מִן הָאֲדָמָה
מִפְּנֵי שֶׁלֹּא נֵפְקוּ לָהֶם הַשָּׁרָשִׁים הַמַּתְאִימִים.

הֲלֹא מוּזָר הוּא, כִּי דַּוְקָא הַבַּחוּרִים הָאֵלֶּה, שֶׁכָּל-כָּךְ
הֵיטִיבוּ לְהַבְחִין בְּכָל פְּקֻדָּה
אִם מְבַקְשִׁים לְהוֹלִיכָם אֶל הַתָּאִים הַמַּחֲנִיקִים, אֶל הַתַּנּוּר,
אוֹ לַמַּחְצָבָה, שֶׁבָּהּ הָעֲבוֹדָה עוֹשָׂה אוֹתְךָ חָפְשִׁי
וָחַי; שֶׁכֹּה הֵיטִיבוּ לֶאֱגֹר
קְרוּמִים שֶׁל לֶחֶם וּקְלִפּוֹת שֶׁל תַּפּוּדִים, עָלִים שֶׁל לֶפֶת

In hiding like little mice or like hamsters—
And in not dying. Of water
There had been no shortage:
Neither in Auschwitz or Sobibor had a single Jew died of thirst.

One time, one time only did they walk in the fields
And one time it is but proper to remember them
Yet the thing is not easy. First of all,
Many of them were not supplied with the new papers
And had also lost all of their old acquaintances.
So what can you engrave on the tombstone of such a Gahalez
For whom there is no name... and no family— the number
Which the S.S. had imprinted on his forearm? And secondly,
In whose memory would he live? He has no parents
Who would make pilgrimage to his grave, throughout the seasons,
To keep it green
And he has no friends who would tell about him, nor a widow
Who would give his name to her son.

There is no good without bad, as they say:
If one is to die for our country, this is the proper way:
To die without being a nuisance, without becoming burdensome
To others, without killing
Slowly, oh so slowly, those who might remember.   ❧

Concerning the Rehabilitation of the Disabled From The Wars Of Israel
Aryeh Sivan

No one disputes that it is our duty to provide for the rehabilitation of
The disabled from our wars: our duty
To ourselves and, no doubt, to them;
And I, who did not leave behind me on the battlefields
A single hair of my body, I wish
To contribute toward the rehabilitation of our disabled
One idea, please.

לְהַסְתִּיר כְּמוֹ עַכְבָּרִים קְטַנִּים אוֹ כְּמוֹ אוֹגְרִים
וְלֹא לָמוּת. בַּמַּיִם
לֹא הָיָה מַחְסוֹר:
בַּצָּמָא לֹא מֵת אַף יְהוּדִי בְּאוֹשְׁוִיץ אוֹ בְּסוֹבִּיבּוֹר.

פַּעַם אַחַת וִיחִידָה הֵם הָלְכוּ בַּשָּׂדוֹת
וּפַעַם אַחַת מִן הָרָאוּי לְהִזָּכֵר בָּהֶם
וְהַדָּבָר אֵינֶנּוּ קַל.   רֵאשִׁית,
רַבִּים מֵהֶם לֹא נִרְשְׁמוּ בַּנְּיָרוֹת הַחֲדָשִׁים
וְגַם אָבְדוּ אֶת כָּל מַכָּרֵיהֶם הַיְשָׁנִים.
מָה אֶפְשָׁר לַחְרֹת עַל מַצַּבְתּוֹ שֶׁל גַּחֲלַץ כָּזֶה
שֶׁאֵין לוֹ שֵׁם וְאֵין לוֹ מִשְׁפָּחָה? אֶת הַמִּסְפָּר
שֶׁהָאָס אָס טָבְעוּ לוֹ בִּזְרוֹעוֹ? וְהַשֵּׁנִית,
בְּזִכְרוֹנוֹ שֶׁל מִי יִחְיֶה? אֵין לוֹ הוֹרִים
שֶׁיַּעֲלוּ לָרֶגֶל אֶל קִבְרוֹ, לְאֶרֶץ הָעֲוֹנוֹת,
יַשְׁקוּ אֶת שָׁרָשָׁיו
וְאֵין לוֹ חֲבֵרִים שֶׁיְּסַפְּרוּ עָלָיו, לֹא אַלְמָנָה
שֶׁתַּעֲנִיק אֶת שְׁמוֹ לְבֵנָהּ.

אֵין רַע בְּלִי טוֹב, כְּמוֹ שֶׁאוֹמְרִים:
אִם לָמוּת בְּעַד אַרְצֵנוּ, זוֹ הַדֶּרֶךְ הָרְאוּיָה:
לָמוּת בְּלֹא לִהְיוֹת מִטְרָד, בְּלֹא לְהַכְבִּיד
עַל אֲחֵרִים, בְּלֹא לְהָמִית,
לְאַט-לְאַט, אֶת הַזּוֹכְרִים.

הַצָּעָה לְשַׁקֵּם נְכֵי מִלְחֲמוֹת יִשְׂרָאֵל
אריה סיון

לֵית מָאן דְּפָלִיג, שֶׁעָלֵינוּ לְשַׁקֵּם
אֶת נְכֵי הַמִּלְחָמוֹת שֶׁלָּנוּ:   חוֹבָתֵנוּ
לָנוּ וְלָהֶם, לָהֶם וְלָנוּ, בְּלִי סָפֵק;
וַאֲנִי, שֶׁלֹּא הִשְׁאַרְתִּי אַחֲרַי בִּשְׂדוֹת-הַקְּרָב
גַּם שַׂעֲרָה מִשְּׂעַר גּוּפִי, אֲנִי רוֹצֶה
לִתְרֹם לְשִׁקּוּמָם שֶׁל הַנְּכִים שֶׁלָּנוּ
רַעְיוֹן אֶחָד, בְּבַקָּשָׁה.

The idea is taken from an acquaintance of mine
Who was injured in the spine by hand-grenade shrapnel
And since then (many years, now) he has been paralyzed
In both legs, but with his own hands
He started-up a factory which manufactures wheelchairs
(The kind that you ride in from the kitchen
To the living room, to the bathroom, to the bed).

I am not an economist, but in my lay opinion
That initiative has proven itself
Better than anticipated. In fact, the business is flourishing.
(Although its owner does not have full satisfaction as a result of his success
Because among other things
He doesn't and will never have children
To leave his business to.)

In accordance with this precedent I suggest
That the ones with gouged-out eyes manufacture glass eyes, the leg-amputees
Make prostheses, and so on and so forth.
For this purpose, I think, it will be worthwhile
To build them a city
Of their own, where these factories
Will be concentrated in one place, and if the area
Of the land available proves too small, it would be feasible
To build high, nineteen, twenty stories,
Why not? Nice, clean elevators,
Steel and glass fibers,
Would glide in complete silence
From the underground parking garages
All the way to the roof.

And we shall stroll there in the streets beneath them and, in autumn, let's say,
The season with which nothing compares in softness and pleasantness along the
     coastal plains
We will go down to the beach, to draw
Into the orbits of our eyes the last
Thighs before the winter, and at night
We will undulate into our wives, to make sons
In our likenesses.   ∽

הָרַעְיוֹן לָקוּחַ מִמַּכָּר שֶׁלִּי
שֶׁנִּפְגַּע בְּשִׁדְרָתוֹ מֵרְסִיסֵי רִמּוֹן
וּמֵאָז (שָׁנִים רַבּוֹת) הוּא מְשֻׁתָּק
בִּשְׁתֵּי רַגְלָיו, וּבְיָדָיו
הֵקִים מִפְעַל הַמְיַצֵּר עֲגָלוֹת-נָכִים
(מֵאֵלֶּה שֶׁנּוֹסְעִים בָּהֶן מִן הַמִּטְבָּח
אֶל הַסָּלוֹן, לַשֵּׁרוּתִים, אֶל הַמִּטָּה).

אֵינֶנִּי כַּלְכָּלָן, וְלִדְעַת-הַהֶדְיוֹט שֶׁלִּי
הוֹכִיחָה אֶת עַצְמָהּ אוֹתָהּ יָזְמָה
מֵעַל לַצִּפִּיּוֹת. עֲבָדָה, הָעֵסֶק מְשַׂגְשֵׂג.
(אִם כִּי לִבְעָלָיו אֵין נַחַת-רוּחַ מְלֵאָה בְּגִין הַצְלָחָתוֹ
וּבֵין הַיֶּתֶר מִשּׁוּם כָּךְ
שֶׁאֵין וְלֹא יִהְיוּ לוֹ יְלָדִים
לְהוֹרִישׁ לָהֶם אֶת מִפְעָלוֹ).

לְפִי הַדֶּגֶם הַזֶּה אֲנִי מַצִּיעַ
כִּי נְקוּרֵי-הָעַיִן יִיַצְרוּ עֵינֵי-זְכוּכִית, קְטוּעֵי-רַגְלַיִם
יַעֲשׂוּ פְּרוֹטֵזוֹת, וְכֵן הָלְאָה, וְגוֹמֵר.
לְצֹרֶךְ זֶה, אֲנִי סָבוּר, כְּדַאי יִהְיֶה
לְהַעֲמִיד לָהֶם קִרְיָה
מִשֶּׁלָּהֶם, בָּהּ יְרֻכְּזוּ
הַמִּפְעָלִים הָאֵלֶּה בְּמָקוֹם אֶחָד, וְאִם יֵצַר
הַשֶּׁטַח עַל הָאֲדָמָה, אֶפְשָׁר יִהְיֶה
לִבְנוֹת לַגֹּבַהּ, תֵּשַׁע-עֶשְׂרֵה, עֶשְׂרִים קוֹמוֹת,
מַדּוּעַ לֹא? מַעֲלִיּוֹת נָאוֹת וּנְקִיּוֹת,
מַתֶּכֶת וְסִיבֵי-זְכוּכִית,
תְּחַלֵּקְנָה בִּדְמָמָה שְׁלֵמָה
מִמַּרְתְּפֵי-הַחֲנָיָה
עַד לְקוֹמַת-הַגַּג.

וַאֲנַחְנוּ נְטַיֵּל לְמַטָּה, בָּרְחוֹבוֹת, וּבְעוֹנַת הַסְּתָו, נֹאמַר,
זוֹ הָעוֹנָה שֶׁאֵין כָּמוֹהָ לְרַכּוּת וּלְנֹעַם בִּשְׁפֵלַת הַחוֹף,
נֵרֵד אֶל שְׂפַת-הַיָּם, לִשְׁאֹף
אֶל אֲרֻבּוֹת-עֵינֵינוּ יְרָכִים
אַחֲרוֹנוֹת לִפְנֵי הַחֹרֶף, וּבַלַּיְלָה
נֵלָפֵת בִּנְשׁוֹתֵינוּ, לַעֲשׂוֹת בָּנִים
בִּדְמֵיוֹתֵינוּ.

Teacher Of Defeated Hebrew Language
Eitan Kalinski

For thirty years
I have been a teacher of Hebrew
I have adorned the speech of my students and children
With golden apples
Coming out of their mouths, pendant
As in silver ornaments
When their words are fitly spoken…

For thirty years
I have been a teacher of Hebrew
I have embellished the language of my students and children
With musings from the tongue of Rabbi
Shneour Zalman of Lyadi
This language— the quill-pen of the heart
Poetry— the quill-pen of the soul.

Thirty days
In the alleys of Shechem and Jenin,
And all the adornments of my tongue
Were driven retrograde
Halted afar
Floundering-foundered at every street corner were the quills of the heart
And the quills of the soul could not ensue.
In Shechem and Jenin
I am a defeated teacher
Of a defeated Hebrew language.

Today
I am a teacher of defeated Hebrew language
An instrument whose strings ruptured in the casbah of Shechem
With its cracked shrill melody
Disgorging from its perforated cavities
"Stinkin' Arab,
Turn to the wall!
Shut up,
You hunka shit!
You freak!" ഔ

מוֹרֶה לְלָשׁוֹן עִבְרִית מוּבֶּסֶת
איתן קלינסקי

שְׁלֹשִׁים שָׁנָה
אֲנִי מוֹרֶה לְלָשׁוֹן עִבְרִית
קִשַּׁטְתִּי לְשׁוֹנָם שֶׁל תַּלְמִידַי וִילָדַי
בְּתַפּוּחֵי זָהָב
הָעוֹלִים מִפִּיּוֹתֵיהֶם תְּלוּיִים
כְּבְמַשְׂכִּיּוֹת כֶּסֶף
עֵת דְּבָרִים דָּבוּר עַל אָפְנָיו ...

שְׁלֹשִׁים שָׁנָה
אֲנִי מוֹרֶה לְלָשׁוֹן עִבְרִית
קִשַּׁטְתִּי לְשׁוֹנָם שֶׁל תַּלְמִידַי וִילָדַי
בַּהֲגִיגֵי לְשׁוֹנוֹ שֶׁל רַבִּי
שְׁנֵיאוֹר זַלְמָן מִלַּאדִי
הַלָּשׁוֹן — קֻלְמוֹס הַלֵּב
הַשִּׁירָה — קֻלְמוֹס הַנֶּפֶשׁ.

שְׁלֹשִׁים יוֹם
בְּסִמְטָאוֹת שְׁכֶם וְגִ'ינִין
הוּסְגוּ אָחוֹר
כָּל קִשּׁוּטֵי לְשׁוֹנִי
מֵרָחוֹק נֶעֱמְדוּ,
כָּשְׁלוּ בְּכָל קֶרֶן רְחוֹב קֻלְמוֹסֵי הַלֵּב
וְקֻלְמוֹסֵי הַנֶּפֶשׁ לֹא יָכְלוּ לָבוֹא.
בִּשְׁכֶם וּבְגִ'ינִין
אֲנִי מוֹרֶה מוּבָּס
לְלָשׁוֹן עִבְרִית מוּבֶּסֶת.

הַיּוֹם
אֲנִי מוֹרֶה לְלָשׁוֹן עִבְרִית מוּבֶּסֶת
שֶׁמֵּיתְרֶיהָ נִקְרְעוּ בַּקַּסְבָּה שֶׁל שְׁכֶם
וּנְגִינָתָהּ הַסְּדוּקָה וְהַמִּצְמַרְרֶת
מְמַלֶּטֶת מִנִּקְבֶּיהָ הַמְחֻרָרִים
עַרְבֵי מַסְרִיחַ
סִ'תּוֹבֵּב לַקִּיר
אוּסְקוּט
יָא חָרָא
יָא מָאנְיָאק.

1936–1986
Eitan Kalinski

At the end of 1936 I reported to duty, a day-old baby in diapers
In hot fire, groping in the darkness of embers
In 1949 I wore the festive attire of my Bar Mizvah
The frontlets of 1948 binding the brands of my people onto my flesh,
In the month of Heshvan 1956 I again wore festive uniform— that which my father
Had taken off in 1948— to bury my youthful comrades in Kadesh. To them
I returned in the month of Iyar 1967, and to the altar of sand
To give it a libation— the survivors of 1957.
In the month of Tishrey 1973 I was called to sprinkle bloody bridegrooms,
To whom 1967 had allowed six more years of life.
From 1982 to 1984 I was called to go up
Crowned with gray hair, from the desert, to bury within the gates
Of Tyre and Beirut the rearguard of my youth
And from my bosom a new sacrifice— an offering out of my own loins.
By the time of my golden jubilee in 1986
From the blended potion of despair I will take to the road
To revive the blood vessels of my altar
So that never again shall anyone blend on it coursing humors
Crowned with golden curls.   ℘

A Siren Of Love
Asher Reich

From behind the gas mask
The world looks suddenly
Narrow and tight like a sealed room.

A sleepy woman emerges from it
Like a wildflower. I cling to her
As to a safety kit. Morning advances
Like writing on the wall.

Is our fate an ancient heritage?
Behind the house

תרצ"ו - תשמ"ו
איתן קלינסקי

בְּשַׁלְהֵי תרצ"ו הִתְיַצַּבְתִּי בְּחַתּוּלֵי בֶּן יוֹמוֹ
בְּמִכְווֹת הָאֵשׁ מְגַשֵּׁשׁ בַּאֲפֵלַת גַּחֶלֶת
בְּתש"ט לָבַשְׁתִּי מַחְלְצוֹת בְּרִית מִצְווֹת
טוֹטָפוֹת תש"ח בִּבְשָׂרִי כּוֹרְכוֹת אוֹדֵי עַמִּי,
בְּיֶרַח חֶשְׁוָן תשי"ז כְּבָר עָטַרְתִּי מַחְלְצוֹת מַדִּים, שֶׁפָּשַׁט
אָבִי בְּתש"ח — לְהַטְמִין עֲלוּמֵי רֵעַי בְּקֹדֶשׁ אֲלֵיהֶם
שַׁבְתִּי בְּיֶרַח אִיָּר תשכ"ז לְהַגְמִיא
בְּמִזְבַּח הַחֲלוֹלוֹת נְצוּלֵי תשי"ז.
בְּיֶרַח תִּשְׁרֵי תשל"ד נִקְרֵאתִי לְהָזוֹת חַתְנֵי דָמִים,
שֶׁתּשכ"ז נָתְנָה לָהֶם עוֹד שֵׁשׁ שְׁנוֹת חַיִּים.
בְּתשמ"ב עַד תשמ"ד נִקְרֵאתִי לַעֲלוֹת
עֲטוּר שֵׂיבָה מֵהַמִּדְבָּר לְהַטְמִין בְּשַׁעֲרֵי
צֹר וּבֵירוּת מַאֲסְפֵּי עֲלוּמַי
וּבְחֵיקִי קָרְבָּן חָדָשׁ — מַתַּת חַלָצִי.
לְעֵת יוֹבְלִי בְּתשמ"ו
מִמֶּסֶךְ יֵאוֹשׁ אָבוֹא בַּדְּרָכִים
לְדוֹבֵב עוֹרְקֵי מִזְבָּחִי
בַּל יִמְסְכוּ בּוֹ עוֹד קְלוּחִים
עֲטוּרֵי תַּלְתַּלִּים זְהֻבִּים.

צְפִירַת אַהֲבָה
אשר רייד

מִבַּעַד לַמַּסֵּכָה
הָעוֹלָם נִרְאָה פִּתְאֹם
צַר וְנָעוּל כְּחֶדֶר אָטוּם.

אִשָּׁה יְשֵׁנָה בּוֹקַעַת מִתּוֹכוֹ
כְּפֶרַח בָּר. אֲנִי נִצְמָד אֵלֶיהָ
כְּאֶל עֶרְכַּת מָגֵן. הַבֹּקֶר עוֹלֶה
כִּכְתֹבֶת עַל הַקִּיר.

הַאִם גּוֹרָלֵנוּ הוּא תּוֹרָשָׁה עַתִּיקָה?
מֵאֲחוֹרֵי הַבַּיִת

The sea turns to us its dark, winter-like back.
The streets are empty, the houses dark and locked. The city
Is splendidly turned off. We

Move heavily like crude oil through water,
Weaving slowly like a pair of cormorants.
From behind the masks we seem
Even to our children so strange and scary.
How life goes by here
Like hearsay

From behind the masks we and this enchanted time
Like a pair of lovers, are breathing the world
Through the radio, and our darkened breaths
Are the breaths of emotion. We hold hands
In our sleep and await a heavy hot weather which does not
Come. Only the siren of love is a repose
And it is she that saves us from the clutch of these days.   ∽

War Night 6
Ilan Sheinfeld

Stifling atmosphere impelled me away from home to the sea.
The raging sea was overstated, like an exaggeration. Like
A cover-up of a lie, or a parable, nothing more.
Jaffa had built up high
All the missile-minarets of Allah, threatening
To rise from their stone. Was lying sealed, like a pad
For launching the barbarians of Islam.

A golden light of divine revelation swept enticingly through
Sealed panes of the heavens. Within the aquarium of the world
I opened my mouth and tightly closed it. A small land-fish.
A sardine with a gas mask, resting on the rocks.

Birds flew off of the water into
God's red pits of mercy.
With the growing darkness rose the level of fear. I went back home,

הַיָּם הִפְנָה אֵלֵינוּ אֶת גַּבּוֹ הַשָּׁחוֹר, הֶחָרְפִּי.
הָרְחוֹבוֹת רֵיקִים, הַבָּתִּים חֲשׁוּכִים וּנְעוּלִים. הָעִיר
כְּבוּיָה לְתַלְפִּיּוֹת. אֲנַחְנוּ

נָעִים בִּכְבֵדוּת כְּמוֹ נֶפְט דֶּרֶךְ מַיִם,
מְדַדִּים לְאִטֵּנוּ כְּזוּג קוֹרְמוֹרָנִים.
מִבַּעַד לַמַּסֵּכָה אֲנַחְנוּ נִרְאִים
אֲפִלּוּ לִילָדֵינוּ כֹּה זָרִים וּמַפְחִידִים.
אֵיךְ עוֹבְרִים כָּאן הַחַיִּים
כִּשְׁמוּעָה

מִבַּעַד לַמַּסֵּכָה אֲנַחְנוּ וְהַזְּמָן הַמְכֻשָּׁף
כְּזוּג אוֹהֲבִים, נוֹשְׁמִים אֶת הָעוֹלָם
דֶּרֶךְ מַקְלֵט הָרָדְיוֹ וּנְשִׁימוֹתֵינוּ הַחֲשׁוּכוֹת
הֵן נְשִׁימוֹת רֶגֶשׁ. אֲנַחְנוּ מַחְזִיקִים יָדַיִם
בִּשְׁנָתֵנוּ וּמְצַפִּים לְשָׁרָב כָּבֵד שֶׁאֵינוֹ
מַגִּיעַ. רַק צְפִירַת הָאַהֲבָה הִיא מַרְגּוֹעַ
וְהִיא שֶׁמַּצִּילָה אוֹתָנוּ מִיָּדָם שֶׁל הַיָּמִים הָאֵלֶּה.

לֵיל מִלְחָמָה 6
אילן שיינפלד

מַחֲנַק חִלֵּץ אוֹתִי מִבַּיִת אֶל יָם.
הַיָּם גָּעַשׁ מֵפָרָז כְּגִזְמָה. כְּעֵין
מַעֲטֶה שֶׁל כָּזָב אוֹ מָשָׁל, וְדָבָר מִלְבַדָּם.
יָפוֹ זְקָרָה מַעְלָה מַעְלָה
אֶת כָּל הַטִּילִים שֶׁל אַלְלָה, מַאֲמִים
לִנְסֹק מִן הָאֶבֶן. נָחָה אֲטוּמָה, כְּכֵן
לְשִׁגּוּר הַבַּרְבָּרִים שֶׁל הָאִסְלָם.

אוֹר זָהוֹב שֶׁל הִתְגַּלּוּת אֵלֶהּ שָׁטַף וּפִתָּה בְּעַד
זְגוּגִיּוֹת שָׁמַיִם אֲטוּמוֹת. בְּתוֹךְ אַקְוַרְיוּם הַתֵּבֵל
פָּעַרְתִּי פִּי וְחָשַׁקְתָּיו. דָּג יַבָּשָׁה קָטָן.
סַרְדִּין עִם מַסֵּכַת גַּזִּים נָח עַל סְלָעִים.

הַצִּפֳּרִים דָּאוּ מִתּוֹךְ הַמַּיִם אֶל
בּוֹרוֹת הַחֶמְלָה הָאֲדֻמִּים שֶׁל אֱלֹהִים.
כְּכָל שֶׁהֶחְשִׁיךְ גָּאָה מִפְלַס הַפַּחַד. חָזַרְתִּי הַבַּיְתָה,

Hurrying to write another poem before the shelling started,
Putting close to hand the black rubber
Skull, to relieve myself somewhat
Of fear of Zyklon.

All and all it was a wonderful day.
I dared to listen to a violin concerto by Mozart
Instead of waiting for the siren. I ate, I wrote.
Now I will close myself for the night in my sealed room,
With the haunting voices which came to visit me
From the time we were burnt in Auschwitz.   ❧

(8th day of Shevat, 5751)

At Nightfall, 1/27/91
Pinhas Sadeh

Night lowers upon the city, upon the deserted streets.

Winter skies darken.

The trees beyond my window are engulfed in blackness. The birds, in their nests,
    sink into somnolence.

In the darkness, somewhere among the bushes, a deadly viper lies in wait.

Once, some place, I read that Napoleon, when he stood near the Pyramids had
    said to his soldiers:

Four thousand years of history are now gazing at you.

At us, now, something other peers. Deeper, more lofty, than Pyramids.

At us, the eyes of our fathers and mothers are gazing.

Innumerable eyes, for two thousand years now, from the ghettos of Worms and
    Mainz,

Toledo, Nemirov, Kishinev, Treblinka, Auschwitz.

And their eyes— what do they say? Their eyes are saying: Children of ours,
    grandchildren, happy are you.

For you do not dig grave-holes for yourselves in the snow, nor burn in furnaces of
    fire, like us.

For you are not torn apart by the teeth of dogs, nor impaled within your
    mother's belly.

For you have power, and you dwell upon your own land.

You are our consolation… insofar as any kind of consolation is possible.   ❧

מְמַהֵר לִכְתּוֹב עוֹד שִׁיר לִפְנֵי הַהַפְגָּזָה,
מֵנִיחַ בְּטַוַּח-יָד אֶת גֻּלְגֹּלֶת הַגָּמִי
הַשְּׁחוֹרָה, לְהִתְנַחֵם מְעַט
מִפַּחַד הַצִּקְלוֹן.

בְּסוֹפוֹ שֶׁל דָּבָר הָיָה יוֹם נִפְלָא.
הֶעֱזְתִּי לְהַאֲזִין לְקוֹנְצֶרְט לְכִנּוֹר שֶׁל מוֹצַרְט
בִּמְקוֹם לְהַמְתִּין לְאַזְעָקָה. אָכַלְתִּי, כָּתַבְתִּי.
עַכְשָׁו אֶסְתַּגֵּר בְּחַדְרֵי הָאָטוּם,
עִם קוֹלוֹת הָרְפָאִים שֶׁבָּאוּ לְבַקְּרֵנִי
מִן הַזְּמָן שֶׁשְּׂרַפְנוּ בְּאוֹשְׁוִיץ.

ח׳ בשבט התשנ״א

עִם רֶדֶת הַלַּיְלָה, 27.1.91
פנחס שדה

לַיְלָה הוֹלֵךְ וְיוֹרֵד עַל הָעִיר, עַל הָרְחוֹבוֹת הַנְּטוּשִׁים.
שְׁמֵי הַחֹרֶף הוֹלְכִים וַחֲשֵׁכִים.
הָעֵצִים מוּל חַלּוֹנִי נֶעֱטָפִים בָּאֲפֵלָה. הַצִּפֳּרִים, בְּקִנֵּיהֶן, נִרְדָּמוֹת.
בַּחֹשֶׁךְ, אֵי שָׁם בֵּין הַשִּׂיחִים, אוֹרֵב נַחַשׁ צֶפַע.

פַּעַם, בְּמָקוֹם כָּלְשֶׁהוּ, קָרָאתִי כִּי בְּעָמְדוֹ לְרַגְלֵי הַפִּירָמִידוֹת נַפּוֹלֵיאוֹן אֶל חַיָּלָיו
אָמַר:
אַרְבַּעַת אַלְפֵי שְׁנוֹת הַהִיסְטוֹרְיָה צוֹפוֹת בָּכֶם עַתָּה.
בָּנוּ, עַתָּה, צוֹפֶה דָּבָר-מָה אַחֵר. עָמֹק יוֹתֵר, נִשָּׂא יוֹתֵר, מִפִּירָמִידוֹת.
בָּנוּ צוֹפוֹת עֵינֵי אֲבוֹתֵינוּ וְאִמָּהוֹתֵינוּ.
עֵינַיִם אֵין-סְפוֹר, מִזֶּה אַלְפַּיִם שָׁנָה, מִגְּטָאוֹת וְרַמְיָזָה וּמָגֶנְצָא,
טוֹלֵדוֹ, נֵמִירוֹב, קִישִׁינֶב, טְרֶבְּלִינְקָה, אוּשְׁוִיץ.
וְעֵינֵיהֶם מָה אוֹמְרוֹת. עֵינֵיהֶם אוֹמְרוֹת: בָּנִים שֶׁלָּנוּ, נְכָדִים, אַשְׁרֵיכֶם.
שֶׁאֵינְכֶם חוֹפְרִים בּוֹרוֹת-קֶבֶר לְעַצְמְכֶם בַּשֶּׁלֶג, וְלֹא נִשְׂרָפִים בְּכִבְשָׁנִים שֶׁל אֵשׁ,
כָּמוֹנוּ.
שֶׁאֵינְכֶם נִקְרָעִים בְּשִׁנֵּי כְּלָבִים, וְלֹא דְּקוּרִים בִּמְעֵי אִמְּכֶם.
שֶׁאֵינְכֶם אֹבְדֵי עֵצָה וְחַסְרֵי אוֹנִים תַּחַת הַשָּׁמַיִם, כַּאֲשֶׁר הָיִינוּ.
שֶׁבְּיֶדְכֶם הַכֹּחַ, וְאַתֶּם יוֹשְׁבִים עַל אַדְמַתְכֶם.
אַתֶּם הַנֶּחָמָה שֶׁלָּנוּ, עַד כַּמָּה שֶׁנֶּחָמָה כָּלְשֶׁהִי אֶפְשָׁרִית.

LIKE BEIRUT
Haiim Gouri

I was like Beirut,
Made out of the different within the same
And of the complete opposite.
Heavens, request mercy
For me too.

I heard when they said unto me that this is a treasure maintained for my benefit,
That life is more interesting in these infested streets,
In the labyrinth of burrows of my subconscious.
There the rival militias, from Haiia Sulum to Ashrafiyah,
Gain, by the last drop of my blood,
The joy of the believers.

Because I was urban war,
Watching, face half-hidden, from the upper stories,
Crossed by no man's lands, attentive as a continuous alert for coming attacks.
A soot-covered vow: even some more.

I also heard that out of the opposites within souls comes the hidden power
Which usually makes beautiful things.
Behold there is another dark woman, very beautiful, her hands on her head,
Crying in me at the foot of the house,
Saying something in garbled English to the reporters.

Like Beirut I worship other gods,
Half-destroyed.
Growing deaf, growing gray.
And there is no sign in me of a cease-fire, of a short respite,
Of sharpshooters' repose.

৪ว

כְּמוֹ בֵּירוּת
חיים גורי

הָיִיתִי כְּמוֹ בֵּירוּת,
עָשׂוּי מֵהַשּׁוֹנֶה שֶׁבַּדּוֹמֶה
וּמֵהַהֶפֶךְ הַגָּמוּר.
שָׁמַיִם בַּקְשׁוּ רַחֲמִים
גַּם עָלַי.

שָׁמַעְתִּי בְּאוֹמְרִים לִי שֶׁזֶּהוּ עשֶׂר הַשָּׁמוּר לְטוֹבָתִי,
שֶׁהַחַיִּים מְעַנְיְנִים יוֹתֵר בָּרְחוֹבוֹת הַנְּגוּעִים הָאֵלֶּה,
בְּלַבִּירִינְתְּ הַמְּחִלּוֹת בְּתַת הַכָּרָתִי.
שָׁם הַמִּילִיצְיוֹת הַיְרִיבוֹת, מֵחַיָּה סוֹלוּם עַד אַשְׁרַפִיֶּה,
זוֹכוֹת בִּי עַד טִפַּת דָּמִי הָאַחֲרוֹנָה
בַּאֲשֶׁר הַמַּאֲמִינִים.

כִּי הָיִיתִי לְחִימַת הַשֶּׁטַח הַבָּנוּי,
צוֹפֶה, חֲצִי פָנִים, מֵהַקּוֹמוֹת הָעֶלְיוֹנוֹת,
חֲצִי שְׁטָחִי הֶפְקֵר, קָשׁוּב כְּכוֹנְנוּת סְפִינָה נִמְשֶׁכֶת.
נֶדֶר מְפֵיחַ: עוֹד קְצָת יוֹתֵר.

וְכֵן שָׁמַעְתִּי כִּי מִן הַהֲפָכִים שֶׁבַּנְּשָׁמוֹת עוֹלֶה הַכֹּחַ הַגָּנוּז
הָעוֹשֶׂה לָרֹב דְּבָרִים יָפִים.
הִנֵּה עוֹד אִשָּׁה שְׁחוֹרָה, יָפָה מְאֹד, יָדֶיהָ עַל רֹאשָׁהּ,
בּוֹכָה בִּי לְרַגְלֵי הַבַּיִת,
אוֹמֶרֶת בְּאַנְגְּלִית עֶלֶגֶת מַשֶּׁהוּ לַכַּתָּבִים.

אֲנִי כְּמוֹ בֵּירוּת עוֹבֵד אֱלֹהִים אֲחֵרִים,
חָרֵב לְמֶחֱצָה.
הוֹלֵךְ וְנֶחֱרָשׂ, הוֹלֵךְ וּמַאֲפִיר.
וְאֵין בִּי שׁוּם סִימָן לְהַפְסָקַת אֵשׁ, לַהֲפוּגָה קְצָרָה,
לִמְנוּחַת הַצַּלָּפִים.

ℭℜ

Notes

Initial numbers refer to pages; references to Biblical passages are given in the form of book.chapter:verse number.

2 **Haiim Gouri**: *Prayer*
Like many of Gouri's poems from 1948, this one is frequently recited in memorial services held for fallen soldiers.

4 **Haiim Gouri**: *Behold, Our Bodies Are Laid Out*
did not break faith (*or, did not betray*)— a common expression denoting the utmost loyalty and bravery (see note to Alterman's *The Time and the Response*).
Mountain Platoon— a unit of thirty-five soldiers under the command of Dani Mas. All fell in battle in 1948 during a mission of assistance to the embattled Ezion Block area southwest of Jerusalem.

8 **Hillel Omer**: *To the Memory of a Comrade*
Quite a number of poems written during that period were dedicated to the memory of Haiim ben Dor who died in the War of Independence.
pillar of love— an allusion to the pillar of cloud and the pillar of fire which led the Israelites on their way from Egypt, see Ex.13:22 and elsewhere.

10 **Hillel Omer**: *Words from the Gray Soldiers*
myrrh and aloes— Can.4:14.
when struck by a staff— allusion to Ex.17.6.
Mountain of God— Mount Sinai, as referred to in Ex.3:1 and elsewhere.
Negev— the southern, desert region of Israel.
Break for us ... gardens— allusion to Can.4:12.

14 **Hillel Omer**: *A Squad in the Land*
Palmach cap— a knitted stocking-cap which became one of the symbols of the Palmach (see note to Alterman's *Around the Campfire* below).
Not the army of Goliath ...— this and following images allude to I Sam.17.

18 **Nathan Alterman**: *Around the Campfire*
The Palmach— an elite unit within the Haganah, the pre-State military force. Symbols of youth, determination, and leadership, its members dominated early Israeli politics and defense forces, and some made a mark in its literary world where they have been referred to as the "Palmach generation." The poem celebrates the establishment of the unit in May of 1941.
Nisan 5708— May 1948. Nisan is a spring month in the Hebrew calendar.
shofar— a ram's horn, used in ancient days for sounding a battle call.

20 **Nathan Alterman**: *The Silver Platter*
Haiim Weizmann— the first president of the then-future State of Israel.
Written in prophetic, semi-Biblical style, this is one of the best-known war poems in Israel. It is often recited in memorial services, especially those held by school children.

22 **Uri Zvi Greenberg**: *Memorial*
  After pilot David Tamir fell in 1971 this poem, which originally appeared in
  1949, was republished and dedicated to him.
  IDF— Israeli Defense Forces.

24 **Uri Zvi Greenberg**: *Splendor from the Splendid*
  The image of David— used in reference to King David, a symbol of power,
  strength, and national independence.

24 **Uri Zvi Greenberg**: *Poem of Blessing*
  Negev— the southern, desert region of Israel.
  they have lifted ... mountains— paraphrase of Ps.121.1.
  ascent of Ephraim— a reference to the hilly area within the ancient land of
  Ephraim, a tribe which settled in Judea.

26 **Uri Zvi Greenberg**: *The Ones Living by Their Virtue Say*
  David the lad ...— see I Sam 16:11ff.
  the Temple-Mount and the Rock— references to the holy sites in Jerusa-
  lem, where, according to Jewish tradition, the Rock (also called "the Drink-
  ing Rock," "the Cornerstone") was located in the middle of the holiest
  chamber within the Temple.
  The Dust, here referred to as holy because of the location, is an allusion to
  Ps.30:10.

26 **Uriel Ofeq**: *Hagomel*
  Hagomel— a blessing traditionally recited after deliverance from danger.
  in the thicket ... horns— allusion to Gen.22:13.

28 **Amir Gilboa**: *And My Brother Was Silent*
  And his blood ... cries— Gen.4:10.

30 **Yehoshua Zafrir**: *Forced March in Summer*
  sukkah (booth, tabernacle)— "a sukkah of peace" is a traditional term de-
  noting divine protection.

30 **Haiim Hefer**: *The Sappers*
  This poem, set to music as a march, is very popular in Israel, especially in
  times of war or military alert.

32 **Haiim Hefer**: *We Left Slowly*
  Set to music, this love poem is frequently sung in Israel, especially on Memo-
  rial Day.

32 **Moshe Tabenkin**: *Eulogy*
  revolves ... like a sword— allusion to Gen.3:24.
  [Mount] Gilbo'a, the spring of Harod, and the Valley of Izre'el— sites in
  the lower Galilee.
  putting forth its figs— Can.2:13.
  ever-burning flame— allusion to Lev.6:6 (12 in some versions).

36 **Yehudah Amichai**: *Two Poems About the First Battles*
Onto my tired face ... the other— the scene builds upon Jacob's dream,
Gen.28:11–19.

38 **Yehudah Amichai**: *Rain on the Battlefield*
Dicki— the commander of the Palmach squad of which the poet was a member, he is mentioned in a number of poems by Amichai.

38 **Yehiel Mohar**: *An Anonymous Squad*
Set to music as a march, this poem is very popular in Israel, especially in times of war or military alert.
Strong like hewed stone— allusion to I Kgs.5:31 and elsewhere.
its banner is love— Can.2:4.
Eilat— a port on the Red Sea, the southermost city in Israel.

40 **Yehiel Mohar**: *Between Sickle and Sword*
The poem alludes to the scene of the building of Jerusalem's wall in Neh.4. The sickle and the sword are combined in the emblem of the Nahal, a functional command within the Israeli Defense Forces, whose mission combines regular military duties with settlement, especially of border outposts.

42 **Ayin Tur-Malka**: *Heralds of New Jerusalem*
Ariela— a nickname for Lea Prizant, a member of the Lechi underground group, who fought in the battle for Jerusalem and was killed in an explosion in 1948.
Heralds of New Jerusalem— Isa.41:27.
Pray for the ... Jerusalem— Ps.122:6.

44 **Ayin Tur-Malka**: *Mirror of the Battle*
Facing the sun ... Gibeon— this and the following images allude to the battle described in Josh.10:12ff.

46 **Nathan Alterman**: *The Time and the Response*
Uri Ilan, a soldier who was captured by the Syrians, took his own life lest he might disclose military secrets to his interrogators. He and his message "I did not betray" became a symbol of heroism in Israel and have been held up as an inspiration for its young people.
outspread net— Prov.1:17.
set as a seal— Can.8:8.

50 **Nathan Yonathan**: *Without the Boy*
Reuven Yaron— Yonathan's student and friend and a talented lyricist, fell in battle in 1956.
The places mentioned are all in the area of the eastern Sinai and the Gulf of Aqaba.

54 **Naomi Shemer**: *On Silver Wings*
Dedicated to the Israeli Air Force, the poem (which has also been set to music by the author) draws from Ps.68:34–35, Ps.114:5, Job 5.7, and Can.2:4.
The seven heavens— allusion to ancient cosmology referred to in *Devarim Rabah*, a homiletic commentary on the book of Deuteronomy.

56 Haiim Hefer: *Parade of the Fallen*
    Hefer is known for a Friday column of rhymed pieces written in response to
    current events. *Parade of The Fallen, The Paratroopers Are Weeping, The Other
    Days,* and *The Young Dead Soldiers* are from that column.

56 Haiim Hefer: *The Paratroopers Are Weeping*
    This poem captures a historical moment during the Six Day War in which the
    paratroopers who liberated the Wailing Wall stood before it, many of them
    weeping.
    Rabbi Judah Halevi— a medieval philosopher and poet who, according to
    Jewish tradition, made a dangerous pilgrimage to the Land of Israel and,
    while kissing the ground of Jerusalem, was trampled to death by an Arab
    horseman.
    If I forget ... Jerusalem— Ps.137:5, a traditional oath of remembrance to
    Jerusalem.
    chariot of fire— allusion to 2 Kgs.2:11–12.
    In which we haven't even had a wall ...— Jews were denied access to
    their holy places when East Jerusalem was under Jordanian rule.

62 Eli Alon: *In The Mount of Final Repose*
    The Mount of Final Repose— a Jerusalem cemetery.
    Amnon [Harodi] and Hanan [Buch]— both from kibbutz Ein Shemer, they
    fell in the battle for Jerusalem..

66 Eli Alon: *Always in Anguish*
    and not betray— see note to Alterman's *The Time and the Response.*

68 Abba Kovner: *My Comrades*
    a waste howling wilderness— Deut.32:10.
    the name and the place— Hebrew puns on common references to God.

68 Yehudah Amichai: *My Child Smells of Peace*
    And in all the land ...— reference to Revelations 18.22.
    the caves of Machpelah— a paraphrase of the name of the cave in Hebron
    in which the Biblical matriarchs and patriarchs are traditionally held to
    have been buried (Gen.23:9 and elsewhere).

70 Yehudah Amichai: *We Have No Unknown Soldiers*
    Yonathan Yahil— fell in battle in 1967.
    One-of-a-name— a term of admiration, and a pun on the name of the Has-
    sidic tzadiq, Israel Baal Shem Tov.
    Ein Gedi— a kibbutz on the shore of the Dead Sea.

72 Yehudah Amichai: *Wildling Peace*
    wolf with lamb— Isa.11:6.
    beating swords into plowshares— allusion to Isa.2:4.

72 Zelda: *A Place of Fire*
    a king, foreign ...— King Hussein of Jordan, in reference to Jews being de-
    nied access to their holy places in East Jerusalem when the city was under
    Jordanian rule.

Zelda: *A Place of Fire* continued

Sapphires, turquoise, and rubies— Isa.54:11–12.

City of David— Jerusalem, in reference to its status as King David's capital.

76 Haiim Gouri: *On a Stone Pillow*
The poem alludes to Gen.28:11–19. See Gouri's *Current Account*, p. 110.

78 Yonathan Gefen: *Setting Up Camp*
Kuneitra— a city in the Golan Heights, on the road to Damascus.

78 David Avidan: *Settlement*
Moshe Dayan— an Israeli Chief of Staff and political figure, widely recognized by the black patch over one eye.
Maskit— a well-known line of Israeli textile-for-export products, the fabrics often decorated with traditional patterns. The irony of the statement is enhanced by the fact that Ruth Dayan, Moshe Dayan's wife, was the general manager of the company producing it.

80 Dan Pagis: *Twenty Years in the Wadi*
The setting is the road from the coastal plains to Jerusalem. This road was the site of major battles, and some of the burnt armored vehicles were left by its side as memorials to the 1948 war. In the late 1960s the road was widened to allow faster access to Jerusalem, and those vehicles were moved from their original resting places, which created great furor in Israel.

82 Anadad Eldan: *When You Grow Up*
Out of these … cry— allusion to Ps.130:1.
What do you see— Jer.1:13.

82 Yehiel Hazak: *Dead in a Bereft Horah*
horah— the archtypical Israeli folk-dance.

84 Yehiel Hazak: *Wake*
Hagai Ronen— from kibbuz Afikim, he fell in battle in 1969.
southern wind supporting— a pun on a military term denoting favorable weather conditions.

84 Meir Wieseltier: *Military Call-Up*
Antoine de Saint Exupéry's *The Little Prince* (1943) is very popular among youngsters in Israel, and the image of the innocent, inquisitive boy often appears in war poems. The prince, the sheep, the planet, the hat, the elephant, and the lamplighter are all drawn from the book.

86 Meir Wieseltier: *Love is Progressing*
Where has … turned aside— Can.6:1.
do not covet— Ex.20:14 (17 in some versions).
A damsel or two— Jud.5:30.

88 T. Carmi: *Memorial Day, 1969*
matriculation exams— comprehensive examinations, given to Israeli students during the last two years of high school, which determine eligibility for university admission.

92   Haiim Hefer: *The Young Dead Soldiers*
      The poem is based on MacLieshe's well-known one by the same name.

92   **Reuven ben Yoseph**: *On the Readiness for Sacrifice*
      Kineret— the Hebrew name of the Sea of Galilee (also known in English as
      the Lake of Gennesaret).

98   **Yair Hurvitz**: *Around the Water, Near the Birds*
      crimsoned garments— Isa.63:1.
      molten seas— I Kgs.7:23.
      pommels of her chapiters— I Kgs.7:41.

104   **T. Carmi**: *Military Funeral in the Heat of Day*
      Joseph Ha'efrati— Carmi's friend, a scholar of literature who fell in battle
      in 1974.
      The angel ... second time— reference to a folklore tradition that children
      learn everything while they are still in their mother's womb. Just before
      they are born an angel taps their lip and makes them forget all they know.
      strangers in a strange land— Ex.2:22.
      mezuzah— an amulet which Jews place on their door-post to invite divine
      protection.
      Each man to his own mezuzah and to his own mailbox— perhaps a
      sarcastic paraphrase of I Kgs.5:5 (4:25 in some versions), which conveys
      an image of peace and tranquillity.

108   **Yehiel Hazak**: *I Saw You*
      the spirit will return— Ecc.12:7.

110   **Haiim Gouri**: *Current Account*
      my brothers ... distress— a paraphrase of Ps.118:5.
      stone pillows and ladder— allusions to Gen.28:11–19. See Gouri's *On a
      Stone Pillow*, p. 76.
      Elul— a summer month, the last month in the Hebrew calendar.
      the mountain drip ... it— Am.9:13 and elsewhere.
      God's eye— (*hamsa* in Arabic) a traditional Middle Eastern amulet shaped
      like the palm of a hand with an eye in the middle.

112   **Yehudah Amichai**: *Since Then*
      Ashdod— a southern coastal city which was the scene of fierce battles be-
      tween the Egyptian and Israeli armies during the War of Independence. A
      series of failed attacks on the Egyptian troops and the large number of ca-
      sualties resulted in a national trauma which is reflected in the poem.
      Negbah and Yad Mordechai— two kibbutzim in southern Israel.
      of blessed memory— a Hebrew pun on a traditional phrase uttered when
      the name of a deceased is mentioned, see dedication to Omer's *To the
      Memory of a Comrade*, p. 8.
      God avenge my blood— a Hebrew pun on a traditional phrase uttered
      when the name of a fallen soldier is mentioned, see dedication to Tur-
      Malka's *Heralds of New Jerusalem*, p. 42.
      Look not upon me ... alive— a paraphrase of Can.1:6.

116 Yehudah Amichai: *From the Songs of the Land of Zion and Jerusalem*
The Land of Zion and Jerusalem— the concluding line of the Israeli na-
tional anthem, *Hatikvah*, "The Hope."
Joseph Trumpeldor— a legendary fighter killed in 1921 during the battle
for Tel Chai, a Jewish settlement in the upper Galilee, which was attacked
by Arabs from neighboring villages. His reputed last words, "It is good to
die for our country," became an inspiration and later a target of cynical
criticism.

116 Raiah Harnik: *Your Socks*
Harnik's son, Guni (1956–82), was killed in the 1982 battle for the Beaufort,
a fortress in southern Lebanon (see p. xxiii). This is also the context of
Harnik's *And At Night*.

120 Eli Alon: *Coffins*
The place names and station code-numbers mentioned in the poem are sites
in Southern Lebanon.
military rabbinate— the Israeli Chaplains' Corps.
moshav— an agricultural settlement in which land and property are pri-
vate or leased to individuals (as opposed to a kibbutz, which is collective).
A long, long row— allusion to Gouri's *Behold, Our Bodies Are Laid Out*, p. 4.

122 Amichai Israeli: *Eulogy*
the Sharon War— a term used in reference to the Lebanon War, implying
that the war was a personal ambition and responsibility of the Minister of
Defense, Ariel Sharon, who was eventually forced to resign.
the rent in the garment— reference to a custom of mourning in Jewish
tradition.

122 Nathan Yonathan: *Friends*
The opening lines of the poem allude to the Joseph story in Gen.37.
Sephi (Joseph Shauman)— a close friend of Yonathan's son Leeor who was
killed in the 1973 war, he himself fell in 1982.
Ayelet and Ofir— Sephi's children.
that handsome lad of ours— reference to Yonathan's son, Leeor.

124 Ramy Ditzanny: *My Hand is Extended for the Peace of the Galilee*
Peace of the Galilee— the official name of the Lebanon War, as well as the
justification attached to it.
Come to me ... butterfly— from a well-known Israeli children's poem.

126 Ramy Ditzanny: *Legging Behind*
The Hebrew word for "unfortunately," the title of the original poem, has the
same base as the word for "millipede" and the poem is constructed
around this pun on legs.

128 Ramy Ditzanny: *A Brand Plucked from the Anti-tank Fire*
A Brand Plucked ... Fire— a paraphrase of Zach.3:2.
a black hat-coat-vest— characteristic garb of ultra-Orthodox Jewish men.
Gemara— a compilation of Jewish Oral Law.
Siddur— the Jewish prayer book.

Ramy Ditzanny: *A Brand Plucked from the Anti-tank Fire* continued
Here I am, my son— Gen.22:7.
Kiddush (sanctification)— a traditional blessing recited over a cup of wine.

130 Ramy Ditzanny: *Complicated and Innovative Orthopedic Surgery*
The poem is written as a mock rabbinical discourse, which results in a strong sarcastic tone.

132 Ramy Ditzanny: *Piggy-Back*
Levenstein House— a rehabilitation center.

134 Dahlia Ravikovitch: *You Don't Kill Babies Twice*
Sabra and Shatila— Palestinian refugee camps in Lebanon. In 1982 a unit of Lebanese Christian militia killed hundreds there, and the Israeli troops, whose help was sought by residents of the camps, made no attempt to stop the massacre. Although their troops were not directly involved in the event, Israelis used it as a rallying point of opposition to their government's involvement in Lebanon (see p. xxii.)

136 Alex L.: *At a Time Like That*
Amalfi— a port city in southern Italy, associated with beautiful scenery and romance.
Sidon— a port city in southern Lebanon.
Rosh Hanikrah— a kibbutz in northern Israel, near the Lebanese border.

140 Aryeh Sivan: *To Live in the Land of Israel*
Abraham on Mount Moriah— allusion to Gen.22:11 ff..

142 Aryeh Sivan: *To Wither Like Weeds in an Easterly Wind*
In May of 1948 a Gahal (acronym for recruits from abroad) unit, consisting of new immigrants, many of whom came from refugee camps in Europe and Cyprus, participated in a futile attempt to capture the police post of Latroun overlooking the road to Jerusalem in the Valley of Ayalon. The members of this unit were not properly trained, and many suffered severe dehydration and confusion. Some 200 of them perished in the battle, which became a subject of bitter debate and criticism. The battle for Latroun was fought as part of a larger military maneuver called "Operation Ben Nun" after the battles of the Biblical leader Joshua ben Nun, some of which were fought in the area.
the sun of Ayalon— allusion to Josh.10:12.
work would make you free— allusion to *Arbeit macht frei*, the motto over the main gate of Auschwitz.
Auschwitz and Sobibor— death camps in Poland during the Holocaust.
one time only did they walk in the fields— allusion to a well-known novel by Moshe Shamir, one of the writers of the "Palmach generation" (see note to Alterman's *Around the Campfire*). The novel, *He Walked in the Fields* (1948), revolved around the character of Elik, Shamir's brother, who fell in the War of Independence and became the archetype of a mythical Palmach fighter. Eventually this mythical character became the target of cynical criticism, which is also evident in Sivan's choice of words.

Aryeh Sivan: *To Wither Like Weeds in an Easterly Wind* continued

the number ... forearm— camp inmates were tattooed for identification. The S.S. was the elite security police and military unit in Nazi Germany.

If one is to die for our country— reference to Trumpeldor's last words (see note to Amichai's *From the Songs of the Land of Zion and Jerusalem*, p. 116.).

144 Aryeh Sivan: *Concerning the Rehabilitation of the Disabled ...*

The poem probably bears a relationship to Jonathan Swift's "A Modest Proposal for Preventing the Children of Poor People in Ireland from Being a Burden to Their Parents or Country, and for Making Them Beneficial to the Public" (1729).

to make sons in our likenesses— paraphrase of Gen.1:26.

148 Eitan Kalinski: *Teacher of Defeated Hebrew Language*

golden apples ... silver ornaments— an allusion to Pr.25:11; conventionally used in reference to well-polished words of wisdom.

Shneour Zalman of Lyadi— the 18th century founder of the Chabad Hassidic movement.

Shechem (Nablus) and Jenin— cities in the West Bank area.

150 Eitan Kalinski: *1936-1986*

Heshvan ... Iyar ... Tishrey— the second, eighth, and first months of the Hebrew calendar. All dates in the poem are based on that calendar. For the sake of immediate recognition by the English-speaking reader, the translation gives the corresponding years according to the general calendar.

Kadesh— the Hebrew name of the Sinai desert (and the 1956 war fought in that area).

bloody bridegrooms— allusion to Ex.4:25.

Tyre— a port city in southern Lebanon.

150 Asher Reich: *A Siren of Love*

safety kit— the anti-chemical-warfare kit distributed to Israelis during the Gulf War.

splendidly turned off— a pun on the Hebrew for "built for an arsenal" (or "splendidly built") of Can.4.4.

cormorants— a prominent symbol of the Gulf War, the oil-covered cormorants off the shores of Kuwait.

heavy-hot-weather *(sharav-kaved)*— a code phrase for an air-raid siren.

152 Ilan Sheinfeld: *War Night 6*

Jaffa— a Tel Aviv suburb which had a large Arab population.

Zyklon— the Zyklon B gas used by the Nazis in their gas chambers.

Auschwitz— a death camp in Poland during the Holocaust.

Shevat— the fifth month in the Hebrew calendar; the date was January 23, 1991 in the general calendar.

154 Pinhas Sadeh: *At Nightfall*

deadly viper— allusion to *nachash tsefa* (a viper), one of the code phrases for air-raid sirens.

Pinhas Sadeh: *At Nightfall* continued

Worms and Meinz (Germany), Toledo (Spain), Nemirov and Kishinev (Russia)— cities which had large Jewish populations, sites of persecution and pogroms from medieval to modern times.

Treblinka and Auschwitz— death camps in Europe during the Holocaust.

156 **Haiim Gouri:** *Like Beirut*

Heavens, request mercy— reference to a well-known poem by Haiim Nachman Bialik, *On the Slaughter*.

I heard when they said to me ...— a pun based on Ps.122:1.

Haiia Sulum and Ashrafiyah— militia strongholds in Beirut.

Biographical Information

Eli Alon (1935–), who writes as A. Eli, was born in the Land of Israel and lives in kibbutz Ein Shemer. His first collection, *Such Were the Generations of Jacob*, was published in 1966. *The Mount of Final Repose* appeared in 1969.

Nathan Alterman (1910–70), born in Poland, immigrated to the Land of Israel in 1925 and settled in Tel Aviv. A poet, playwright, translator, and essayist, he became a prominent and influential figure in the pre-State, and later the Israeli, literary circles. His poetry is characterized by frequent use of rhythm, rhyme, and alliteration, and by extensive use of imagery. *Stars Outside,* his first collection, was published in 1938. Volumes of his collected work were published in the 1960s and 1970s.

Yehudah Amichai (1924–), born in Germany, came to the Land of Israel in 1936. He served in the British Army's Jewish Brigade in WWII and later in the Palmach (see note to Alterman's *Around the Campfire*) and the Israeli Defense Forces. His poems became well known in the 1950s, with his first collection, *Now and in the Other Days,* appearing in 1955. Amichai's work in poetry and prose is widely translated and he has been a recipient of numerous literary prizes, among them the Israel Prize for Literature.

David Avidan (1934–95), born in the Land of Israel, lived in Tel Aviv. He began having poetry published in the early fifties. His idiosyncratic style was controversial and his experimental work in various fields of writing was highly publicized. His initial poetry collection, *Lipless Faucets,* was published in 1954. Two later collections, *Poems of War and Protest* (1976) and *The Last Gulf: Poems of Desert Storm* (1991), were composed of war poetry. He won several literary prizes.

Reuven ben Yoseph (1937–), born in New York, immigrated to Israel in 1959 and settled in Jerusalem. His first collection, *Waiting Seagulls,* was published in 1965. A collection of war poetry entitled *Voices in the Golan Heights: Poems of the Yom Kippur War* appeared in 1976. He has won several literary prizes.

T. Carmi [Carmi Tcherni] (1925–94), was born in New York and immigrated to the Land of Israel in 1947. He fought in the War of Independence and settled in Jerusalem. *Blemish and Dream,* his first collection, was published in 1950. A poet and translator widely recognized by his first name, Carmi won several literary prizes.

Ramy Ditzanny was born in Israel and lives in Jerusalem. His initial collection, *Poems from the Ward of the Crippled in Spirit,* which reflected the horrors of the 1982 war and his hospitalization experience following it, was published in 1984. His war poetry has received enthusiastic critical acclaim, and he has won several literary prizes.

Anadad Eldan (1924–) was born in Poland. His first collection, *Streaming Darkness and Fruit,* appeared in 1959.

Yonathan Gefen (1947–), born in the Land of Israel, has produced poetry collections, verses for children, and political satire. His first collection, *Poems Which Anat Especially Loves*, was published in 1969.

Amir Gilboa (1917–84), born in the Ukraine, immigrated to the Land of Israel in 1937, and in 1942 joined the British army. He fought in North Africa and with the Jewish Brigade of the British Army in Italy. Many of his early poems reflect his war experience and the horrors of the Holocaust. His first collection, *For a Sign,* was published in 1942, and by the late 1950s he was established as a prominent young poet. He won many literary awards including the Israel Prize for Literature.

Haiim Gouri (1923–), born in the Land of Israel, served in the Palmach (see note to Alterman's *Around the Campfire*). He spent some of the post-WWII years on rescue missions in displaced-persons camps in Europe. *Flowers of Fire,* his first collection, appeared in 1949, and since then he has established himself as one of Israel's most prominent poets. Gouri, also a novelist and an active journalist, has won numerous literary prizes, among them the Israel Prize for Literature.

Uri Zvi Greenberg (1896–81), born in Galicia, served two years as a soldier in the Austrian army during WWI. In 1924 he immigrated to the Land of Israel, where he became active in the Revisionist party. In 1949 he was elected to the parliament, representing the right-wing "Herut" party. His strong political stance led to rejection of his poetry by the general public. The strength of his work, however, achieved recognition late in his life, and he received numerous literary awards. His first Yiddish collection was published in 1915, and his first in Hebrew, *A Grave Threat and the Moon,* in 1925.

Raiah Harnik (1933–), born in Germany, saw her initial collection, *Poems for Guni,* published in 1983. Her collection *Poems of the Herzl Mountain* appeared in 1987. Both reflect the experience of the bereaved and point to the cruelty and senselessness of war.

Yehiel Hazak (1936–) was born in the Land of Israel. *Basalt Stones,* his first collection, was published in 1961.

Haiim Hefer (1925–), born in Poland, had his first collection, *Light Munition,* published in 1949. His weekly pieces of rhymed prose, published regularly since the 1960s, typically respond to political and social events, and include many references to war and the political and human situations associated with it.

Yair Hurvitz [also Horowitz] (1941–88) was born in Tel Aviv. His collection *In Mute Distress* appeared in 1961, and his collected works in 1974 and 1988.

Eitan Kalinski is a resident of Tel Aviv who has taught Hebrew in a number of countries around the globe, currently (1995) in St. Petersburg. His book, *Teacher of Defeated Hebrew Language,* appeared in 1989.

Mati Katz (1944–64), born in Tel Aviv, fell in battle in 1964. Poems of his were included in a posthumous collection (1981) featuring four young Israeli poets.

Abba Kovner (1918–87), born in the Crimea, was one of the leaders of the Vilna Ghetto revolt and later an organizer of post-war emigration of Holocaust sur vivors. After he himself immigrated, he wrote his epical *While There is Still Night* during imprisonment by the British as an illegal immigrant (1947). He fought in the War of Independence and settled in kibbutz Ein Hachoresh. Kovner, also a novelist and an essayist, was awarded the Israel Prize for Literature.

Karmela Lakhish (1935–), born in Haifa, has produced three books in prose, her first being *The Diary 1947–1948* which appeared in 1988.

Alex L. [Alex Liban] (1942–), born in Tel Aviv, is a member of kibbutz Rosh Hanikrah. His first collection, *To Write Longings*, was published in 1987.

Yehiel Mohar (1921–69), born in Galicia, immigrated to the Land of Israel in 1937. *From Heart and Landscape*, his initial collection, was published in 1951.

Uriel Ofeq (1926–87), born in the Land of Israel, was a scholar of children's literature. His collection *To the Ears of the Tree* appeared in 1954.

Hillel Omer (1926–90), who wrote as "Ayin Hillel," was born in the Land of Israel. A well-known architect and environmental activist, he wrote children's poems and light satirical verse. His collection *Land of Noon* was published in 1950.

Dan Pagis (1930–86), born in Romania, spent part of his childhood in a concentration camp. Escaping in 1944, he arrived in the Land of Israel in 1946. A professor of Hebrew Literature, he published studies in modern and medieval Hebrew poetry. His first poetry collection, *The Shadow Dial*, was published in 1959.

Dahlia Ravikovitch (1936–), born in Tel Aviv, began having poetry published in the late 1950s, and her initial collection, *The Love of an Orange*, appeared in 1959. Ravikovitch also wrote for children as well as translating poetry and children's literature into Hebrew. She has received several literary prizes.

Asher Reikh (1937–) was born in Jerusalem. His collection *In the Seventh Year* was published in 1963. A poet and an editor, he has received a number of literary prizes.

Gideon Rosenthal (1950–73), born in Tel Aviv, fell in battle during the Yom Kippur War. A collection of his original and translated poetry was brought out posthumously in 1975.

Pinhas Sadeh (1929–94), born in Galicia, arrived in the Land of Israel in 1934. A poet and a translator, he also compiled an anthology of Hassidic legends. His first poetry collection, *Burden of Dumah*, was published in 1951.

Yoseph Sarig (1944–73), born in kibbutz Beyt Hashita, was a prolific writer and musician. He fell in battle in the Yom Kippur War, and his collection *Twenty Poems* was issued posthumously in 1975.

Ilan Sheinfeld (1960–), a poet, literary editor, and teacher, had his first collection, *Bewitched Lizard*, published in 1981.

Naomi Shemer (1931–), born in the Land of Israel, has been very popular since the 1960s for both her lyrics and melodies. Her major collection, *All My Songs*, appeared in 1967.

Aryeh Sivan (1929–), born in Tel Aviv, fought in the War of Independence and has been a teacher of Hebrew language and literature. *Poems of Armor* (1963), his first collection, includes many war poems.

Moshe Tabenkin (1917–79), born in the Land of Israel, lived in kibbutz Ein Harod. His first collection, *Poems*, was brought out in 1943.

Ayin (Alizah Gurevitch) Tur-Malka (1926–), born in Jerusalem, was a member of the Lechi underground group. Her first collection, *Nest of Twigs*, was in 1963. The widow of Uri Zvi Greenberg, she is largely responsible for the recent publication of his collected works.

Meir Wieseltier (1941–), born in Russia, came to Israel in 1949. His initial collection, *Chapter A Chapter B*, was published in 1967. Wieseltier was a leading figure among young poets of the 1960s and 1970s.

Nathan Yonathan (1923–), born in Russia, was brought to the Land of Israel in 1925. His collection *Dirt Roads* was published in 1951.

Natan Zach (1930–), born in Germany, came to the Land of Israel in 1935. A poet, translator, editor, and critic, he became a prominent outspoken advocate of rebellion among the young generation of poets in the 1950s. His initial collection, *First Poems*, appeared in 1955, since when he has received numerous literary awards, including the Israel Prize for Literature.

Yehoshua Zafrir [*né* Liebliech] (1928–), was born in Poland. After being liberated from the Buchenwald camp he came to the Land of Israel in 1946 and settled in kibbutz Mishmar Hanegev. A collection of his poems entitled *I Dream a Well* was published in 1984.

Zelda [Mishkowsky] (1914–84), who wrote under just her first name, was born in the Ukraine and arrived in the Land of Israel in 1925. Her poetry is characterized by extensive religious imagery. Her first collection, *Leisure*, was published in 1967, and she received a number of literary prizes.

Bibliography

Sources of Poems (Hebrew):

Alon, Eli. *The Mount of Final Repose.* Tel Aviv: Sifriyat Poalim, 1969.

Alterman, Nathan. *The Seventh Column.* 2 Vols. Tel Aviv: Hakibbutz Hameuchad, 1975.

Amichai, Yehudah. *Now in the Din Before the Silence: Poems, 1963–1968.* Jerusalem: Schocken, 1968.

_____. *Not Just to Remember.* Jerusalem: Schocken, 1971.

_____. *Poems, 1948–1962.* Jerusaelm: Schocken, 1963.

_____. *Great Tranquility: Questions and Answers.* Jerusalem: Schocken, 1980.

Avidan, David. *Practical Poems.* Jerusalem: A. Levin Epstein, 1973.

Avinoam, Reuven, ed. *Parchments of Fire.* Tel Aviv: Israel Ministry of Defense, 1970.

ben Yosef, Reuven. *Voices in the Golan Heights: Poems of the Yom Kippur War.* Jerusalem: Dvir, 1976.

Carmi, T. *Selected Poems 1951–1969.* Tel Aviv: Am Oved Publishers, 1970.

_____. *At The Stone of Losses.* Jerusalem: Dvir, 1981.

Ditzanny, Ramy. *Poems from the Ward of the Crippled in Spirit.* Tel Aviv: Domino, 1984.

Eldan, Anadad. *By Himself in the Heavy Stream.* Tel Aviv: Hakibbutz Hameuchad, 1971.

Gilboa, Amir. *Poems.* 2nd printing. Tel Aviv: Am Oved, 1971.

Gouri, Haiim. *Flowers of Fire.* Merhaviah: Sifriyat Poalim, 1949.

_____. *Movement to Touch.* Tel Aviv: Hakibbutz Hameuchad, 1968.

_____. *Awesome.* Tel Aviv: Hakibbutz Hameuchad, 1979.

_____. *Poems (The One Who Comes After Me).* Tel Aviv: Hakibbutz Hameuchad, 1994.

Greenberg, Uri Zvi. *Collected Works.* Vol. 7. Jerusalem: Mosad Bialik, 1994.

Hazak, Yehiel. *Bereft Horah.* Tel Aviv: Eked, 1970.

_____. *Betrayal.* Tel Aviv: Hakibbutz Hameuchad, 1982.

Hefer, Haiim. *Light Munition: Song Poems.* 2nd printing. Tel Aviv: Hakibbutz Hameuchad (1949), 1978.

_____. *Friday Columns.* Jerusalem: Idanim, 1978.

Hever, Hanan, and M. Ron, eds. *No End to Battles and Killing.* Tel Aviv: Hakibbutz Hameuchad, 1982.

Horowitz [*also* Hurvitz], Yair. *Poems 1960–1973.* Tel Aviv: Siman Kri'ah, 1974.

Kafri, Yehudit, ed. *Border Crossing: Poems from the Lebanon War.* Tel Aviv: Sifriyat Poalim, 1983.

Kalinski, Eitan. *Poems (Teacher of a Defeated Hebrew Language)*. Tel Aviv: Sifriyat Poalim, 1989.

Kovner, Abba. *A Canopy in the Desert*. Tel Aviv: Sifriyat Poalim, 1970.

Ofek, Uriel, ed. *From the Wars: Prose and Poetry*. 2nd printing. Tel Aviv: Keter, 1970.

Omer, Hillel. *As Far As Here*. Tel Aviv: Hakibbutz Hameuchad, 1983.

Pagis, Dan. *Transformation*. Ramat Gan: Agudat Hasofrim, 1970.

Reich, Asher. "Love Siren." *Maariv*, 8 February 1991.

Rozenthal, Gideon. *Poems and Translations*. Tel Aviv: Sifriyat Poalim, 1975.

Sadeh, Pinhas. "At Nightfall, 1/27/91." *Maariv*, 2 January 1991.

Sarig, Yoseph. *Twenty Poems*. Tel Aviv: Hakibbutz Hameuchad, 1975.

Sheinfeld, Ilan. "War Night 6." *Yediot Acharonot*, 8 February 1991.

Shemer, Naomi. *All My Songs*. Tel Aviv: Yediot Acharonot, 1967.

Sivan, Aryeh. *To Live in the Land of Israel*. Tel Aviv: Am Oved, 1984.

Tamir, Nahman, ed. *The Six Days*. Tel Aviv: Tarbut Vechinuch, 1967.

Tur-Malka, A. *The Wells' Song*. Jerusalem: Agudat Shalem, 1971.

Wieseltier, Meir. *Tiens*. Tel Aviv: Siman Kri'ah, 1973.

_____. *The Concise Sixties*. Tel Aviv: Siman Kri'ah, 1984.

Yonathan, Nathan. *Songs Along the Shore*. 3rd edition. Tel Aviv: Sifriyat Poalim, 1974.

Zelda. *Leisure; The Invisible Carmel; Do Not Go Far*. 8th printing. Tel Aviv: Hakibbutz Hameuchad, 1978.

Articles Cited (Hebrew):

Avidan, David. "War Poetry as Political Poetry." *Maariv*, 2.1.1991.

_____. "War Poetry (3) as Passive Stepping in One Place." *Maariv* 2.15.1991.

Bartana, Orzion. "The Great Noise." *Maariv*, 2.8.1991.

ben Shaul, Moshe. "What Happened to the Gulf Muse." *Maariv*, 3.1.1991.

Dorman, Menahem. "The War Poetry Controversy." *Mozna'im*, 64:8 (1990): 47–48.

Edeliest, Ran. "The Disgrace of Men-of-Spirit." *Yediot Acharonot*, 11.23.1990.

Hameiri, Irit. "Writers and Books in Days of Confusion." *Yediot Acharonot*, 2.8.1991.

Yonathan, Nathan "Thoughts at Night." *Yediot Acharonot*, 2.8.1991.

Selected Reference:

Alter, Robert. *After the Tradition*. New York: Dutton, 1969.

Andersen, Elliot, ed. *Contemporary Israeli Literature*. Philadelphia: Jewish Publication Society, 1977.

Bargad, Warren and S. F. Chyet, eds. *Israeli Poetry: A Contemporary Anthology*. Bloomington: Indiana University Press, 1986.

Bernhard, Frank, trans. *Modern Hebrew Poetry.* Iowa City: University of Iowa Press, 1980.

Birman, Abraham, ed. *An Anthology of Modern Hebrew Poetry.* London: Abelard-Schuman, 1968.

Burnshaw, Stanley, T. Carmi, and E. Spicehandler, eds. *The Modern Hebrew Poem Itself.* New York: Schocken Books, 1966.

Carmi, T., ed. *The Penguin Book of Hebrew Verse.* New York: Penguin Books, 1981.

Dor, Moshe, Barbara Goldberg, and Giora Leshem, eds. *The Stones Remember: Native Israeli Poetry.* Washington, DC: World Works, 1991.

Featherstone, Simon, ed. *War Poetry: An Introductory Reader.* London and New York: Rutledge, 1995.

Foss, Michael, ed. *Poetry of the World Wars.* New York: Peter Bedrick, 1990.

Glazer, Mira, ed. *Contemporary Israeli Women Poets: Burning Air and a Clear Mind.* Athens: Ohio University Press, 1981.

Halkin, Simeon. *Modern Hebrew Literature: Trends and Values.* New York: Schocken Books, 1950.

Hayisraeli, Amram et al., eds. *The Seventh Day: Soldiers Talk About the Six-Day War.* Middlesex, England: Penguin Books, 1971.

Johnston, John H. *English Poetry of the First World War.* New Jersey: Princeton University Press, 1964.

Keller, Adam. *Terrible Days: Social Divisions and Political Paradoxes in Israel.* Amstelveen, The Netherlands: Cypres, 1987.

Kravitz, Nathaniel. *3,000 Years of Hebrew Literature.* Chicago: Swallow Press, 1972.

Minz, Ruth F., ed. *Modern Hebrew Poetry: A Bilingual Anthology.* Berkeley: University of California Press, 1968.

Miron, Dan. *Facing the Silent Brother: Essays on the Poetry of the War of Independence* (Hebrew). Jerusalem: Keter, 1992.

Penuely, S., and A. Ukhmani, eds. *Anthology of Modern Hebrew Poetry.* Jerusalem: Institute for the Translation of Hebrew Literature, 1966.

Silk, Dennis, ed. *Fourteen Israeli Poets: A Selection of Modern Hebrew Poetry.* London: Andre Deutch, 1976.

Stokesbury, Leon, ed. *Articles of War: A Collection of American Poetry About World War II.* Fayetteville: University of Arkansas Press, 1990.

Author Index

About Esther Raizen

Esther Raizen grew up in Israel, and came to the United States in 1982. She received her Ph.D. from the University of Texas, where she now teaches in the Hebrew program of the Department of Middle Eastern Languages and Cultures. Her dissertation entitled "Romanization of the Hebrew Script: Ideology, Attempts and Failure" received the University of Texas Outstanding Dissertation Award in 1988. She is a recipient of the 1993 Texas Excellence Teaching Award. She lives in Austin with her husband and three children.

DATE DUE